T0305648

Industrialization and Economic Diversification

Economic diversification entails a shift away from a single income source towards multiple income sources from an increasing spectrum of sectors and markets. A persistent concern for some Asian and African economies is their reliance on commodity exports and how they are exposed to the risk of export volatility and income instability. The Covid-19 pandemic and previous oil crashes have demonstrated the adverse impact on such economies. This book provides a systemic analysis of sustainable economic development through economic diversification.

The book analyses diversification and development experiences from comparative perspectives of Asia and Africa. It also investigates determinants of export diversification differentiated by commodities-dependence versus manufactured products and looks at the roles of various institutions and governance of institutions in export diversification.

This book will provide policy insights into how different degrees of specialisation in exports across countries have affected outcomes in terms of living standards, economic growth, and employment.

Banji Oyelaran-Oyeyinka is currently Senior Special Adviser to the President on Industrialization at the African Development Bank (AfDB). He served within the United Nations (UN) system for 20 years as Director, Regional Office for Africa, Chief Scientific Advisor, UN-HABITAT, and Director, Monitoring & Research Division. He was Senior Economic Adviser, UN Centre on Trade and Development (UNCTAD) and is currently Visiting Professor at the United Nations University-MERIT, Maastricht, the Netherlands and the Open University, UK. He is a Fellow of the Nigerian Academy of Engineering and Fellow of the Nigerian Academy of Chemical Engineering. His publications include *Resurgent Africa: Structural Transformation in Sustainable Development* (Anthem Press, 2020); *From Consumption to Production: The Why and Ways Out of Failed Industrialization in Nigeria* (Kachifo Limited, 2017); *Structural Transformation and Economic Development* (Routledge, 2017).

Kaushalesh Lal is Professorial Fellow at United Nations University-MERIT, Maastricht, the Netherlands. Dr Lal earned his PhD from Erasmus University Rotterdam, the Netherlands. Prior to joining the United Nations University,

Maastricht in 2003, Dr Lal was with the Institute of Economic Growth, Delhi. He has published more than 30 articles in peer-reviewed journals. His areas of research interest include Economics of Technical Change, ICT, Globalisation and Technological Change, Industrialisation and Economic Development. Dr Lal is on the panel of reviewers of several renowned international journals. Dr Lal has several books published by renowned international publishers to his credit. His prominent books are: *Knowledge Infrastructure and Higher Education in India* (Routledge, 2020, with Shampa Paul); *Structural Transformation and Economic Development* (Routledge, 2017, with Banji Oyelaran-Oyeyinka); *Servitization, IT-ization and Innovation Models* (Routledge, 2013, with Hitoshi Hirakawa, Naoko Shinkai, and Norio Tokumaru).

Routledge Studies in Development Economics

For more information about this series, please visit: www.routledge.com/series/SE0266

Industrialization and Economic Diversification

Post-Crisis Development Agenda in Asia and Africa

Banji Oyelaran-Oyeyinka and
Kaushalesh Lal

Routledge
Taylor & Francis Group

LONDON AND NEW YORK

First published 2022
by Routledge
4 Park Square, Milton Park, Abingdon, Oxon OX14 4RN

and by Routledge
605 Third Avenue, New York, NY 10158

Routledge is an imprint of the Taylor & Francis Group, an informa business

© 2022 Banji Oyelaran-Oyeyinka and Kaushalesh Lal

British Library Cataloguing-in-Publication Data
A catalogue record for this book is available from the British Library

Library of Congress Cataloging-in-Publication Data
Names: Oyelaran-Oyeyinka, Banji, 1955- author. | Lal, Kaushalesh, 1955-
author. Title: Industrialization and economic diversification : post-crisis development agenda in Asia and Africa / Professor Banji Oyelaran-Oyeyinka and Kaushalesh Lal.
Description: Abingdon, Oxon ; New York, NY : Routledge, 2022. | Series: Routledge studies in development economics | Includes bibliographical references and index. |
Identifiers: LCCN 2021052997 | ISBN 9781032156866 (hardback) | ISBN 9781032156859 (paperback) | ISBN 9781003245322 (ebook)
Subjects: LCSH: Diversification in industry–Africa. | Diversification in industry–Asia. | Economic development–Africa. | Economic development–Asia.
Classification: LCC HD2756.2.A35 O94 2022 | DDC 338.6--dc23/eng/20211029
LC record available at https://lccn.loc.gov/2021052997

ISBN: 9781032156866 (hbk)
ISBN: 9781032156859 (pbk)
ISBN: 9781003245322 (ebk)

DOI: 10.4324/9781003245322

Typeset in Galliard
by Deanta Global Publishing Services, Chennai, India

To all Covid-19 warriors who have scarified their lives for the cause of humanity and to those who have survived

Contents

Figures

Tables

Preface

Why would we write another book on economic diversification? There are several reasons. Five to six decades after independence, African countries remain the least economically diversified and consequently extremely dependent on Natural Resources (NR) for export earnings. The Covid-19 pandemic exposed the dangers of such dependence in ways not experienced in the past. The yoke of Africa's colonial past of being the supplier of raw materials rather than a processor of commodities condemned the region to a beggar for vaccines in the face of vaccine nationalism, unable to access critical life-saving drugs and even ordinary masks as the pandemic ravaged the world. The legacy of resource-dependence has translated to an African production ecosystem dominated by foreign oil and foreign mineral multinationals whose sole purpose is to explore, extract, and export resources with zero value addition in situ. Africa imports about 90% of its medical supplies from India and China as the pharmaceutical markets in Africa have, over the process of time, evolved into an arena dominated by Western pharmaceutical companies after independence. This production space has since in part been replaced by Indian, Chinese, and Bangladesh firms among others. While there are a few firms making genuine efforts to produce, the majority are either distributors of imported pharmaceutical products, or manufacturers of a small range of product baskets based on low technology and low skill.

Second, we believe Africa is at an inflection point; a critical juncture such as this is the opportune time to renew the call for a strategic development change. We have done so by analysing the contrasting development experiences of Asia and which countries travelled a difference pathway of using NR as an enabler of industrial manufacturing. We hope African leaders including policy makers will re-examine and reconfigure the focus of their development agenda heretofore. Asia provides an inspiration that the reversal of African fortunes could be turned in a far shorter period than happened when Europe, for example, industrialised.

Third, there are inevitable changes to the global industrial and social order. It points to a scenario that if Africa does not speed up its industrialisation process, the world will further leave the region behind and the ensuing dynamics will disengage it and its people even from the onrushing global trading and production systems. One such inevitability is *energy transition*, a fundamental structural change of energy systems. This will bring about a paradigmatic shift in energy systems that will radically transform the energy landscape everywhere. At various points in history, human societies progressed from depending on straw as a source of energy to relying on wood, then coal, and, eventually, fossil fuels such as oil and gas. Technological innovation, economic or social changes, as well as demands and availability of energy resources, are all drivers of energy transitions. Given that nearly all nations of the world have committed to the goals of the Paris Agreement to reduce CO_2 emissions and lower global atmospheric temperatures to 1.5°C, oil-producing countries must now transform their energy systems from a fossil fuel-based system to a zero-carbon system while still meeting their energy needs for economic growth and development. The transition from one energy system to another entails significant changes in the entire energy system, which includes the market, stakeholders, policies, and institutions, as well as the mindset or behaviour of energy users. Nigeria, Angola, DRC, and Algeria among others are big oil exporters with large natural gas reserves. They derive between 80–95% of export earnings and 50–70% of public revenue from fossil fuel. For Africa, this is another imperative for diversification. In sum, heavy dependence on the fossil fuel industry for economic development entailing investment in hydrocarbon-based oil and gas infrastructure built over 60 years requires deep-going changes. Africa's inflection point, including energy transition, is brought into stark relief by the pandemic; all converge at the crossroads of three major challenges – energy security, economic diversification, and climate change. Covid-19 adds intriguing complexities to the confluence of existing socio-economic factors, posing additional hurdles towards achieving a successful energy transition in Africa, resolving the poverty, inequalities, and health and human challenges in places like Nigeria and in much of the Sahel region.

Fourth, oil-dependent nations will face gradually declining investment flows in their hydrocarbon industry as pressure to meet global emission targets intensify. For example, at the global level, the electric car (EC) is growing exponentially according to the World Economic Forum. Three million vehicles are now being sold annually as at 2020 and automobile manufacturers now offer both the hybrid and full plug-in electric vehicles (EVs) at commercial scale. Projections show that 54% of new car sales worldwide and 33% of the global car fleet will be electric respectively. The implications for oil producers, non-oil producers and the African region that lack the industrial base to participate at any point in the EV value chain will be hugely significant. We discuss this in Chapter 1.

Long before its independence, Nigeria had relied almost solely on agriculture export; it was the largest exporter of palm oil and palm kernel. Demand for both had soared due to World War I. Nigeria made £9.5 million from exports in 1918, the highest since its amalgamation four years earlier – 61% was from palm oil and palm kernels. The pandemic of 1918 struck and disrupted trade in raw materials; as it was then, so it remains now that Nigeria did not plan for the aftermath of an external shock.

Export revenues from palm oil and palm kernels were the main source of income for the colonial government. Then as now, Nigeria relied on a single commodity, which is petroleum oil. Before World War I, Nigeria exported palm oil to Liverpool to make soap, and shipped palm kernels to Germany to make cattle feed and the oil extracted from them was sold to the Dutch who made margarine from it. The demand for palm oil and palm kernel ended abruptly in 1920. This affected many big and small British merchants and companies, subsistence farmers, and their families, in the south-east and Niger Delta. As it was then, the economy lacked diversification, there was no infrastructure to spur growth in other sectors after the crisis subsided, demand for oil had collapsed.

This is not just a Nigerian story. It is Africa's pathology of oil and mineral dependence. This pathology spawns another, which is the paradox of underdevelopment, amidst natural resources abundance. Africa ships away its resources; other countries got rich by adding value through manufacturing; 100 hundred years after, nothing has changed.

The top two oil and minerals exporters in Africa share the unfortunate distinctions of been poorly economically diversified, in addition to their similar poverty and inequality profiles. In 2018, 92.4% of the total exports from Angola were hydrocarbon fuel. Oil rents accounted for 25.6% of the country's GDP (Gross Domestic Product). In 2019, the country ranked 148th out of 189 countries in the UN's Human Development Index. Similarly, Nigeria's oil exports in 2018 were 94.1% of total exports, oil rents amounted to 9% of GDP. In terms of quality of life, in 2019 it ranked 161st on the Human Development Index .

In the Democratic Republic of the Congo (DRC), *mineral rents* constituted 13% of total GDP and DRC HDI (Human Development Index) value for 2019 is 0.480 – which puts the country in the low human development category – positioning it at 175 out of 189 countries and territories. Clearly, without exception, minerals and oil producers in sub-Saharan Africa tend to have low HDIs and widespread inequality that are related closely to dependence on minerals and oil exports.

This pathology is the theme of our book. Asian nations have become rich over the last five decades by manufacturing and exporting to others including high-quality goods and services. Poor African countries remain poor because they continue to produce raw materials for those who engineered the transformation of their economies. For example, 70% of global trade in agriculture is in semi-processed and processed products. Africa is largely absent in this market while the region remains an exporter of raw materials to Asia and the West.

The book carries out a systematic identification of the problems by analysing export data of major economies in the two regions. Consistent with much of the findings in the vast literature on the subject, we found that countries that are rich in natural resources such as oil, over time experienced very unstable export income. At the times of oil shocks, these countries witnessed negative growth rates from which recovery proved difficult even when peak demand returned. We agree with recent scholarship that natural resources can be a blessing or a curse depending on a country's history, institutions, and political orientations. The book presents comparative empirical evidence from countries that have converted natural resources to blessings and those whose dependence turned to a curse of underdevelopment. We quantitatively identify and analyse such factors; these factors could be broadly categorised into political, governance, quality of institutions, and innovation capacity, among others.

The more diversified a country's export becomes, the more it gains from globalisation and integration into the global trading system. The successful Asian countries acquired capabilities in manufacturing resulting in significant export earnings and overall economic performance.

The role of technological competence takes a pivotal position in global integration. A country with high levels of technological competence will likely achieve a greater degree of integration with the world economy. On the other hand, a country with low levels of technological competence should strive for greater market diversification even at a relatively low income, as Korea and others have successfully demonstrated.

To substantiate our empirical findings, we have detailed case studies of countries that have converted their natural resources into blessings and those that have failed to do. What is quite evident is that there is no universal formula applicable to all countries and for all times. Those countries that converted natural resources into assets treated them as an opportunity, and deployed resource rents to build infrastructure to support other sectors such as manufacturing and services. The policy process put them into a virtuous circle of prosperity and development. Such countries developed competencies needed for successful industrialisation and successfully diversified; vertically as well as horizontally. On the other hand, those that treated natural resources as everlasting resources and remained dependent on such resources failed to diversify. The industrial clustering approach in general and development of product- and market-specific clusters have been the common policy instruments for diversification and growth.

We agree that cross-country comparisons are fraught with dangers of data, cultural contexts, and interpretations. However, we see clear broad evidence of a reversal of Africa's fortune and contrasting progress in Asian countries. Although Africa has made good progress in improving aspects of governance and developing some quality institutions, a condition necessary for export diversification, the region needs to increase the pace of improvements. The indisputable conclusion of the book is that Africa needs to wean itself of the pathology of natural resource-dependence. African countries need to make greater technological efforts in value addition in order to export processed agri-products and processed hydrocarbon and minerals rather than exporting primary products. At the root of all these are historically derived institutions and contemporary policies – that we have identified no matter how imperfectly – that the continent needs to develop and build.

Acknowledgements

We conceived this book during the Covid-19 pandemic. The pandemic brought the lockdown and, for the most part, my wife bore the brunt of my obsession with the subject matter of this book. I thank her most sincerely for her continuing encouragement and support.

I thank the following colleagues for assisting with case studies and other relevant materials, Professor Magnus Onuoha, Professor Ayo Olukotun, Dr Oluyomi Ola-David. We are grateful to Professor Arup Mitra for providing deep understanding of industrial policies implemented by several countries. Our sincere thanks are due to Dr Shampa Paul for her contributions in the book.

We thank the editors of Routledge who have been patient with us as we work on the book.

Abbreviations

ADB	African Development Bank
AFDB	African Development Bank
APEC	Asia-Pacific Economic Cooperation
CAGR	Compound Annual Growth Rate
CPIA	Country Policy and Institutional Assessment
DRC	Democratic Republic of the Congo
EPDI	Export Product Diversification Index
EMDI	Export Market Diversification Index
FDI	Foreign Direct Investment
FT	*Financial Times*
GDP	Gross Domestic Product
GII	Global Innovation Index
GMM	Generalized Method of Moments
HDI	Human Development Index
HHI	Herfindahl–Hirschman Index
ICMM	International Council on Mining and Metals
ICT	Information and Communication Technologies
ISP	Internet Service Provider
IVA	Industry Value Added
LDC	Least Developed Country
MENA	Middle East and North African
MNC	Multinational Corporation
MVA	Manufacturing Value Added
NEXIM	Nigerian Export-Import Bank
NIE	Newly Industrialising Economy
NR	Natural Resource
R&D	Research and Development
ROK	Republic of Korea
SME	Small and Medium-Sized Enterprise
SITC	Standard International Trade Classification
TC	Technological Competence
USAID	United States Agency for International Development

USGS	United States Geological Survey
VA	Value Added
WDI	World Development Indicators
WGI	World Governance Indicators
WTO	World Trade Organization

1 Asia's Industrial Progress and Africa's Reversal of Fortune

1.1 Introduction

The early years of the 20th century were very challenging for the Asian continent; extreme poverty was rife as countries struggled through wars (Vietnam, Korea, Japan), waded through catastrophic economic decisions (China's Great Leap Forward cost at least 20 million lives), and struggled through colonial restructuring (partition in India and Pakistan). Decades later, these countries have completely transformed their economies and societies. Shedding the grips of colonial and stringent communist influences, countries marshalled private funding, sourced foreign direct investment, and repositioned themselves to maximise their comparative advantages. Small countries with little natural endowment (Hong Kong, Singapore, Taiwan) rebranded themselves as port cities and financial hubs, and larger countries harnessed their large populations to become manufacturing hubs (China, Vietnam). The average Asian who in 1950 had almost half as much income as the average African was twice as rich by 2016. The income of the average Asian had risen to 80% of that of the average global citizen. Meanwhile, Africa wallowed in poverty with its average citizen worse off, at only 40% of the worldwide average.[1]

In the early years, the Republic of Korea (ROK) was almost completely dependent on donor support for food and consumption goods, as well as raw materials and military assistance. Analysts compare its success with the rebirth of the phoenix from the ashes and destruction from the Korean War. Korea's economic breakthrough is described as the "miracle on the Han."[2] "At the time, South Korea was considered as the hellhole of foreign assistance and as a bottomless pit for money and assistance."[3] Korea had been transformed from a "bottomless pit" (as a USAID [United States Agency for International Development] report in the mid-1960s had termed it) and an "economic basket case" (as it was referred to in all too many works in development studies) to one of the world's most successful economies. From a per capita income less than Ghana's during the time of that Plan, its phenomenal growth had led it to joining the exclusive club of the world's most affluent industrial economies, the OECD, in 1996.[4] The country achieved and sustained high growth for over two decades against overwhelming odds: political turmoil; heavy defence burdens; international

DOI: 10.4324/9781003245322-1

insecurity; the world's third highest population-to-land ratio; and the highest per capita-to-farmland ratio in the world, excluding the city-states like Singapore.

On the contrary, Africa possesses huge amounts of minerals including strategic minerals. According to the United States Geological Survey (USGS) data on global mineral reserves,[5] Africa hosts cobalt (52.4%), bauxite for aluminium production (24.7%), graphite (21.2%), manganese (45.7%), and vanadium (16%).[6] According to the AfDB (African Development Bank), the current figures are just the tip of the iceberg because current exploration activities in Africa are delineating huge strategic mineral deposits.[7] Industrial products from these minerals are assuming even greater importance as demand heightened during the transition to the low carbon future including for cobalt, copper, lithium, manganese, graphite, nickel, aluminium, steel, zinc, and rare earth elements.

For example, expectedly, battery demand from electric vehicle manufacturers will increase more than nine times between 2020 and 2030. Thus, the growth of battery demand within both the continent and elsewhere represents an opportunity for developing the strategic mineral value chains in Africa based on the abundant mineral resources for battery storage technologies and electric vehicles.[8] From the current near-tragic socio-economic condition of the Democratic Republic of the Congo (DRC) and of much of Africa, the possession of minerals and raw materials is hardly the best pathway to growth and clearly has not been the basis for African development. For example, the DRC is already supplying 70% of the world's cobalt production,[9] but the bulk of the gains across the value chain have been appropriated by countries with the technological capabilities and industrial production capacity. China controls the battery chemical industry, with the biggest market share for all the five main battery metals. Diversifying the global supply chain would require significant investment from regions such as Europe and North America.[10] The economic backwardness of Africa's mineral-dependent countries in the midst of metals and minerals abundance has been due to the lack of critical scientific infrastructure, investment, and human skills.

As a commodity exporter still locked in the mining and mineral-processing stage, Africa is at the bottom of the global battery and electric vehicle value chain, expected to reach US$8.8 trillion by 2025.[11] For more than five decades, African countries have watched helplessly unable to break the vicious cycle of excessive dependence on the export of mineral resources. Asia on the other hand has extended its reach globally, including by creating multiple value chains on the continent; it did so by strengthening its productive capabilities and aggressive accumulation of technological capabilities. For example, to meaningfully participate in this market, African producers of battery minerals have to invest in stronger backward linkages between the extractive sector and other sectors of the local economy. Domestic production will demand localised procurement value chain and promote resource-driven industrialisation, including the production of battery precursors (US$271 billion by 2025), battery cells (US$387 billion by 2025), cell assembling (US$1.18 trillion by 2025), and, ultimately, electric vehicles (US$7 trillion by 2025).[12] Better integration of African battery mineral producers into global value chains will not only contribute to the achievement of the

SDGs (Sustainable Development Goals) and enlarge the share of wealth that is retained locally but also strengthen the competitiveness of local SMEs (small and medium-sized enterprises) and enable the creation of decent jobs for the youth.

This book posits that, fundamentally, Asian countries have achieved spectacular success due in large part to their pursuit of industrialisation and technological acquisition. The strategy has consisted of industrial (vertical) diversification as well as horizontal diversification in agriculture. African countries on the contrary took the low road in exporting minerals and raw agricultural commodities with little value addition. For this reason, Africa has experienced a reversal of fortune.

The rest of the chapter is organised as follows:

Section 1.2 presents income disparity among sample countries particularly African and Asian countries. Not only income disparities in recent times but also the section delineates varying growth trajectories between Asia and Africa. In the following section, we discussed how natural resources could be converted into blessings or curse, the role of governance, long tern vision for economic development, quality of institutions, and the presence of corruption in use/misuse of natural resources. Section 1.4 explains Africa's reversal of fortune while the next presents interpretation of the theoretical literature on natural resource-dependence and implications for industrialisation and economic diversification. Section 1.5 outlined stylized facts on how we interpret theoretical literature on natural resources dependence, its implications to industrialization, economic diversification and long-term development of African economies. Section 1.6 discusses how natural resource-dependence harms horizontal diversification and industrial agriculture. Finally, summary of the chapter is presented in Section 1.7.

1.2 Growth trajectory of countries

While Asian countries – many without natural commodities – were forced to creatively innovate to maximise their competitive advantages, most African countries have remained reliant on the easy money from resource exports. As fluctuating commodity prices have made volatility the norm of African countries unstable in the last decade, many have turned to their Asian counterparts for loans and aids to sustain economies that have fallen far behind. Asian nations assimilated manufacturing technologies and other aspects of the value chain that multiply the value of resources and create higher value jobs. The success of Asia proves that in less than three decades, focused leadership and sustained industrialisation can drag nations out of poverty.

Some scholars of underdevelopment posit that while African economies were awash with revenue in the 1950s from their vast commodities, the legacy of colonialism and slave trade meant there was inadequate labour to build new industry. For two centuries, between 1650 and 1850, Africa's population barely grew,[13] meaning national economies could only support monoculture exporting, needing external input for knowledge capital, technology implementation, and products processing. This is, however, no longer the case but perhaps there is an argument to be made for path-dependent institutional rigidities and mental modes that perhaps still hold Africa backwards. According to the United Nations database, the Africa population as at 2020 is estimated at be over 1.3 billion people, and expected to almost double to 2.4 billion by 2050. Of this, over 60% are currently classified as youth representing an unquantifiable potential resource.[14]

However, harnessing the potential of this latent force of youth demands both the right policies, within the right institutional setting and the right leadership mindset. In the words of Douglas North: "History demonstrates that ideas, ideologies, myths, dogmas and prejudices matter." *Institutions, Institutional Change and Economic Performance.* Cambridge: Cambridge University Press, North, D. C. (1990).

Evidently, ideas influence human behaviour which derives from a mindset, generated as thought-patterns, rational or irrational sets of assumptions, beliefs, values, or mental models of individuals, groups, societies, and even nations. Informal institution as mindset shapes development in profound but insidious ways. When society or a person loses confidence in their own ability and capacity to accomplish goals, a sense of dependency sets in. A powerful but corrupt decision-maker with a wrong motive unchecked by formal institutional rules could make choices and decisions that may send millions into poverty and deprivation.

Institutions, governance, and human behaviour explain in large part what has shaped the history of the DRC. As with most nations, endowed and resource rich; greed abounds, and corruption permeates the fabric of society. This relationship has its roots in colonialism in the case of the DRC. The DRC was once a colony of Belgium's King Leopold II, who exploited the colony's abundant resources. In 1960, the Belgian government abruptly awarded the colony its independence, resulting in a nation without the experience to govern itself efficiently. In its infancy, the nation suffered from civil war and dictatorship, both of which drained natural resources.

The bloody conflicts that have stained the DRC's postcolonial history have been funded largely by mineral wealth. In the eastern part of the DRC, illegal trade of minerals, especially coltan and gold, helps finance rebel groups. The combination of ineffective governance and abundant mining opportunities have made it relatively easy to fund insurgency, especially in this region.

Coltan is indispensable to the creation of all modern technological devices. The mineral is refined in tantalum powder, which is used to create heat-resistant capacitors in electronic goods of mass consumption, laptops, cellphones, such as mobile phones, laptops, and videogame consoles, whose profits have fuelled the largest conflict in modern African history,[15] and electric cars. Congo holds 80% of global coltan deposits, most of which are located in Kivu and Orientale, and produces 60% of the world's supply. The rise of digital technology during the last decade drives demand for coltan and will evidently persist as long as no alternative materials are found for these technological devices. The eastern part of the Democratic Republic of the Congo (DRC) is extremely rich in coltan (columbite-tantalite) and rife with conflicts.

For over ten years, companies in industrialised countries have purchased coltan despite war and lawlessness in the DRC, and they became profitable sources of foreign currency for a multitude of state and non-state actors, including rebel forces, Rwandan and Ugandan governments (and their armies), licensed companies, and poor communities with no employment opportunities.

The resulting power struggles over this valuable ore combined with the weakness of the Congolese state provoked conflict and political turmoil in the country. The war in the DRC has reached a level of complexity to the point that it has been renamed the "African World War", having involved eight African nations and 25 rebel groups and caused the highest death toll since World War II. Even though coltan is not the only cause of the Congolese war, it has been a core problem with neighbouring countries.

1.3 Africa's reversal of fortune

In order to capture the performance of Asian and African economies, average per capita income[16] of all major economies of Asia (Bangladesh, Bhutan, China, Dem. People's Rep. of Korea, India, Indonesia, Japan, Malaysia, Maldives, Myanmar, Nepal, Pakistan, Philippines, Republic of Korea, Sri Lanka, Singapore, Thailand, and Vietnam) is estimated. Similarly, the average per capita income of sub-Saharan African countries was generated from WDI (World Development Indicators) data followed by the relative movement of income in both continents. Figure 1.1 depicts the movements of relative per capita income. From the figure, it is clear that on the one hand the average income of African economies is declining, while the relative per capita income of Asian countries is increasing on the other.

Reversal of Africa's fortune manifests in economic, social, technological, and industrial conditions. Compared with comparator Asian countries, by analysing the disparities in development metrics, particularly the levels and rates of growth of national incomes and the Human Development Index (HDI), the differences

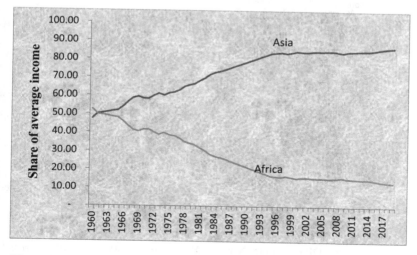

Figure 1.1 Share of average income in Asia and Africa.

are stark. For detailed analysis of major economies in both the continents we consider three 20-year periods namely: 1980, 2000, and 2019 averages. Figure 1.2 presents trends of per capita income of a few sample countries. Income has been measured as GDP per capita in USD constant at 2010. The figure presents trends of 1980, 2019, and 2000.

The Republic of Korea (ROK) has the highest GDP/capita in 2019 ($28,605.73), almost double that of 2000 (US$15,414.29), two decades earlier. The figure increased sevenfold in the 40 years from 1980 ($3679.11). On the

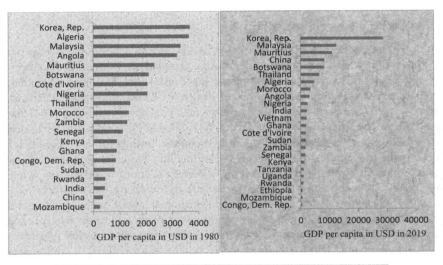

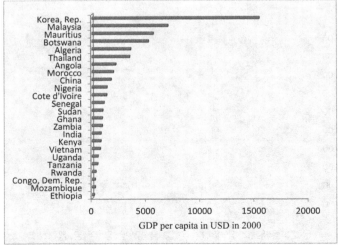

Figure 1.2 Trends in GDP per capita. Note: GDP data are constant at 2010; Source: WDI.

contrary, the GDP/capita for DRC was $845 in 1980, declined to $290 20 years later, and then rose to $424 in 2019.

All the Asian countries in the sample recorded continuous growth rates and some very rapidly while African countries increased relatively slowly and some declined. By the year 2019, the income of ROK was six times that of Algeria and nine times that of Angola, whereas all three, i.e., Algeria, Angola, and ROK had similar income levels in 1980. Forty years ago, Nigeria's income was six times that of China while Sudan had almost 2.5 times the income of China. In 2019, Chinese income became almost 3.45 times that of Nigeria and 4.79 times to that of Sudan. The widening disparities are truly shocking to say the least.

Another very important observation for poorer countries is the wide fluctuations and sudden and significant changes in growth rates, in either direction of rising and falling. Historically countries suffer reversals in fortune due to political upheavals, civil wars, and, more commonly for mineral-dependent countries, fluctuations in commodity prices.

On the other hand DRC that had far higher income ($844.50) than Mozambique ($ 37.83) in 1980 receded to third position from the bottom with an income of $289.99 in 2000. Although the income of DRC marginally improved after 2000, it remained the lowest income country (among the sample) having GDP of $423.64 in 2019. Although Rwanda's position did not change much, it had fourth position and continued to hold this position even in 2019, its income declined from 1980 to 2000 at the rate of –1.0% annually and picked up during 2000 to 2019. The economy grew at 8.25% annually in the later period. The GDP of Rwanda has been $440.31, 352.50, and 904.74 in 1980, 2000, and 2019 respectively.

1.4 Explaining Africa's reversal of fortune

The central thesis of this book is that Africa fell behind because it relied on the low-growth pathway of commodity extraction and export while Asia made spectacular progress as it took the high road of learning and mastering of technologies that undergird industrialisation. The possession of natural resources has been imputed for the thesis of resources curse. Of the 15 least diversified countries in the world, eight are in Africa.[17] Clearly, not much diversification appears to take place in Africa even among those with relatively higher income levels due largely to continuing and high dependence on natural resources of many middle-income African countries. At current estimation, natural resources account for more than one-fifth of GDP in five of the ten African countries with GDP per capita of more than $5,000.

Our basic proposition in this book is that Natural Resource (NR) abundance is not by itself a curse or a blessing. What determines the development trajectory and development outcome of NR assets including the nature of policies and the institutional context within which a country operates?

Conversion of NR assets into opportunities or curse is determined by country-specific factors that could be broadly categorised into political stability, governance, quality of institution, and economic policies. Natural resources are converted into opportunities by countries that have vision for long-term economic development while others just see NR as everlasting resources and remain solely dependent on these resources. The prevalence of rent-seeking policies results into resource curse while the use of NR as a means for development leads to resource blessings.

We have witnessed the uneven growth in wealth between the two regions. Clearly, the state and institutional capabilities underlying the generation and diffusion of knowledge and how that underlies the development dynamics are central. In the following sections and chapters, we analyse factors that separate the countries that made rapid progress in "catching up" and those that tend to be stagnating and "falling behind".

In what follows, we outline the stylised facts of how we interpret the theoretical literature on NR-dependence, implications for industrialisation, economic diversification, and what it all means for long-term development of African economies. Economic diversification induced by structural transformation is undergirded by industrial and technological capacity-building resulting in a shift towards higher productivity sectors, higher skills employment, and shrinking informal sector.

1.5 Stylised facts

1.5.1 Natural resource curse or blessing?

Are natural resources a "curse" or a "blessing"? The empirical evidence suggests that the trajectory of a country's development creates the resultant outcome: blessing or a curse. We have learnt from history that countries that make successful use of natural wealth by converting such into assets for their citizens do so by constructing a framework of sustainable macroeconomic policies, equitable governance system, intolerance of corruption, etc. For example, countries such as the United Arab Emirates, Norway, Singapore, and Malaysia among others, have turned their natural resources into blessings due to obligatory focus on human resource development policies, and expansion of physical and technological infrastructure. Subsequently these countries went into a virtuous circle of economic growth which helped to raise the living standard of citizens.

On the other hand, some other countries, namely, DRC, Nigeria, Venezuela, Iran, and Libya, among others, have witnessed their natural wealth turned into a resource curse due to lack of long-term vision of development, unequal distribution of income leading to social unrest, bad governance, presence of high levels of corruption, and lost opportunity for industrialisation. These countries have allowed an environment that fosters rent-seeking activities rather than creating institutional structures that turn their natural resources into assets. Dependence on oil exports tends to exacerbate inequality in society and increases the number of poor people. Examples confirming this assertion are Nigeria, DRC, and Angola, where in recent decades the number of poor people has increased significantly.

This section summarises the key findings from the literature including qualitative and quantitative surveys on the issue of resource abundance and its relationship with key parameters. We put these forward as stylised facts that will be articulated in subsequent chapters as to why a set of countries enjoys their natural resources while others suffer.

There are two broad sets of explanatory variables, firstly political factors focusing on the notion of resource curse (rentier state theories, rent seeking, conflict, corruption, among others.) The second set is economic variables (volatility of commodities cycles, Dutch disease, and exchange rate fluctuations among others). What is becoming clear is that these factors do not point to some inevitability of bad outcomes resulting from resource abundance.

The most prominent set of issues relates to resource boom, commodity super cycle, and how these induce volatility and appreciation of the real exchange rate. Other notions include the connection of resource-dependence and rent-seeking behaviour; the triggering of civil conflict, ethnic fractionalisation particularly in the context of dysfunctional institutions, and prevalence of corruption.[18] Finally, and most critical for long-development, is that resource-rich developing economies tend to forgo industrialisation and technological acquisition and as well experience the least diversification and structural transformation. This is an issue that is not often treated in the literature, which we will take up more systematically in Chapter five.

1.5.2 Natural resource-dependence undermines industrialisation and innovation

A key finding resonating in the literature on resource abundance is the role of institutions in explaining resource blessing or curse. First, that within strong institutional contexts, it is possible for policies to prevent the Dutch disease effect; however, this has been very rare in the experience of developing countries and hardly so in the African experience, except for Botswana.

The conventional wisdom on resource-abundance much earlier was that of a "blessing" not a "curse". Several scholars attributed economic development of earlier industrial nations to their mineral and commodities abundance as the driver of economic development.[19] Latecomer countries that pursue technology-driven horizontal and vertical diversification especially at the low-income stage such as Malaysia and Vietnam have proved that *resource-abundance*, as opposed to *resource-dependence* could supply the needed investment capital for latecomer economies to achieve sustainable growth.[20] In other words, the development outcome of a country possessing abundant natural resources, including improvements in economic and human development, is not as a result of the asset itself but rather on the rate and direction of technologies applied, the structure of knowledge institutions, and the technological capabilities that a country explicitly invest in.

The economic growth of the United States (US) for example was, in part, made possible by resource-based industrialisation in the 20th century, through the manufacturing of iron ore, coal, lead, nickel, zinc, antimony, copper, and oil (Wright and Czelusta 2007). However, this was because the US had built a relatively strong industrial and technological base; it invested in research, innovation, and technologies that enabled resource extraction and beneficiation. This was supported by strong state knowledge institutional structures such as engineering universities and the US Geological Survey; these provided the knowledge, skill, and training in mining, minerals, and metallurgy, (Andersen, 2012).

In other words, unlike the low levels of scientific and technological human capital, and weak knowledge systems with which poorer resource-dependent African countries started at independence, the experiences of more advanced resource-rich countries that had accumulated pertinent technology, skills, and knowledge were different. The extant capabilities within these countries enabled the NR sector to lead the industrialisation drive. By these the technologies fostered backward and forward linkages of the natural resource sectors through new oil and mineral discovery, extraction, and resource-processing technologies and processes, as well as moved the countries into new industries related to the resource sectors. The European experiences, as well as the Scandinavian and Australian, among others, were not dissimilar; in other words, resource-based industrialisation has to be underpinned by a strong legal, knowledge institution, and requisite technological capabilities. Absent these critical pillars, perverse institutions that retard industrialisation tend to develop and entrench. In the same manner, Sweden in the early phases of its development exported a boom of cereals and sawn wood and later, pulp, paper, and iron ore from the mid-19th century, (Blomström and Kokko, 2007). The country embarked subsequently on diversification by the acquisition and adoption of technologies, through learning, adaptation, and subsequently innovation, particularly by investing in dynamic domestic knowledge clusters. These comprised networks of private sector-led research institutes, universities, firms, and public investment in industry-oriented skills formation.[21]

Australia is another country that invested heavily in human capital and engineering skills to harness its abundant natural resources such as bauxite, nickel, silver, copper, and gold dating back to the 1960s. The investment consisted of training in engineering education and R&D (Research and Development) with mining accounting for 20% of total R&D in 1995/1996 (Wright and Czelusta, 2007). Today, Australia is a world leader in mining software systems, home to global mining exploration ventures, and an important global supplier of high-tech services and equipment to meet the demand for safer and cleaner mineral extraction and processing processes.

The country experiences reviewed above show that investment in domestic technological capabilities underlined the success of resource-based industrialisation (downstream, upstream, and horizontal). Investment in education and training especially engineering and vocational skills; strong public–private partnerships, and alignment of different policy tools, including industrial strategy ones, emerge as recurrent factors. Ultimately, these hinged on the countries' policy frameworks and institutional capabilities.

In an advanced economy with a strong industrial technological foundation, proceeds from hydrocarbons tend to flow into the productive sector of a country's economy to develop infrastructure that further supports critical sectors' design of manufacturing equipment, as well as research and development (R&D). All these investments in the long run strengthen the export base of developed nations and reduce their volume of imports leading to a favourable balance of trade. In Canada for instance, the extractive industry (mining sector) contributed $109 billion or 5% of Canada's total nominal GDP and the industry's direct and indirect employment accounts for 71,9000 jobs in 2019.

Unlike the experiences of the advanced industrial countries cited, today's mineral-rich African countries have not succeeded to industrialise. Studies including Auty and Evans provide evidence that mineral exports are negatively correlated with growth. While the slew of reasons given for the inability of countries to effectively transform natural resources to growth, namely, the Dutch disease; rent seeking and conflicts; corruption and compromised political institutions; lack of technological and industrial capabilities lead to low economic diversification and unsuccessful structural transformation. For example, Africa's oil and gas sector makes only a small contribution to GDP despite generating the majority of export earnings, as it is a highly technology and capital-intensive industry that employs few people. The materials and equipment used in the exploration and production are not produced in-country and therefore it has limited horizontal interconnection to the domestic economy. There is minimal domestic manufacturing input in the oil sector, especially in the oil product refining. The local content makes up about 5% in goods and services. The same situation applies for Zambia's cooper, for example.[22] The International Council on Mining and Metals (ICMM) estimated that domestic manufacturers supplied a very small share of Zambian mining inputs. Domestic procurement was estimated to be around US$1.75 billion annually, of which 5% (or US$87 million) represents locally manufactured goods. The reasons for the weak systemic capacity include low horizontal integration of local suppliers, lack of competitiveness, and relative technological capabilities to meet standards.

The economic growth experienced by developing nations is tied to the income generated from rents and sales of the resources in the international markets. However, exports of fossil fuels and minerals even when they lead to annual growth in GDP, do not translate to improved human capital, and manufacturing value added.

As we demonstrate in subsequent chapters, Africa's industrial performance, measured in terms of the industry value added (IVA) and manufacturing value added (MVA) in GDP, has been lagging far behind comparator countries in Asia. MVA, which measures the degree of industrial processing remain low in Africa, signifying the lack of industrial dynamism. This is consistent with the continent's reliance on exports of its abundant natural resources, especially mineral and agricultural resources.

The phenomenon of the Dutch disease also points to the reason for poor industrial growth. The reason is that whenever there is a resource boom, the extra revenue accruing from the sale of natural resources (oil and minerals) triggers appreciation of the real exchange rate and subsequent contraction of the traded sector (Corden and Neary, 1982; Corden, 1984).

1.5.3 Natural resource-dependence jeopardises technological learning and economic growth

We will show in Chapter 5 of this book that economic development is driven largely by industrial manufacturing and that the key requirement is technological learning, the driver for economic diversification and structural transformation. Countries that are locked in to resource extraction and trade tend to record decline in the traded sector once they begin to enjoy resource trade boom. Studies show that higher resource revenue leads to movement of labour from the traded (manufacturing at core) to the non-traded sector. Given that manufacturing grows through learning-by-doing, there is a progressive diminishing of technological capital and, by implication, overall rate of industrialisation. According to Esanov: "the resource boom permanently lowers the rate of growth. One can show that non-resource GDP falls on impact after a resource discovery if the traded sector is capital-intensive."[23]

An important reason why oil-producing countries experience technical lock-in is the difficulty of spillovers into other sectors due to the unique processing techniques and skills that underpin petroleum refining. Therefore, there is weak horizontal connection through the learning-by-doing process that occurs in the oil sector. This is echoed by the "product space" framework whereby countries find it relatively easier to diversify by deploying capabilities acquired from other products they had specialised in to master new sectors requiring the same skills and technical capabilities.[24]

History shows us that nations accumulated wealth only from the accumulation of technological capacity that enables both horizontal and vertical diversification through learning to produce a more complex and wider set of innovation-driven products, goods, and services. However, the negative externalities from resource boom almost always impact the traded sector (manufacturing) which is the engine of growth and the greater beneficiary from learning-by-doing and other positive externalities. Prolonged and non-mitigated influence of the extractive economy on non-resource export sectors impacts the process of learning and competitiveness which is a long-term process.

For example, the academic literature seems to suggest that resource boom impact and mineral dependence tend to manifest in negative outcome largely in poor countries. The most poignant evidence is that these countries, after several decades of independence, remain dependent on multinational oil and mineral companies in both upstream and downstream activities. This is contrary to the experiences of the more developed economies and that of more advanced Asian economies that have achieved significant diversification; the latter over the last 40 years. In the early years of the 20th century the United States dominated the global trade and production of almost all major industrial minerals, surpassing nations with bigger mineral reserves due to its superior technical capacity.[25]

In regional comparative perspective with Africa, Asian countries like Malaysia, Korea, and, lately, Vietnam have diversified significantly despite its significant deposit of natural resources. Malaysia's GDP and exports comprise significant manufacturing activities that drove the increase in GDP per capita. Over time, the share of low technology such as food and textiles in this country has reduced while machinery accounts for a very significant share and both machinery and other manufactures comprise a large majority of the value added originating from the manufacturing sector.

Malaysia through deliberate policy actions, diversified its export over the last five decades while a country like Nigeria with very similar agricultural endowment did not diversify. Exports of manufactures by Malaysia reached 80% of total exports by 2000 with the electronics sector accounting for a large share of the country's manufactured exports. Additionally, it succeeded with horizontal diversification of its rich agro-business sectors namely, rubber, palm oil, and petroleum industries that contributed to its dynamic industrial base.

Vietnam is endowed with other natural resources such as coal, phosphates, rare earth elements, bauxite, chromate, copper, gold, iron, manganese, silver, zinc, offshore oil and gas deposits, timber, hydropower. The natural resources diminished after 1980 and its contribution to GDP fell substantially. Subsequently, the country's focus shifted to manufacturing and services from agriculture and crude oil exports; it succeeded to diversify economic activities rather than depending on natural resources. Subsequently, the percentage GDP contribution of mineral and oil resources gradually reduced and is now relatively small as far as mineral, crude oil, and natural resources are concerned. The GDP contribution of natural resources was highest (14.18%) in 2008 while in case of crude oil it was less than 10% (8.98% in 2006).

Clearly, resource-rich economies may turn such assets into a curse by relying exclusively on these commodities as sources of export revenue which exposes them to a regime of volatility and foreign exchange shocks. The blessing is lost when countries fail to develop autonomous capabilities for processing such as oil refining by which systemic learning is forgone. Investment in minerals-related knowledge seems a legitimate component of a forward-looking development programme.

In sum, the prevalence of resource curse is a peculiar feature of some but not all countries, especially developing countries that discovered minerals and oil resources in the absence of the pertinent technological and human capabilities to explore, extract, and process them. Second, the phenomenon of resource curse, in terms of time frame, has become prominent only in the last 50 years, which correspond roughly to the period when most of these countries that bear the burden of a "curse" attained independence. We suggest that a combination of relatively strong knowledge system including universities and vocational education assets, legal and political institutions, and the right technologies underpinned the resource blessing of the older nations.

1.5.4 Good institutions underpin resource blessing, bad institutions foster resource curse

Institutions in Africa exhibit profound ineffectiveness in responding to development challenges.[26] The most telling recent examples have been the current and past outbreaks of pandemics, commodity prices boom and busts, and locust invasions, among others. The devastating impacts of these profoundly damaging crises could not trigger short- and longer-term strategic solutions as there have been no institutions for responding to crises including production of medicines and vaccines. It is hard to find scientific organisations and institutions with comparable capacity as comparators outside the continent. When coupled with poorly functioning policy-making bureaucracies, Africa can be said to be characterised by lack of both broad and specific competencies in their coordination functions. For the most part, we have a situation in which policy coordination is largely politically driven in the absence of strong market coordination.

A critical institutional gap is the lack of industrial and development finance structures dedicated to long-term industrial development. Poor financial commitment for meeting organisational goals results in disillusionment of scientists and policy researchers over time leading to migration and brain drain. We also have here a lack of private sector trust in collaborations with public sector institutions; this has jeopardised the rise of a vibrant private sector since organisations that promote the growth of private sector firms are missing. Their inefficiencies give rise to the poor coordination of knowledge and economic production functions, leading to imbalances in the demand and supply for skills of the right kinds, quantity, and quality mix at sectoral levels and over time.

Oil wealth tends to become a barrier to building and nurturing quality institutions that undergird industrial and scientific dynamism. Bureaucratic and political elites are entwined in corruption practices, patronage, and granting of import licences and other privileges to friends and associates. Bad governance and corruption seem to be far more debilitating and explain in large part why oil bonanzas over several decade have undermined the performance of the Nigerian economy (Sala-i-Martin and Subramanian, 2003).

The race to occupy political office has meant that resource abundance engenders the appetite and propensity to vie for power; it is no secret that the path to high-level political office is strewn with all manner of financial voter inducement in low-income countries. Extractive economic regimes so run, ensure that politicians have zero accountability to the electorate; the voters once bribed, lose the right to "democracy dividends". Given the lack of accountability pressure, government business is not managed by competence and the beneficiaries are not those who build factories. In this way, natural resources abundance is a culprit in blocking the evolution of technological and institutional structures.[27]

Another reason why bad institutions undermine industrial growth is that natural resource windfall rather than promote traded sectors, pushes productive entrepreneurs into rent seeking. Clearly, there are differences between countries with "production-friendly institutions and others with rent grabbing-friendly institutions" (Mehlum et al., 2006).

When resource-rich countries are blessed with requisite strong institutions such as with Australia, Canada, the US, New Zealand, Iceland, and Norway, and also Botswana (Acemoglu et al., 2003), wealth becomes a blessing. However, if institutions are dysfunctional, and the legal system is subject to the whims of the powerful, rent seeking becomes far more profitable than manufacturing and other similar businesses requiring hard work. Evidently, weak institutions may explain poor performance of oil-rich states such as Angola, Nigeria, Sudan, and Venezuela, diamond-rich Sierra Leone, Liberia, and Congo, and drug states Columbia and Afghanistan. There, institutions are themselves products of long historical and colonial origins.

1.5.5 Natural resource-dependence harms horizontal diversification and industrial agriculture

An important historical difference between Asia and Africa is the achievement of the Green Revolution by the former followed closely by different levels of industrial revolution. Africa achieved neither. Agricultural productivity growth propelled by structural transformation depends in large part on the industrial manufacturing sector, especially its capital goods subsector, which could generate other productive inputs. The development of capabilities in industrial agriculture would determine productivity and ultimately long-term development performance of economies.

The significant difference in productivity undergirds the wide income per worker of farmers working in rural areas and those employing modern methods. What distinguishes the subsistence and modern industrialised agriculture is fundamentally in the productivity gaps, which transmits to, and is reflected in, differences in their living standards. This large and persistent difference in agricultural productivity gaps in 2020 is striking given that Arthur Lewis (1955) pointed it out[28] in his 1954 *Manchester School* paper: Lewis summarised a part of his argument thus:

> The main sources from which workers come as economic development proceeds are subsistence agriculture, casual labour, petty trade, ... and the increase in population. In most but not all of these sectors, ... the marginal productivity of labour is negligible.

Development economists have stressed the pivotal role of manufacturing and clearly recognise its inextricable link with agriculture. The lesson of history is that the development process is fundamentally linked to the reallocation of workers out of agriculture and into "modern" economic activities.[29] When the transition through structural transformation does not occur, it leads to the misallocation of workers across agriculture and non-agriculture that explains in large part the international income and productivity differences. Oyelaran-Oyeyinka and Lal

(2017) made the point with empirical evidence that the reallocation of capital and labour to the most productive sectors through structural change fuel economic growth, and significantly raise per capita income in low-income African and Asian countries.

The main sources of productivity growth are the adoption of advanced technologies and upgrading of endogenous skills of the workforce; both inputs are expected to result in higher productivity.

According to an OECD-FAO projection, the top three exporters of rice by the year 2025 remain India, Thailand, and Vietnam – these countries have been responsible for over 65% of total exports. By 2025, Vietnam is expected to overtake India, making Vietnam the largest exporter. In this period, the export share of the top three exporters will drop to less than 60% due to the emergence of Cambodia and Myanmar as major rice exporters.

1.5.6 Africa's slow transition from subsistence to industrial agriculture

From the forgoing, there are two broad concepts of agriculture, namely, industrialised agriculture and subsistence agriculture. Industrial agriculture is underpinned by modern scientific and technological techniques designed to produce crops and livestock on a large scale and distributed based on modern supply chain logistics. One of the most important objectives of industrial agriculture is to increase crop yield, which is the amount of food that is produced for each unit of land.

Industrialising agriculture therefore involves the mastery of the applied sciences that encompass the full range of agro-industry including crop production horticulture, livestock, fisheries, and forestry. The management dimension includes the art, science, and business of producing crops and livestock for economic purposes. Central to raising yield is the application of a broad range of science and technologies such as crop breeding, production techniques, crop protection, and economics among others. The investment in, and mastery of, the above technologies, is what separates modern agriculture business from subsistence practices which characterise the life of the rural population.

Industrialised agriculture is therefore designed to realise economy of scale driven by mechanisation – replacing animal and labour – leading to production of large quantities of food at lower costs. The adoption of industrialised agriculture involves the utilisation of farm machines, investment in large irrigation systems, and use of chemical fertilizers, improved seed varieties, and pesticides.

The agriculture sector accounts for a large percentage of employment and value added in developing countries. Usually, agriculture's share of employment is higher than its share of value added, meaning that value added per worker is higher in the non-agriculture sector than in agriculture. Also, as with most developing countries, measured Value Added (VA) per worker is ordinarily relatively lower in agriculture compared with other sectors of the economy such as manufacturing and services. In theory, based on simple two-sector models the prediction is that value added per worker should be equal in agriculture and "non-agriculture".[30] However, value added per worker for most developing countries, is four times higher in non-agriculture than the agriculture sector. In sub-Saharan Africa, the difference is much larger; it could be as high as with a factor of ten.

These large agricultural productivity differences imply that African countries lag other regions by much wider gaps in agriculture than in non-agriculture, Vollrath (2009). In addition, the failure to modernise agriculture suggests that the problem of Africa's economic development is fundamentally connected to not just poor adoption of modern technological methods but also the dysfunction associated with "misallocation" of workers across sectors, with too many workers in the less productive agriculture sector.[31] There continue to be high contribution of the agricultural sector to GDP, which points to the poor diversification of most African economies. On average, in the region, agriculture contributes 15% of total GDP, but this average masks the wide variations across the countries.

Figure 1.3 shows the trend in agriculture value added as a share of GDP in sub-Sahara African countries compared to that of the rest of the world comparatively 2000 and 2019. The analyses show that agriculture value added as a percentage of GDP is higher among sub-Sahara African countries than the rest of the world. The values in 2000 range from 2.79% (Botswana) to 44.67% (Ethiopia) in 2000 in sub-Sahara Africa and from 0.86% (United Kingdom) and 21.61% (India) in 2000 for the developed countries. The high agriculture value added recorded for sub-Sahara African countries shows lack of diversification into

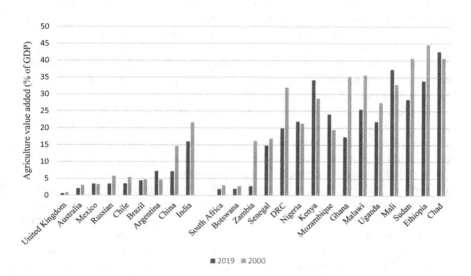

Figure 1.3 Agriculture value added (% of GDP) – 2000/2019. Source: World Development Indicators, World Bank, 2020.

high-value high-productivity products, which means Africa continues its reliance on non-processed agriculture.

In 2019, sub-Sahara African countries maintained higher values than the rest of the world, with values ranging from 1.89% (South Africa) to 42.59% (Chad) while values in the developed countries ranges from 0.61% (United Kingdom) to 15.97% (India). We plotted the values in 2000 against that of 2019. The chart shows that the share of agriculture value added in GDP declined for all the developed countries considered except Argentina in 2019 compared to that of 2000, whereas for some of the sub-Sahara African countries such as Kenya, Mozambique, Mali, and Chad the values of 2019 increased above the values in 2000.

The implications are myriad. First, the current structure of agriculture suggests that workers such as farmers and, in general, agricultural households specifically, would continue to endure lower living standards compared with workers in manufacturing. Second, low productivity and limited value addition to agricultural commodities means low GDP contribution of agriculture to the economy, as well as limited sectoral employment opportunities for rural dwellers including women. Third, as the main source of income for Africa's rural population – estimated to represent 64% of the total – low VA perpetuates mass poverty.

Fourth, Africa has and would continue to suffer persistent and high incidence of undernourishment, far higher than other regions of the world as it continues to import food staples estimated at around US$50 billion a year. Africa's rural farming population is made up predominantly of a high percentage of smallholder farmers (80%) who cultivate low-yield staple food crops on small acreages of land. These farmers do not use quality inputs such as seed and fertilizer.

The situation of low productivity applies across the full value chain both at the farm level (low crop yield) and at the manufacturing processing level and constitutes a barrier to structural transformation which requires that rising productivity frees up labour to move out of agriculture into manufacturing. In other words, the level of value addition and crop processing of agricultural commodities is low and post-harvest losses in sub-Saharan Africa average 30% of total production, meaning that the region loses over US$4 billion each year.

For the forgoing reasons, the human capabilities and technological infrastructure to increase farm yields as well as manufacturing value added (MVA) are extremely important especially as global demand for high-value agricultural products including processed and packaged food increases relative to raw materials. Value added processing activities in agro-processing create end-to-end, on-and-off farm jobs, raise incomes and, more broadly, the quality of life of rural dwellers especially smallholder farmers. In addition, new techniques of production serve to raise the technical capacity of hitherto unskilled workers while integrating them into the virtuous circle of more modern and efficient value chains.

To improve workers well-being, explicit policy steps have to be taken to improve Africa's agricultural productivity, which is currently ranked the lowest in the world, with US$335 of VA per worker. Achieving higher labour productivity and growth in yield to meet that of Asia and other regions would require investments in education and training of farmers as industrialised agriculture is knowledge driven. Urgent actions are required in the face of rapid technological and scientific advances and applications and, as well, the challenges of climate change that equally threaten further negative effects on yield growth.

1.6 Malaysia: a case of successful horizontal and vertical diversification

Malaysia is a typical example of an economy that though endowed with abundant natural resources has been successful in diversifying its economy over its five decades of post-independence growth and development. Since the country gained its independence from Britain in 1957, the economy has diversified beyond agriculture and primary commodities. The economy shifted from being one dominated by tin, agriculture, and exports of agricultural commodities to an economy that is more industrialised. Its manufactured exports now constitute a sizable share of total exports and GDP while agriculture's share of GDP dropped from about 26% in 1971 to about 10% in 1995 and 8% in 2005.

Malaysia's growth record has not been a uniform one as the country has experienced volatile growth in its economic history. Over the course of its post-independence years, it has experienced periods of slow and fast growth. In the late 1970s, public investment played a more active role in the economy to support affirmative action policies. Economic growth of the 1980s was relatively higher compared to the 1970s and this growth was engineered by the drive for industrialisation, introduction of pro-growth policies and a push for heavy industries that began in the second half of the 1980s. During the 1990s, growth averaged more than 8% per annum up until the verge of the financial crisis where there was more liberalisation, greater foreign direct investment inflows and an expanded role for private investment.

From 1991, export diversification become intensified and at a fast pace as the export of goods and services grew at 17% per annum. The trade intensity ratio, which was about 86.9% of GDP in 1970, increased to about 228.9% by 2000. Malaysia's export structure has witnessed dramatic change from the export of tin, rubber, and palm oil, which dominated its export in the 1950s and 1960s to exports of manufactured goods such as electronics and electrical products. Imports of intermediate goods were on the increase due to their importance in manufactured export. The basis for this export-led growth in the manufacturing sector is due to the industrial policy approach adopted by the Malaysian government, which supported exporters by providing tax holidays and creating export processing zones. The government also used tariffs, import restrictions, and government procurement of locally produced goods to promote exports and protect domestic manufacturers.

Economic growth has been accompanied by the greater importance of trade to the Malaysian economy and the growth of the manufacturing sector from the 1980s to date. Foreign direct investment (FDI) played a central role in the diversification of the economy and the growth of the manufactured exports has contributed much to the diversification of Malaysia's exports. Generally, Malaysia has kept its economy relatively open. Subsequently, Malaysia's industrial policy approach has been incorporated in its industrial master plans and long-term planning documents designed to promote specific manufacturing industries of which the most recent is that which covers the period from 2016 to 2020. Ideally, these plans have identified various manufacturing industries that could be promoted, be they resource-based or non-resource based manufacturing industries. In effect, Malaysia's economic diversification is a typical example of a combination of horizontal and vertical diversification, where horizontal diversification entails the policies that promote increasing the production of an existing export commodity while vertical diversification involves adding value to the existing product or production of new products. This is evident in Malaysia's rubber export, as it also manufactures rubber products like tyres and gloves, making it the biggest producer of rubber gloves, diversifying into higher-end products of medical gloves for the health sector.

In sum, the Malaysian government actively implements policies and strategies they set after conducting research on the global economy and assessing the impact of global competition on the domestic economy. However, their policy goal is directed towards becoming a high-income economy and a developed country by 2020. Hence, the New Economic Model spanning from 2011 to 2020 incorporates the period of the Tenth Malaysia Plan, 2011–2015. This recent diversification policy maintains the openness of the economy to international trade and exploits the trade opportunities in the new markets for Malaysian export in Asian and non-Asian countries (Yusof, 2010).

1.7 Summing up

The main thrust of the chapter has been on the causes of reversal of Africa's fortune. The chapter brings out empirical evidence to show that four decades ago many "Asian Tigers" had income several times less than many African countries and by the second decade of the 21st century they converted themselves to world leaders with income several times higher than their African counterparts. For instance, Nigeria's per capita income in 1980 was six times that of China and per capita income of China is almost three and half times that of Nigeria in 2019. On comparing average per capita income of Asia with Africa we found that Africa was ahead of Asia before the 1960s. Thereafter relative average per capita income in Asia has been increasing while in Africa it has been declining and the ever-increasing gap has been enormous in both the continents in recent times.

The chapter also brings out the possible reasons for this scenario. It is evidently established that endowment of natural resources is Africa has proved to be a curse for the region while it has become a blessing for Asia. The conversion of natural resources into opportunities or curse is reliant on country-specific factors that could be broadly categorised into political stability, governance, presence of corruption, quality of institution, and economic policies. Improvement in these factors in Asia has put the region in a virtuous circle of prosperity and development. On the other hand, Africa has treated natural resource assets as an everlasting resource and has been engaged in rent-seeking activities. Consequently, the region has gone into a vicious circle of poverty and underdevelopment.

Finally, it is recommended that Africa needs to change its mindset and embark on policies that focus on diversification in manufacturing, the agro-processing industry, and the services sector rather than relying on production and exports of products based on natural resources. The successful implementation of such policies is expected to bring out the region from a vicious circle. That would not only ensure economic stability in the region but also enable it to have more sustainable development regime.

Notes

1 *Quartz*, January 23, 2018; Preeti Varathan, 'Reversal of fortune: The recent history of the global economy, in one chart', (https://qz.com/1183308/the-economic-reversal-of-asia-and-africa-in-one-striking-chart/); accessed October 10, 2020.
2 Koen (1977); Woronoff (1983).
3 This was an answer to what Korea was like in the 1970s, development economist Irma Adelman's response to Professor David Zilberman, who conducted the interviews, asked Irma about her first impressions of Korea at the time. Cited in: https://mdp.berkeley.edu/history-biography-and-the-miracle-on-the-han/; accessed July 2, 2021.
4 https://thewire.in/economy/the-bitter-taste-of-failure; accessed July 2, 2021.
5 U.S. Geological Survey (2021).
6 Cobalt (DRC – 51%, Madagascar – 1.4%); bauxite for aluminium production (Guinea – 24.7%); graphite (Madagascar – 8.1%, Mozambique – 7.8%, Tanzania – 5.3%); manganese (South Africa – 40%, Gabon – 4.7%, Ghana – 1%,) and vanadium (South Africa – 16%).
7 An example, is the 400 million metric tonnes lithium deposit delineated in the DRC (Manono deposit).
8 Global Battery Alliance (2019).
9 And account for 50% of global cobalt reserves.
10 China controls 80% of the cobalt sulphate market. Four out of the top five producers by nameplate capacity are in China. The exception is Finland's Kokkola refinery, with a 14,500-ton capacity. The remaining four companies have 67,000 tons of capacity in China (BNEF, 2021).
11 Bloomberg New Energy Finance (BNEF, 2020).
12 BNEF (2020).
13 isj.org.uk/africa-rising/.
14 World Bank Database, https://data.worldbank.org/; accessed October 11, 2020.
15 https://reliefweb.int/report/democratic-republic-congo/coltan-and-conflict-drc; accessed July 3, 2021.
16 Incomes are estimated based on constant USD in 2010.
17 International Monetary Fund's Export Diversification Index (2020).
18 van der Ploeg (2011).
19 Innis (1956).
20 Viner (1952), Lewis (1955).
21 www.wider.unu.edu/sites/default/files/wp2016-83.pdf; accessed July 26, 2021.

22 https://thenationonlineng.net/sanusis-critical-treatise-on-state-of-the-nation/; accessed July 28, 2021.
23 Economic Diversification: Dynamics, Determinants and Policy Implications, Akram Esanov.
24 Hidalgo et al. (2007) and Hausmann et al. (2013).
25 The US share of world mineral production in 1913 was far in excess of its share of world reserves; mineral-rich countries like Brazil, Chile, Russia, Canada, and Australia did much worse in developing new reserves and cheaper techniques (David and Wright, 1997).
26 Oyelaran-Oyeyinka and Gehl-Sampath, *Latecomer Development* (2010).
27 Robinson and Acemoglu, 2006, made the point that growth of manufacturing can weaken the power of political elites.
28 Lewis (1955) *Theory of Economic Growth.*
29 Lewis (1955).
30 www.theigc.org/project/the-agricultural-productivity-gap-in-developing-countries/; accessed October 1, 2020.
31 www.theigc.org/project/the-agricultural-productivity-gap-in-developing-countries/; accessed October 3, 2020.

2 Export Diversification in Resource and Non-Resource Rich Asian and African Countries

2.1 Introduction

There has been a long history in the economic development literature articulating the economic development benefits of export-promotion strategies. The importance of trade, particularly exports, for economic growth is widely discussed in the academic literature (Emery, 1967; Keesing, 1967; Michaely, 1977; Feder, 1982; Edwards, 1993). The rationale for export expansion includes the following. First, export development allows the home country to focus investment on those sectors where it enjoys a comparative advantage, consistent with neoclassical trade theory (Heckscher, 1919; Ohlin, 1933; Samuelson, 1948). The resulting specialisation is likely to augment overall productivity. Second, the resulting economies of scale foster a gain of larger international markets, which allows the country to compete in the export sector. Third, global competitive pressures are likely to lead to a reduction in inefficiencies in export production leading to the adoption of relatively efficient techniques in the traded sector. Finally, a larger export sector would avail more of the resources required to import in a timely manner both physical and human capital, including advanced technologies in production and management, and for training high-quality labour (Fosu, 2001b). The above are strong rationale to engage with diversified exports especially for low-income African economies with small internal markets (Fosu, 2001a; Helleiner, 1992; Lussier, 1993).

The importance of trade for growth and development dates back to classical trade theory that stipulates that countries should specialise in producing and exporting commodities in which they have comparative advantage (Heckscher, 1919; Ohlin, 1933; Samuelson, 1948). If countries accept this as a basis of their development, African countries, for example, would continue to export primary products, while importing manufactures. However, recent theoretical and empirical studies have on the contrary emphasised the importance of a broader export diversification, rather than export specialisation (Herzer and Nowak-Lehmann, 2006). This conceptual shift may be traceable to several factors. First, broader export diversification favourably influences the pattern of growth and structural transformation that countries and regions experience. Second, export diversification increases a country's ability to meet such goals as job creation and

DOI: 10.4324/9781003245322-2

improvements in income distribution (Hausmann and Klinger, 2006; Hwang, 2006). Third, export diversification tends to attenuate export revenue instability and volatilities in imports and capital, which tend to be growth inhibiting (Fosu, 1991, 2001). To mitigate particularly the challenges of relative instabilities associated with concentrating in commodity exports, the current view is that countries should consider diversifying.

There is evidence that a strong link exists between the poor state of export diversification and the dismal nature of employment creation in developing countries, especially in Africa (Oyelaran-Oyeyinka and Lal, 2017; FAO, 2004). Creating meaningful and stable employment usually requires relatively high and stable growth, which in turn is dependent on exports diversification that allows a country to spread its risks over a broader number of countries and commodities, and to hedge against real and potential terms of trade shocks emanating from commodity prices (Acemoglu and Zilibotti, 1997). Indeed, it is widely believed that the considerable progress in the structural transformation of leading Asian countries has been the result of the shift towards economic diversification, that is, from primary to labour-intensive manufactured exports, and further to more resource-intensive manufactures (World Bank, 1993; Sarel, 1996).

We organise the rest of the chapter as follows: Section 2.2 provides a selected literature review of export diversification in oil-rich countries compared with non-oil emerging countries in Africa and Asia. We then follow with an analysis of selected oil-rich and non-oil-dependent Asian and African countries in Section 2.3.

2.2 Export diversification in oil-rich countries and emerging economies

Economic diversification is a desirable policy objective amongst most oil-rich countries (Ahmadov, 2014; Alsharif et al., 2016). Theoretical and empirical literature show that economic diversification hedges against the effect of commodity price volatility, which is a major source of fiscal disruption for resource-dependent economies, while aiding employment creation in non-oil sectors, inter-sectoral linkages, and consequent skill transfers – with its potential long-term benefits – to the domestic environment (Auty, 2001; Lederman and Maloney, 2003; Collier and Page, 2009).

There are several and diverse insights from empirical studies which examined the impact of export diversification on the economy of oil-rich countries, (Cadot, Carrere, and Strauss-Kahn, 2013). The mixed results could be due to a wide variety of reasons including the type of data used and scope of coverage (Ross, 2017); it could be an understanding of measurement of diversification-related concepts as well as selection bias problems. In cases of missing or unreliable data on oil-exporting countries, analysis results can be misleading (Ross, 2012). According to Battaile and Mishra (2015), only a handful of oil-dependent countries report impressive growth in exports due to the classification of refined oil products as manufactured output, thus making the level of economic diversification and exports diversification difficult to estimate (McMillan et al., 2014; Alsharif et al., 2016). Measuring export diversification by means of commodity price volatility is also fraught with errors due to the narrow export basket of oil-dependent countries. In panel studies of oil-rich economies, the issue of selection bias may arise. For instance, studies may adopt the IMF's definition of oil-rich economies as one which consists of at least 20% of oil, gas, and other minerals (Ahmadov, 2014; Gelb, 2010). Investigating export diversification through such preselected samples may lead to inferential bias, because oil-rich countries whose exports are diverse will be excluded while those whose exports are more concentrated are included.

For a sample of mineral exporters, including 16 oil exporters, Cadot, Carrere, and Strauss-Kahn (2011) found a trend of export diversification and re-concentration, albeit non-monotonic effects were present and prevalent at higher levels of export concentration (over 70%). Contrariwise, findings from IMF (2014) showed that there was no clear pattern of economic diversification or export re-concentration in oil-rich economies with higher incomes using the Heckscher–Ohlin model, since most resource-rich countries tend towards export specialisation, with an unclear transmission mechanism to export diversification. However, these findings are out of line with expectations of the Prebisch–Singer hypothesis that low-income economies specialising in commodity exports may be faced with trade deficits which make it difficult for export diversification to occur (Prebisch, 1950; Singer, 1950). On the other hand, the staple theory of growth posits that a resource boom tends to attract capital and labour and stimulate investment in local industries that could spur export diversification (Innis, 1956; Watkins, 1963).

Whereas Ferreira (2009) found no long-run impact of export expansion and diversification on economic growth for Costa Rica, because its diversification and expansion policies were rendered ineffective by the weak linkages between multinational corporations in its free-trade zones. Several studies find empirical support for the export-led growth (ELG) hypothesis, which posits that export growth is a key determinant of economic growth. Considering patterns of exports diversification, Stanley and Bunnag (2001) found that Costa Rica and Honduras showed greater stability in foreign exchange earnings due to better diversified export products and export markets in relation to El Salvador and Guatemala. In Matthee and Naudé (2007), South African regions with more diversified exports experienced higher growth rates and increase in share of national export. The observed increments in economic growth rate were mostly due to horizontal export diversification and not vertical diversification. Also, Herzer and Nowak-Lehnmann (2006) found a positive relationship between export diversification and economic growth by identifying positive externalities resulting from learning-by-doing and learning-by-exporting in Chile's manufacturing sector. They also found that vertical export diversification induces rapid expansions in certain resource-based industries such as export of food products and feedstock. The findings by Doki and Tyokohol (2019) also provide empirical support for a positive long-run relationship between export diversification and economic growth for Nigeria using the IMF Theil export diversification index.

Accounting for the effect of institutional frameworks on export diversification patterns amongst oil-rich countries, Omgba (2014) studied the differences between the start of oil exploration and political independence. From this study, the wider the gap in the start of oil exploration and political independence, the greater will be the participation of oil-rich countries in export diversification. Also, it has been shown that an oil boom negatively affects export diversification when the initial level of diversification in the countries was low (Djimeu and Omgba, 2018). However, in another sample of 134 resource-rich countries, an oil boom had no significant impact on countries that had had higher degrees of export diversification. The tendency of oil-rich countries towards export specialisation increases their vulnerability to commodity price shocks, as is the experience of oil-producing states in Africa which have achieved minimal success in export diversification (Ross, 2019). For the United Arab Emirates (UAE) economy, the findings of Haouas and Heshmati (2014) support the resource curse hypothesis with the resultant effects of decline in productivity levels, sensitivity to volatility, negative investment returns, and over-reliance on domestic labour for employment.

Existing literature also documents important determinants of export diversification in East Asian countries. Such factors include domestic investment, foreign direct investment, financial sector development, competitiveness, institutional strength (Lee et al., 2011), and regional economic integration. Therefore, the more diversified a country's export the less susceptible it is to the debilitating effects of exchange rates and tariff rates. Moreover, structural breaks and changing democratic regimes are important factors in export diversification, structural change, and economic growth, as seen in Pakistan (Akbar et al., 2000; Javed and Munir, 2016). A period of economic boom produced a short-run relationship between export diversification and Pakistan's growth pattern. Another Pakistani study found that characteristics of export-oriented manufacturing firms – such as, firm age, level of managerial expertise, type of ownership, and firm size – contribute to high profitability, economic growth, and export diversification (Ghani et al., 2012). For instance, the heterogeneity observed in patterns of export diversification across Brazil indicates that innovation and strategic positioning of firms were more contributory than mere access to resources (Cirera et al., 2015). From the forgoing, since manufactured exports promote economic growth via learning-by-doing, an increase in funding for Research and Development (R&D) could stimulate development of exports from the primary sector to manufacturing sector.

Further evidence from emerging economies indicates that, as observed for oil-rich countries, more diversified economies experience lower output volatility, higher average growth rates, and productivity growth than less diversified economies (Al-Marhubi, 2000; Lederman and Maloney, 2003; Arnold et al., 2018). In an empirical investigation of Taiwan, Mauritius, Finland, China, and Chile, Agosin (2007) found that export diversification through its interaction with per capita volume of export growth was highly significant in explaining per capita GDP growth over the period 1980 to 2003. The findings of Arnold, Mike-Xin, Ke-Wang, and Hanlei-Yun are consistent with traditional economic theories but with the exception that export diversification had a more significant impact on reducing output volatility than improving long-run growth in emerging countries within the context of a cohesive economic development strategy.

In sum, notes from studies of resource-rich countries, and East Asian and emerging economies indicate a gamut of factors contributing to the level of economic diversification and that export diversification is important for all countries. It is also apparent that sustainable growth and development objectives will thrive on the wheels of diversified sources of income from trade in addition to well-directed development finance.

2.3 Asia and Africa in regional comparative perspective

We adopt the sector share of exports approach, which is a well-known proxy of exports diversification to estimate diversification in Asia and Africa. This is a measure of industrial manufacturing and technological capabilities. We examined two sectors, namely, manufacturing and agriculture; we draw data from the World Development Indicators (WDI) database. We will show the export share of both sectors for Asia and Africa in two parts, see Figure 2.1. The selected Asian countries included in the analysis are: Thailand, Vietnam, Malaysia, South Korea, China, and India while African countries are: Algeria, Angola, Nigeria, Sudan, Botswana, Côte d'Ivoire, Ethiopia, Kenya, Mauritius, Morocco, Rwanda, Senegal, Tanzania, Uganda, Zambia, Congo, Dem. Rep. (DRC), Ghana, Mozambique, Libya, Egypt, United Arab Rep., South Africa, and Tunisia.

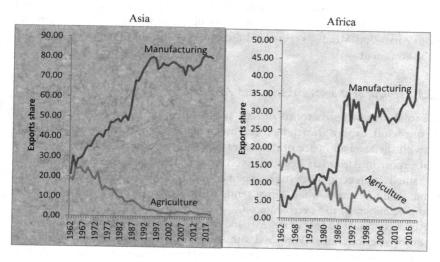

Figure 2.1 Exports shares of manufacturing and agriculture in Asia.

From part one of Figure 2.1, exports share of manufacturing in Asia grew faster and overtook that of agriculture right from the late 1960s, a typical manifestation of positive structural transformation. The gap between the two shares was marginal in the beginning of the study period. For instance, the shares of manufacturing and agriculture were 21.24% and 19.17% respectively in 1962. The gap narrowed down to almost zero in 1964, but has been increasing since then. The shares of manufacturing and agriculture were 79.76% and 3.17% respectively in 1995 and the gap narrowed down slightly but has been increasing since then. Noticeable is the fact that the share of agriculture has been continuously decreasing and share of manufacturing has been increasing. The findings suggest that Asian countries have been diversifying into manufacturing exports consistently leading to higher export share. The proportion of agriculture in overall export has been decreasing as a share of exports. The share of manufacturing exports reached 79.60% while that of agriculture declined to 0.96%.

From part 2 of Figure 2.1 (Africa), until 1975, the share of agriculture export was higher than manufacturing. The situation changed with the share of agriculture declining while that of manufacturing increased for a time. Increase in exports share of manufacturing suggests that some of the countries in Africa did diversify into manufactures.

In comparative perspective, while there was exports diversification in both continents, the pace of diversification in Asia has been at much faster levels and complexities of products than in Africa, and limited to a few countries such as South Africa and Morocco. What distinguishes the two regions is the pace of diversification proxy by export share in manufacturing. For instance, exports share of manufacturing in Asia changed from 21.24% in 1962 to 79.60% in 2018 while in Africa it changed from 6.68% to 47.27% during the same period. From the finding, the pace of diversification in Africa has been far slower compared to Asia; clearly, Africa has a long way to go in reaching the level of diversification recorded in Asia. It may also be worth mentioning that within the African sample, South Africa and Morocco registered greater diversification than other countries in the continent.

2.3.1 Growth of exports in Asia and Africa

The total merchandise exports of Asia as presented in Figure 2.2 show that, on the one hand, export growth has been much higher than Africa, which is consistent with the level and pace of diversification. On the other hand, the growth of total export in Africa has been relatively marginal compared to Asia. Evidently, diversified Asian economies have gained considerably large proportions of global manufactured exports while Africa tends to be stuck with exports of raw commodities, minerals, and petroleum oil.

Africa continues to lag behind Asia and other developing regions in manufacturing exports performance. Compared with Asia, Africa's total export performance has been disappointingly flat over decades measured in value terms (current US dollars) from 1962 (Figure 2.2). Asia gradually took off into a strong export-performing

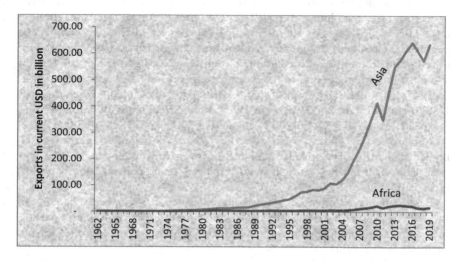

Figure 2.2 Exports growth in Asia and Africa (USD). Source: Authors.

region around the mid-1980s; this sustained growth trajectory has continued. Until the mid-1990s, the pattern of growth of African export was similar to Asia; this was the period of Africa's renewed growth after the disruption caused by the Structural Adjustment Programme (SAP) of the 1980s. Indeed, Africa's best performance in exports growth was in 2000–2005, when it recorded a growth rate of 17%, as compared with Asia's of 15%; alas, the region could not sustain this trajectory.

Consistent with resource-dependent lock-in behaviour, exports from African countries have demonstrated a high degree of dependence on a few primary agricultural or mineral exports. Some have attributed the dominance of agriculture and natural resources in African exports to the region's vast arable land and wealth of mineral resources. We estimate that unprocessed mineral and energy accounts for 80%, on average, of African exports. Agriculture employs between 65 and 80% of the workforce in the region. Consequently, Africa has consistently performed below average on export diversification.

At the root of the poor diversification is the weak performance of these countries in their transition from agrarian societies to industrial nations. Take the case of Indonesia and Nigeria. In the same manner in which industrial diversification shielded countries from volatility, a country like Indonesia equally leveraged the concept of agricultural diversification to reduce risk to individual farmer's income as well as national and regional food supply risk. When a country relies on one or limited number of food crops, it faces direct risks from natural and market shocks as well as other hazards compared with a situation with a more diversified cropping system. In situations of shocks to the economic system, agricultural diversification becomes an important response for attenuating the instability of rural income and therefore fostering rural economic growth and alleviating poverty.

Clearly, structural transformation, in the absence of a modernised industrial agriculture, is incomplete and has left large swathes of African rural areas in poverty. This is illustrated by the contrasting experiences of the two comparator countries, Nigeria and Indonesia.[1] While manufacturing export has helped reduce poverty and fostered wealth creation, a country such as Indonesia, the biggest and most important country in the Asian region, did so by horizontal diversification of agriculture. The country increased its per capita national income from US$200 (at constant 2000 prices) in 1965 to more than US$1,000 in 2005, and is expected to reach US$4200.00 by the end of 2020, and US$4700.00 in 2022. In terms of capita GDP growth over the years 1965–1985, Indonesia ranked higher than any other South East Asian country apart from Singapore. The contrast with Nigeria, where growth stagnated in 1970 and collapsed in the 1980s, is dramatic, Figure 2.3.

Based on export-oriented industrialisation since 1993, more than 50% of Indonesian exports have consisted of manufactured goods; in a sharp contrast, in Nigeria, oil has remained predominantly the most important source of foreign exchange, while industrial exports are insignificant.

What is however notable is the timing of the boom in the Indonesian industrial exports compared with that of the growth of its GDP. Rapid income growth was triggered in 1967 and grew sustainably until 1982, while Indonesia's exports began in 1983 (around 5%) and reached to more than 50% in 1993. In other words, Indonesia's economic take-off had set in way before – by a full 15 years – it emerged as a dynamic industrial exporter. This means there was a clearly another source of GDP growth that preceded manufacturing export, Figure 2.4.

The explanation lies in the innovations made to the agricultural sector, particularly in food-crop agriculture. Between 1968 and 1985 areal yields of rice, the staple food, rose by almost 80% while total rice production grew almost

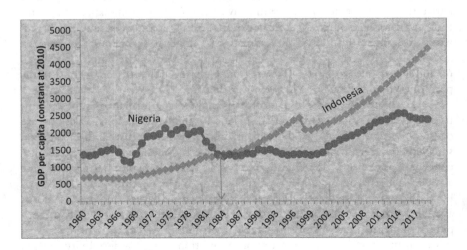

Figure 2.3 Indonesia and Nigeria GDP per capita growth. Source: Authors.

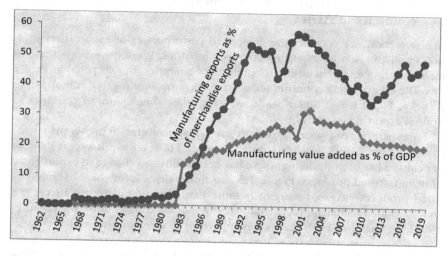

Figure 2.4 Indonesia industrialisation 1962–2019. Source: Authors.

three times faster than population growth. In 1974, Indonesia was the largest rice importer in the world: by 1984, it was self-sufficient. The key factors responsible for the boom in food production were innovations applied to a largely subsistence agriculture base, and consistent application of new technological inputs.

These include higher per hectare use of artificial fertiliser in food-crop farming which increased by a factor of ten in the years 1968 and 1985. The attainment and impact of this Green Revolution was dramatic in raising on-farm incomes and, as well, the prosperity and health of the rural economy.

On the contrary, in Nigeria, neither the initial agricultural nor the subsequent industrial stage of this transformation took place. While there are major ecological differences with Asia, these differences should not be reasons for inaction. There have been significant breakthroughs in maize and cassava breeding, as far back as in the 1970s some of them were achieved on Nigerian soil at the International Institute of Tropical Agriculture in Ibadan. However, in Nigeria as with several other countries in the region, the slow pace of modernisation and lack of investment in innovations including in agricultural extension services, prevented the potential of new varieties from being realised (Holmén, 2005:70).

Clearly relying on economic growth through easy exports of natural raw materials will not be enough to create the base for accumulating national wealth. Sub-Saharan Africa especially will have to address the persistent issue of food imports in the face of land and resource-abundance. The old pattern of prospering solely through commodity trade has been shown to be a sub-optimal strategy compared with specialisation in processed agriculture.

2.4 Comparing oil and non-oil-exporting countries countries in Africa

In this section, we consider the differential performances of export diversification in oil and non-oil exporting countries in Africa. We show exports share of manufacturing and agriculture in both sets of countries, in two parts, in Figure 2.5. The oil exporting countries included in the group are Algeria, Angola, Côte d'Ivoire, Nigeria, and Sudan while we treat other sample African countries as non-oil exporting countries.

From part one of Figure 2.5, export share of agriculture was higher than manufacturing until 1998 in oil-exporting countries. However, while export share of agriculture has been declining, there has been almost no change in export share of manufactured products. Figure 2.5 also shows that export share of manufactured products increased marginally more than that of agriculture after 1998 and continued to remain higher till 2019 in oil-exporting countries. Even after 1998, the shares of both the sectors moved in tandem without much change. The analysis shows that export share of manufactured products did not register much increase during the study period. Rather it declined from 6.85% in 1960 to 6.16% in 2018. Clearly, the findings show that there was no export diversification in oil-exporting countries in Africa.

Exports diversification in non-oil exporting countries in the African continent is depicted in part 2 of Figure 2.5. What we have is the opposite of what applies in oil-exporting countries. Until 1969, the export share of agriculture was higher than that of manufactured products but the shares interchanged positions since then and continued until 2019. Unlike oil-exporting countries, the share of manufacturing has been increasing though at a low pace and small magnitudes relative to Asia. The figure shows a change from 6.59% in 1960 to 53.42% in 2019

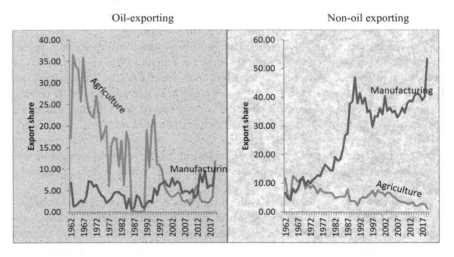

Figure 2.5 Exports shares of manufacturing and agriculture in oil and non-oil exporting countries in Africa. Source: Authors.

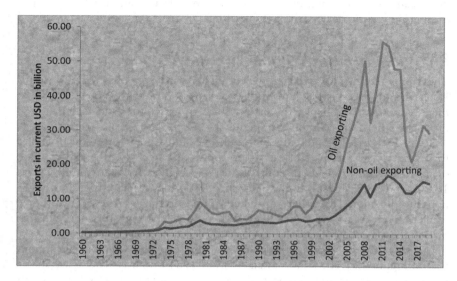

Figure 2.6 Exports growth in oil and non-oil exporting countries in Africa. Source: Authors.

suggesting that export diversification in manufacturing has been taking place in non-oil exporting countries.

Figure 2.6 presents the growth of merchandise exports in oil-exporting and non-oil exporting countries in Africa. The figure depicts a distinguishing aspect of foreign earnings. Exports in oil-exporting countries have been highly volatile while in non-oil exporting countries growth has shadowed with much less volatility. The volatility in total exports in oil-exporting countries is understandable as exports earnings depend on demand and price of oil in international markets, which are highly unpredictable. The volatility exerts strong pressures, in varying degrees, on foreign earnings in oil-exporting countries. Whereas in non-oil exporting countries, fluctuations in demand and price of manufactured products are subject to less fluctuations resulting in relatively regular exports earnings.

In summary, there has been no significant export diversification in oil-exporting countries resulting in highly volatile foreign earnings. Irregular foreign exchange has strong bearing on other development and investment goals that are severely affected by volatility. On the other hand, export diversification has taken place, albeit modestly, in non-oil exporting countries resulting in more stable foreign earning. Stable foreign income allows countries to plan and implement development policies more predictably.

2.5 Analysis of degree of export diversifications

In the following section, we have grouped countries into three categories depending on the extent and intensity of diversification. The purpose of the analysis is to understand the association between exports diversification and total exports and earnings in varying degrees of diversification.

2.5.1 High-level diversification countries in Asia

The sample consists of two high-performing Asian economies, namely South Korea and China. As is well known, these Asian countries have largely diversified their economies. We depict the export share of agriculture and manufactured products in both the economies in Figure 2.7.

From Figure 2.7, export diversification in South Korea started much earlier than China. The first part of the figure shows that by 1962, the export share of manufactured products in South Korea was higher than agriculture: it was 18.20% and 13.35% respectively. Since then, export shares have been moving in opposite directions. The share of manufactured products increased to 87.66% while that of agriculture declined to 0.93% in 2019; a strong structural transformation through diversification.

We show the growth of export shares of the sectors in China in the second part of Figure 2.7. The data is available from 1984 onwards. The figure shows that export share in China has been following a similar trajectory to that of South Korea. However, the export share of agriculture (5.71%) in China was higher than South Korea (0.84%) while shares of manufactured products were 47.65% and 91.22% respectively. Our findings show that South Korea was far ahead with China in terms of export diversification in manufactured products. However, China surpassed South Korea in 2018 in terms of export diversification, as the share of manufactured products (93.37%) was higher than South Korea (87.78%) while agriculture share was lower in China (0.42%) than South Korea (0.95%).

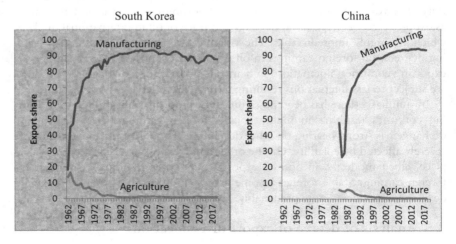

Figure 2.7 Export shares of manufacturing and agriculture in Asian countries. Source: Authors.

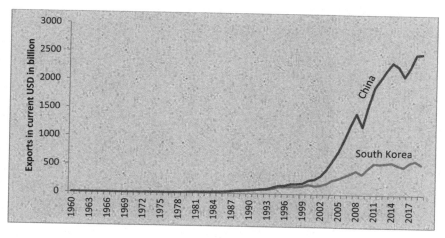

Figure 2.8 Exports growth in South Korea and China. Source: Authors.

In the next graph, we show export diversification as exports earning. We present the total merchandise exports of China and South Korea in Figure 2.8.

From Figure 2.8, we show that export diversification is strongly associated with revenue and foreign income earnings and GDP growth by implication. Until 1990, export earnings of South Korea (US$65.02 billion 1990) were higher than China (US%62.09 billion in 1990). South Korea and China interchanged their position with regard to exports earning after 1990. Although growth of exports earnings has been positive in both the countries, the pace of growth in China accelerated. Consequently, exports earning in China and South Korea were US$2,499.03 and US$542.23 billion in 2019 respectively. The unprecedented growth of exports earnings of China is related to the larger degree of diversification.

2.5.2 Intermediate diversification countries in Asia

We group Indonesia, Turkey, and Malaysia into this category of "Intermediate Diversification". The export shares of these countries are shown in three parts in Figure 2.9. From the figure, the behaviour of export diversification is more or less similar in all the three countries. In the initial period, the export shares of agriculture were higher than manufacturing while the scenario interchanged at an inflexion point and has continued to date.

In the case of Indonesia, until 1981 the export share of agriculture (8.22% in 1981) was higher than manufactured products (3.02% in 1981). The export share interchanged its position since 1982 and share of manufactured products has continued to be higher than agriculture to date. The exports shares not only interchanged their position but travelled in the opposite direction. Consequently,

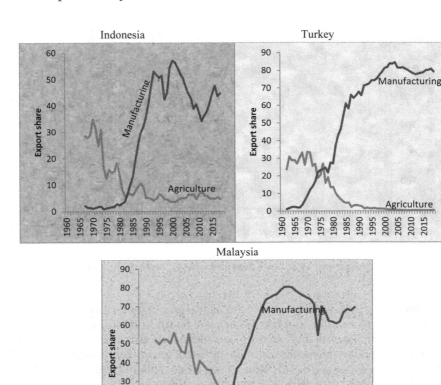

Figure 2.9 Exports shares of manufacturing and agriculture in intermediate diversification countries in Asia. Source: Authors.

the export shares of the sectors in 2019 were 44.72% and 4.65% respectively. The substantial rise in export share of manufactured products suggests that the country achieved considerable success in export diversification.

In the case of Turkey, the intersection points of export shares occurred in 1974 when share of manufactured products (21.91%) rose faster than agriculture (18.79%). Since then the shares have moved in opposite directions. Consequently, manufacturing share rose to 79.24% while agriculture share reduced to 0.54% in 2019. Malaysia followed the same path as that of the other two countries. The intersection point was realised a decade later than that of Turkey in 1983 when share of manufacturing and agriculture crossed the inflection point (24.72 and 24.26% respectively). The share of manufacturing has been rising since then and

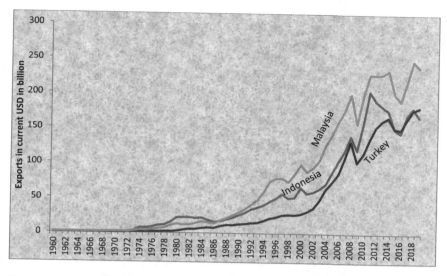

Figure 2.10 Exports growth in intermediate diversified countries in Asia. Source: Authors.

agriculture has been declining. In 2018, the shares reached 69.50% and 1.35% respectively. Although Malaysia diversified its export, the level of diversification is less than that of Turkey: manufacturing export share in Malaysia was 69.50% while it was 80.88% in Turkey in 2018.

The next set of analyses examines the growth of total merchandise exports of these countries; again, we show that export earnings performance is closely related to diversification. Figure 2.10 depicts the trend of exports of these countries. The figure shows that exports in the three countries have been growing but differentially with the degree of diversification. For instance, the degree of diversification is highest in the case of Turkey but the trend in growth of exports is similar to that of Indonesia which has lowest degree of diversification. Clearly, factors fostering diversification such as policy institutions have different impacts on export performance.

2.5.3 Intermediate diversification countries in Africa

We next examine the extent of export diversification in Africa as countries in Africa have also witnessed diversification; three countries are included in the analysis namely: Kenya, Senegal, and Morocco. Figure 2.11 depicts the export shares of manufacturing and agriculture in these countries. Data for Kenya and Senegal are missing for several years leading to discontinuity in graphs.

The analysis of Kenya is presented in the first part of the Figure 2.11. From the figure, based on the availability of data, the share of manufacturing has been

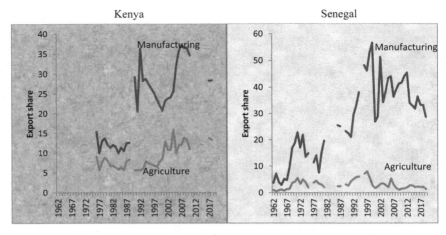

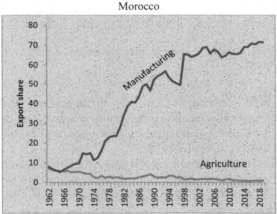

Figure 2.11 Exports shares of manufacturing and agriculture in intermediate diversification countries. Source: Authors.

higher than agriculture. Kenya's diversification offers a unique trend, i.e., the export shares of both the sectors have registered a positive trend. For instance, the shares of manufacturing and agriculture were 15.40% and 9.12% respectively in 1976 and reached to 28.44% and 13.34% in 2018.

Part two of the figure shows that share of manufacturing has been higher than agriculture ever since the availability of data. The shares were 3.75% and 1.03% respectively in 1962. Unlike Kenya, the shares followed a different trajectory. The share of manufactured products increased from 3.75% in 1962 to 28.69% in 2019 while agriculture share marginally increased to 1.29% in 2019. It may be inferred that Senegal witnessed more diversification than Kenya.

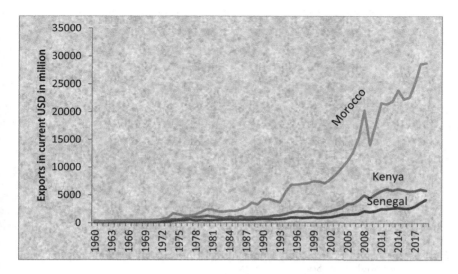

Figure 2.12 Exports growth in intermediate diversification countries in Africa. Source: Authors.

Growth of export shares of Morocco, presented in the third part of Figure 2.11 shows that shares diversified at a high pace. The shares of manufacturing and agriculture were similar (8.02% and 7.03% respectively) in 1962. The export diversification in Morocco has been similar to several countries of Asia. The growth of shares not only moved in the opposite direction but also changed rapidly. Consequently, the share reached 71.42% and 1.02% respectively in 2019.

In order to capture the economic impact of diversification on total merchandise exports, we examine the trend of exports, which is presented in Figure 2.12.

From the above figure, growth of Morocco's merchandise export has been significantly higher than that of the other two countries due to its proportionally high percentage of manufactures compared with Senegal and Kenya whose exports are in non-processed raw materials. The growth of exports is also attributed to its wider degree of export diversification. On the contrary, export growths in Kenya and Senegal are limited and products are rather low technology and low value. Clearly, the higher the degree of diversification the more a country earns from growth of exports.

2.5.4 *Low diversification economies*

Two countries, namely Nigeria and Bangladesh, are examined in this category. We present the analysis of both countries in Figure 2.13.

Figure 2.13 shows the trend in movement of shares of both sectors. In the initial period, the export share of agriculture in Nigeria (16.63% in 1962) was

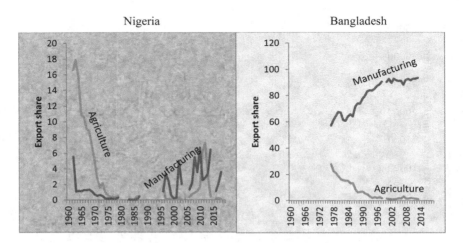

Figure 2.13 Export shares of manufacturing and agriculture in Nigeria and Bangladesh. Source: Authors.

much higher than manufacturing (5.56% the same year). The shares of both the sectors however declined until 1985 (0.04% and 0.03% respectively) and have been fluctuating since then. Given the movement of shares there has been no significant movement towards exports diversification.

On the contrary, Bangladesh, another low-income country, has succeeded somewhat in achieving exports diversification especially in garments and textiles. It can be seen from the second part of Figure 2.13 that growth of shares has been moving in opposite direction in both sectors ever since the availability of data; evidently, the share of manufacturing has been higher than agriculture. The shares were 57.31% and 27.85% respectively in 1977. Since then manufacturing share has been growing and that of agriculture has been declining with the shares reaching 95.80% and 0.75% respectively in 2015. Export diversification in Bangladesh has been far higher than Nigeria.

Depending on the degree of diversification, total merchandise exports will follow different trajectories: exports of both the countries are analysed and trends are presented in Figure 2.14.

Figure 2.14 shows that on the one hand, total merchandise exports of Bangladesh are lower than Nigeria; they have been growing at a steady pace. On the other hand, exports in Nigeria have witnessed a high level of volatility which is considered detrimental to the development process. Moreover, high volume of exports in Nigeria is due to oil exports rather than manufactured products or processed agriculture. Due to the wide swings and crash of the oil market, exports of Bangladesh achieved the same value as those of Nigeria in 2019.

On the other hand, the economic performance of Bangladesh has been very impressive in the last 25 years, it is now a main source of foreign exchange for the

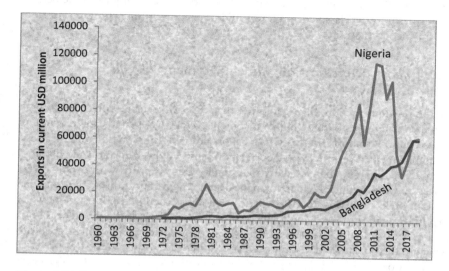

Figure 2.14 Exports growth in Nigeria and Bangladesh. Source: Authors.

country. The sector generates about $5 billion worth of products each year from garment export; it provides employment to around three million workers of whom 90% are women. While the RMG (Ready-Made Garments) sector is not homogenous, Bangladesh has developed a highly advanced manufacturing ecosystem characterised by a high degree of entrepreneurship and innovative management capabilities. Garment firms have invested significantly in productivity-enhancing technologies, automation, continuous improvement, and digitisation.[2]

Its per capita income in 2019 was $1,856, much higher than that of Pakistan ($1,285). In fact it is very much comparable with India ($2,100). The major source of income is from exports of garments, which is roughly 84% of the total exports. The remarkable performance of the sector in international markets is partly a result of investments in manufacturing technologies in the garments sector, its lack of regulation, and the low wages paid to its women garment workers. More importantly, the growth of Bangladesh's RMG sector has been as much a result of improved factory conditions and transparency as it is of the sector's growth through horizontal diversification over the past decade. Bangladesh's success has been achieved through market diversification of its customer countries and more upgrading into more complex products and value added services. The sector thrived by targeting a broader range of European customers and managed market risks through adaptation to the ever-changing demand patterns in the global fashion market.

Improved income has contributed to advances in development indicators. For instance, life expectancy improved from 64.5 years in 2000 to 72.6 years in 2019. Similarly, mean years of schooling went up from 4.1 to 6.2 and the human development index jumped from 0.478 to 0.632 during the same period. Bangladesh is now classified as a lower middle-income country progressing from its low-income status.

2.6 Export diversification and employment in Asia and Africa

In the previous section, we established that export diversification leads to high exports earnings resulting in higher income. Several studies cited earlier including cross-country econometric analysis of export diversification on different measures of employment reveal the strong correlation between diversification and employment. The different analyses show that employment expands with export diversification, while vulnerable employment declines with export diversification. The chapter seeks to answer the following questions: is there a relationship between export diversification and employment broadly and what are the differences in its nature in Africa and Asia? If export diversification fosters employment creation, what are the policies and institutions for creating this positive nexus?

How do we avoid the type of export diversification that leads to jobless growth? The data from which we calculate employment ratio come from the World Development Indicators database. Employment ratio is measured as percentage of employment to total population (15+). Export Diversification Index data has been taken from UNCTAD statistics. The data are available from 1995 to 2019. Hence the analysis presented in this section is limited to 1995 to 2019.

We select four representative countries to understand the association between export diversification and employment generation, South Korea and Bangladesh represent Asia. We select these two countries because South Korea has been diversifying its exports for a long period while Bangladesh is relatively new in its endeavour of export diversification. Similarly, Africa is represented by South Africa and Morocco.

The association between export diversification index and employment ratio in these countries are depicted in Figure 2.15. From the first part of the figure, we observe the best fit between employment and diversification index; in the case of South Korea, it is shown as a parabola of two degrees. This shape of association suggests that employment generation is cyclic in nature. We attribute this to declining share of manufacturing in the country. The decline in exports share could be the reason for declining employment for the last few years resulting in a parabolic association between employment and export diversification index.

The second part of the figure depicts the relationship between the two in the case of Bangladesh. From the figure, the best-fit association is an inverted parabola of order two. Exports diversification in Bangladesh is led by manufacturing of exports of ready-made garments. It is important to understand why Bangladesh could not create much employment though exports increased in the beginning.

The association between diversification index and employment could be better explained in terms of the existence of a quota system imposed by WTO (World Trade Organization). Export of garments was very much governed by the quota

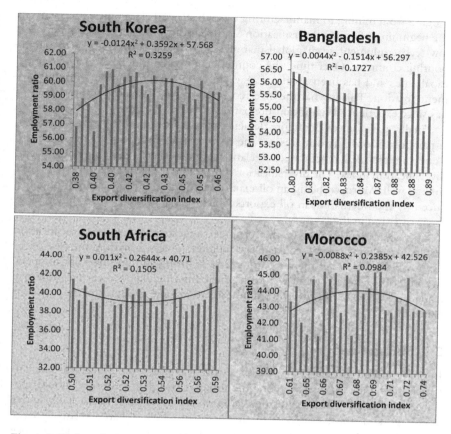

Figure 2.15 Association between employment and export diversification index. Source: Authors.

system of WTO until 2005. Before 2005 firms in Bangladesh may be owned by foreign countries that could have exhausted export quotas from their own land. Such firms did very little diversification resulting in no additional employment creation. And whenever diversification has taken place, it has created more employment. For instance, employment was 54.99% when the diversification index was 0.87 but when it changed to 0.80 the employment changed to 56.42%. The change of diversification index from 0.87 to 0.80 suggests that some diversification took place, meaning that diversification resulted in the creation of more employment.

The third part of the figure depicts the association of employment and export diversification index in South Africa; the relationship is similar to what we found in Bangladesh. It is quite possible that South Africa may equally be engaged in re-export but not necessarily because of any restriction of quota imposed by WTO.

As is well known, South Africa is a manufacturing hub of all kinds of products ranging from mining to manufacturing of sophisticated electronic equipment. In the beginning of export diversification South Africa would import machinery and low-tech equipment from global manufacturers and re-export them to neighbouring countries. Over time, the country acquired considerable manufacturing capabilities and has been able to engage in export diversification with employment creation. This is what the inverted parabola captures although the country has since experienced significant premature de-industrialisation.

Finally, part four of the figure depicts the association in the case of Morocco. A parabola of order two represents the best-fit association. Such a low R-square value suggests that practically no relationship exists between employment and diversification index. The diversification index did not follow a definite trend over time as well. Morocco being an oil-exporting country, the index might be influenced by the fluctuation in oil exports which may be unrelated to the employment situation in the country.

The analysis presented in this chapter suggests that export diversification results in higher foreign earning but it could be jobless growth in the case of re-export. However, if the manufacturing base is strong and products are competitive in global markets, there is greater possibility that export diversification may take place. This kind of diversification leads to income growth and employment generation.

2.7 Summing up

In sum, there has been a significant theoretical shift over the years. The initial classical and neoclassical economic thought was that a country should specialise in producing and exporting a commodity in which it had a comparative advantage and, thus, use more of the factor in which it had a relatively large endowment. That meant that (African) developing countries would produce and export primarily primary products and import manufactures. In contrast, recent theoretical understanding emphasises the need for export diversification into manufacturing in developing countries. Indeed, empirical evidence seems to be in concert with the latter theories, in that those countries pursuing export diversification have performed better in terms of sustained growth and development. Further, the theory of derived demand suggests that such growth would likely result in relatively large demand for labour, leading to higher employment, though the rate of increase would be dependent on the labour-intensive nature of the technology employed.

The recent empirical evidence suggests that economic diversification has become pivotal to sustainability of growth and economic development in all the countries irrespective of richness in natural resources. In fact, the evidence presented in the chapter suggests that export diversification is strongly associated with better economic performance resulting in improvements in development indicators. On the other hand, the countries that could not diversify faced unstable income and reduction in employment resulting in poor economic performance. In general, Asian countries are more diversified compared to their African counterparts.

The manufacturing sector has witnessed more diversification compared to other sectors. Consequently, the export share of manufacturing in total export from leading countries is around 80% in 2019 in Asia compared to less than 50% in Africa. The evidence presented in the chapter suggests that there is strong association between export diversification and employment creation. The chapter concludes that export diversification is one of several instruments that could be applied for better economic performance.

Notes

1 This Indonesian case study draws on Henley, D. (2012). 'The Agrarian Roots of Industrial Growth: Rural Development in South-East Asia and Sub-Saharan Africa', *Development Policy Review*, Vol. 30(51), 525–547.
2 www.mckinsey.com/industries/retail/our-insights/whats-next-for-bangladeshs -garment-industry-after-a-decade-of-growth; accessed July 19, 2021.

3 Oil Dependence and Structural Stability

3.1 Introduction

In this chapter, we examine the direct and indirect impacts of oil dependence on African economies. African countries are not just oil dependent; they are also major exporters of raw materials including oil, natural gas, base and precious metals, and minerals. Consider the revenue of three African oil producers in 2019 before the Covid-19 induced oil price collapse – Nigeria (US$41 billion), Angola (US$32.3), and Libya (US$24.8). Oil prices experienced a major collapse from around US$60 to less than US$20 by April 2020.

We provide empirical evidence showing that continuous concentration on commodities exports is strongly related to relative economic instabilities. For Africa as a whole, the dependency figures are significant and troubling as commodity exports on average account for 80% of total merchandise exports. In almost half of Africa's economies commodity exports earn 90% or more of merchandise export earnings. And for three-quarters of African countries, commodity exports make up 70% or more of export earnings. Due to this lack of diversification, most of Africa's economies remain dependent on the vagaries of commodity prices in the international market and often on the price of a single resource.

Existing evidence show that over the long term, on average, the real prices of most primary commodities produced by African countries (except copper and gold) have trended gently down and exports of these products have declined over time thus impacting export revenues (Figure 3.1). The benefits of technical progress and value addition to these commodities do not therefore accrue to the respective economies.

Economic growth in many African economies continues to rely on primary commodity price movements due to lack of capacity for value addition to export commodities and institutional capacity to diversify economies. This has implications for export revenue mobilisation, fiscal sustainability, debt vulnerability, and capacity to implement expansionary fiscal policy at the scale required to provide adequate support to citizens in times of exogenous shocks, including during disease pandemics such as Covid-19.

Despite the proven natural capital potentials of Africa, especially in agriculture, energy, mining, and other extractives, African countries continue to export

DOI: 10.4324/9781003245322-3

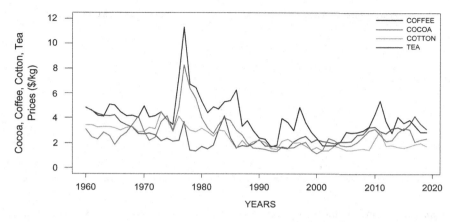

Figure 3.1 Real Prices of cocoa, coffee, cotton, and tea (1960–2020). Source: AfDB-ADI (2020).

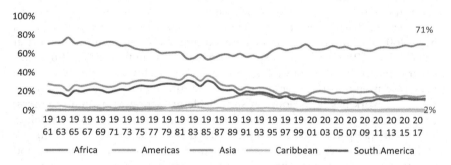

Figure 3.2 Cocoa production in the world, 1961–2017. Source: AfDB-ADI (2020).

primary commodities. With a few exceptions, the degree of processing (value addition) in Africa's commodity exports remains generally low and the share of local labour in their value is relatively small. For example, Africa accounts for 70% of world production of cocoa beans (Figure 3.2).

However, about 80% of Africa's cocoa production is already sold even before it is harvested. Africa accounts for about 21% of the world's cocoa grinding, and at most 1% of the global chocolate market. Raw cocoa exportation is tantamount to exporting jobs from Africa. In 2011 the chocolate industry employed about 70,000 people in the European Union and United States. The chocolate industry retail market in 2017 was valued at US$106.19 billion with 43% utilisation of all cocoa produced. In 2026, its retail market value is expected to rise to US$189.89 billion. Yet, Africa only earns 3–6% of the chocolate industry's retail market value even though it is the main producer of cocoa.

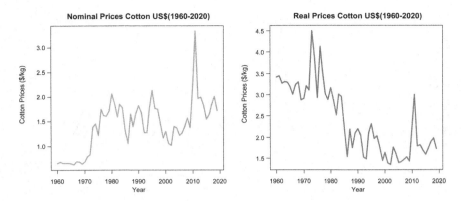

Figure 3.3 Nominal and real prices of cotton in US$ (1960–2020). Source: AfDB-
ADI (2020).

As shown in Figure 3.3, the story about the fluctuation in the nominal prices
of cotton was as true in the times of Mohammed Ali as it is now. Even more telling is the fact that the real price of cotton has tended significantly downwards
since 1960. This means that countries exporting the same quantities of cotton
annually since 1960 receive less export revenue today than they did in 1960. This
further explains the need for building local and regional value chains to enhance
the beneficiation of Africa's natural resources in Africa for the benefit of Africans.

A lot of work has been done on sustainable extraction of natural resources,
beneficiation, corporate social responsibility, gender inclusion, artisanal mining,
and lack of transparency and corruption along the value chain, accounting for
natural capital and reversing the resource curse. However, lack of policies and
institutional capacity to effectively add value, diversify the economies, and implement counter-cyclical measures during commodity price BOOM periods continue to expose resource-rich countries vulnerable to fluctuations in prices and
aggregate demand for key export commodities in the global market. This makes
it very difficult for primary commodity-dependent countries to effectively build
resilient economies that can withstand exogenous shocks such as Covid-19.

There are several avenues and channels through which low oil prices affect
key socio-economic variables. For instance, an unexpected fall in oil prices affects
government revenues and development plans. This is the immediate outcome in
countries like Nigeria and Angola for example wherein oil revenues account for a
substantial portion of total national government revenues,

Second, oil shocks manifest in the pattern instability of African exports which
has been found to be independently growth-inhibiting (Gyimah-Brempong,
1991). This could be through reduced growth rate, which is evident in most countries as the Covid-19 pandemic hits economies, and rising inflation. Instability is
therefore channelled directly through consumer prices for both oil importers and
exporters, and indirectly through trade and other commodity markets.

Third, it may also be transmitted into capital or import instability, either of which could be also growth-inhibiting (Fosu, 1991, 2001b), with long-term adverse implications on employment creation. Africa is particularly vulnerable because its trade largely in agricultural raw materials and minerals is highly concentrated with very limited diversification and exports dominated by primary commodities, consistent with neoclassical trade theory. Economic history has shown that without diversification into manufacturing and services, and away from simple resource extraction, the long-term development prospects of countries are always bleak. The need for economic diversification in the continent is high, more so given that the growth cycle is at a low point.

For the most part, African governments have not taken advantage of the last decade's growth spurt to move towards diversification – neither in their economic structures, nor in their export baskets. Evidently, the effects and the more lasting impacts of oil shocks will vary depending on the capabilities of countries to take discretionary monetary and fiscal measures. While countries with more diversified economies may escape the severe effect ordinarily experienced by low-income and technologically weak nations, both groups of countries may be forced by reduced revenues to cut government spending and imports.

Other immediate and inevitable adjustments in times of lower oil prices are sharp currency adjustments, contraction of the fiscal policy space, and decline in tax revenues from the oil sector. However, a sudden change in oil prices, by increasing uncertainty, does put on hold vital development investments some of which could be irretrievably lost especially where there is prolonged negative growth including a recession. The effect of decling revenue on developing economies could be severe (Kilian, 2014). Similarly, uncertainty generated by sharp movements in oil prices can also hinder the consumption of durable goods (Kilian, 2014). For example, given that oil is a feedstock for critical chemical sectors including petrochemicals, paper, and aluminium, the decline in prices directly affects a wide range of processed or semi-processed inputs. These effects are transmitted to the transportation, petrochemical, and agricultural sectors, and the manufacturing sector broadly.

While the direct impact of falling oil prices on poverty is likely to be limited, the indirect effects may be substantial and largely beneficial. Energy consumption by the poor is low: households in the poorest quintile of the income distribution typically spend well below 10% of their income on fossil fuel sourced energy (Vagliasindi, 2012). As a result, the direct impact of falling oil prices on the poor is expected to be small. However, indirect effects would work through growth and falling food prices. More than 70% of the world's poor live in oil-importing countries, where low oil prices (to the extent they are transmitted into local fuel prices) will support growth and real incomes.

This will benefit the poor as well as the more prosperous. The poor could gain further if falling oil prices allowed expenditures on subsidies to be reallocated to better-targeted pro-poor programmes. However, in oil-exporting countries, easing growth and, in some cases, tightening fiscal policy could weaken prospects for the poor. Falling oil prices also pass through into other commodity prices, in particular food prices: a 45% decline in global oil prices could reduce agricultural commodity prices by about 10% as discussed above. Changes in global food commodity prices will also be reflected in most countries' domestic food prices – even if only with a lag and muted by transport cost and local supply and demand conditions (Cudjoe et al., 2010).

Falling food prices may benefit the majority of the poor but harm the very poorest, despite an adjustment in household behaviour. Many poor households are net food buyers – and would thus benefit from lower food prices. In low-income countries, however, about half of the poor households are only marginal net food buyers and the poorest households tend to be net food sellers (Aksoy and IsikDikmelik, 2008). Hence, while the bulk of the poor may benefit from low food prices, the poorest may see net real income losses. However, poor households will likely mitigate some of the impact of falling food prices by adjusting the hours worked or the number of household members working in employment outside the family farm (Ivanic and Martin, 2014).

3.2 Recovery from oil shocks

Economic growth is measured by the rate of change of real income per capita. In Figure 3.4 we provide the frequency distribution of the growth rate of (several) countries from 1961 to 2019. We divided the decades into five periods that reflect periods before and after major oil crises. Figure 3.4 presents oil crises and their impact on the growth rate of income in various countries.

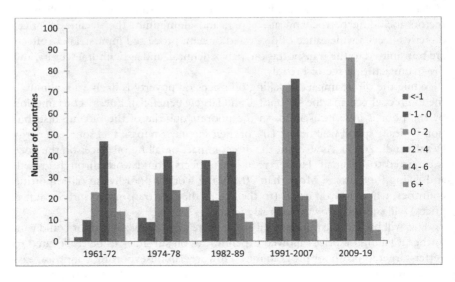

Figure 3.4 Based on growth of GDP per capita. Source: Authors.

We reach the following conclusions:

1. More countries experienced higher growth rates before the crises than after. From the figure, there were just two countries with less than -1.00% growth rate before the 1973 crisis, the number of countries with similar growth increased to 8 and 30 before falling to 17 before the 2020 crisis. When we compare the first three periods the number of countries experiencing decline of income gradually increased. The number of countries recording above 6% growth fell. *Evidently, more and more countries record declining income due to oil crises and more significantly it gets harder to recover from the shocks.*

2. The number of countries with high growth (more than 6%) decreased from 14 before the 1973 crisis to just five before the 2020 crisis. The decrease in number suggests that relatively high-growth developing countries that experienced loss of income growth due to external shocks have the propensity to migrate into the category of lower-income growing countries without taking remedial actions.

3. The simple average rate of growth of all the countries BEFORE the crises were (73:3.27%, 79:2.80%, 90:2.25%, 2008:2.01%) and dropped to (73:1.45%, 79:1.44%, 90:1.51%, 2008:1.37%) after the crises. On the other hand, the average growth rate of major oil-producing countries before the crises were (73:3.30%, 79:3.01%, 90:1.96%, 2008:2.09%) and dropped to (73:1.50%, 79:1.40%, 90:1.70%, 2008:0.68%) after the crises. It is clear that oil shocks lead to greater income disparities between oil and non-oil producing countries.

4. Negative/low growth tends to experience path-dependency: in order to answer the question as to who loses and by what extent, we examine the movement of growth rates within each category band. In-depth analysis suggests that it is not only that the number of countries in the less than -1% growth category increased ever since the 1973 crisis to the 2020 crisis, but that their growth rates also declined.

The growth rates are depicted in Table 3.1. *The table shows that average growth rate before the first oil crises was -1.44% while it declined to -2.76% after the crisis. With every oil crisis, there is a resultant lower growth rate which finally culminated in income growth of -2.93% before the 2020 crisis.* This trend in growth rates is

Table 3.1 Income growth rates due to various oil crises

Growth rates	1961–72	1974–78	1982–89	1991–2007	2009–19
<-1	-1.44	-2.76	-2.41	-2.77	-2.93
-1–0	-0.39	-0.56	-0.56	-0.48	-0.42
0–2	0.99	1.14	1.03	1.22	1.01
2–4	2.98	2.94	2.84	2.82	2.74
4–6	4.64	4.82	4.95	4.68	4.65
6+	7.33	8.98	7.50	7.83	6.88

Source: authors estimation using WDI data

similar but is of exact opposite nature in high-growth countries. For instance, in the category of countries growing at more than 6%, the average growth before the 1973 crisis was 7.33% and continued to increase after each successive oil crisis. The income growth before the 2008 crisis reached to 7.83%. However, it marginally declined before the 2020 crisis. *The findings show that impact of oil crises on low-growing countries is more severe than for high-growth countries.*

Figure 3.5 presents analysis of major oil-exporting countries of Africa and Asia. The list of countries is presented in Appendix 3.1.

From Figure 3.5 the number of countries having income growth of less than -1 increased from the 1993 crisis to the crisis before 2020. For instance, there was only one country, i.e., Chad, in this category before the 1973 crisis; the number increased to four (Angola, Equatorial Guinea, Oman, and South Sudan) before the 2020 crisis. *On the other hand, the number of countries with growth rate between 4% and 6 % increased from five to four. We may infer from the findings that countries with lower income growth are most affected due to various oil crises.*

Table 3.2 presents the movement of income growth from one oil crisis to another. From the table the average growth rate of countries with less than -1

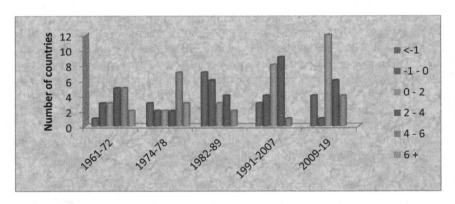

Figure 3.5 Based on growth of GDP per capita of oil-exporting countries. Source: Authors.

Table 3.2 Income growth rates due to various oil crises in oil-exporting countries

Group	1961–72	1974–78	1982–89	1991–2007	2009–19
<-1	-1.21	-3.08	-2.24	-2.84	-4.47
-1–0	-0.17	-0.26	-0.51	-0.63	-0.40
0–2	0.99	0.88	0.48	1.34	0.93
2–4	2.67	3.24	3.13	3.02	2.69
4–6	4.78	4.64	4.50	4.31	4.22
6+	9.38	8.66			

Source: authors estimation using WDI data

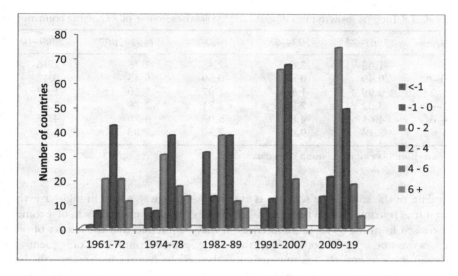

Figure 3.6 Based on growth of GDP per capita of non-oil exporting countries. Source: Authors estimation using WDI data.

was −1.21% before the 1973 crisis and it deteriorated to -4.47% after the 2008 crisis. It seems countries growth experiences a path-dependent trajectory by which low/negative growth tends to be reinforced over time. In this case, growth declined more drastically after each oil crises. On the other hand, average growth increased for the countries that fall within the category of 2–4%. For instance, the average growth before the 1973 crisis was 2.67% and it increased to 3.02% before the 2008 crisis. A decreasing trend is registered in other growth categories, but the rate of decline is much lower in high-growth countries. For instance, in the growth category of more than 6%, the average growth was 9.38% before the 1973 crisis and it recorded 8.66% after the 1973 crisis.

Figure 3.6 depicts the impact of oil crises on oil consumers. The trend is similar to that oil-exporting countries. The number of countries in the lowest growth bracket increased from the 1982 crisis to 2008. There was only one country in this bracket before1973 crisis and number increased to 13 after the 2008 crisis. On the other hand, in the high-growth bracket, it is the other way round. Hence it may be inferred from the results that the impact of oil crises in low-growth countries is more severe than high-growth countries.

Table 3.3 presents average income growth rate of non-oil exporting countries after each oil crisis. It can be seen from the table that although the trend in decline of income growth in low-growth countries (less than -1.00%) is similar to that of oil-exporting countries, the magnitude is much less in non-oil exporting countries than the other. This suggests that the impact of oil crises is more sever on oil-exporting countries rather than oil-importing countries. This is a very important

Table 3.3 Income growth rates due to various oil crises in non-oil exporting countries

Group	1961–72	1974–78	1982–89	1991–2007	2009–19
<-1	-1.68	-2.64	-2.45	-2.75	-2.46
-1–0	-0.49	-0.65	-0.59	-0.43	-0.42
0–2	0.99	1.16	1.07	1.20	1.02
2–4	3.02	2.92	2.81	2.79	2.75
4–6	4.61	4.89	5.03	4.70	4.75
6 +	7.14	9.05	7.50	7.83	6.88

Source: authors estimation using WDI data

finding of the study. The scenario is exactly the other way round in high-growth countries (income growth between 2–4%). In this bracket average growth of income increased from the 1993 to 2008 crises. It may be inferred that the impact of oil crises was not as severe compared to that of low-growth countries. Consequently, loss of income growth was minimal, and they could register higher growth. In absence of oil crises, the income of such countries could have been much higher.

Summary of the findings are as follows: impact of oil crises is more severe on low-growth countries than the other countries. This is true whether a country is an oil exporter or not. Another distinguished finding is that impact of crises is far more severe on oil-exporting countries than oil-importing countries.

The results indicate that not all oil-exporting countries are at the same levels of development and their absorptive capacity and response to oil shocks are different. The literature tells us that while oil shocks do transmit differential asymmetric effects in oil-exporting developing countries, what is not in dispute is that lower oil prices tend to lead to major revenue cuts, cutbacks in social services, and, in extreme cases, lead to stagnation and recession in the economy. What is disturbing in the analysis here is that higher oil prices and accompanying higher revenues do not seem to result into sustained economic growth given the progressively worsening income growth that we see over several decades. We will examine direct and indirect impacts of the shocks on poverty, income growth, and employment and, as well, the differences in their institutional quality, particularly government effectiveness.

3.3 Country-level analysis

Several economies in Africa such as Nigeria, Angola, Algeria, Democratic Republic of the Congo, Brazzaville, and Sudan are predominantly dependent on oil production and exports. They are highly vulnerable to oil price changes in international markets. The chapter analyses the oil price fluctuations and their impact on these economies vis-à-vis the exports of primary agri-products.

The analysis focuses on two decades. The entire period is divided into three sub-periods depending on the oil prices in the international markets. The BOOM period is marked by the sudden jump of oil prices while decline in oil prices is regarded as the BUST period. The period with marginal change is defined as the stable period. It is found that the oil prices in the BOOM period jumped from US$17.54 per barrel in November 1998 to $164.08 in June 2008. They did not witness comparatively much change during the stable period (changed from $144.68 in July 2008 to $108.26 in December 2013). During the BUST period, prices slipped from $106.85 in January 2014 to $46.36 in December 2018. Analysis of each country is presented separately.

3.4 Analysis of Nigeria

The analysis of Nigeria is presented in four parts in Appendix 3.2. Part 1 of the figure presents growth of value added in agriculture during 1998 to 2018. It can be seen from the figure that growth of agriculture, forestry, and fishing value added has been highly volatile during the BOOM period. This could be because of volatility of commodity prices in international markets. The overall trend of value added suggests that it has been decreasing during the study period.

Part 2 of the figure presents the trend of GDP per capita constant at USD 2010 (GDP) during the study period. It can be seen from the figure that GDP witnessed a positive trend up to stable and registered downfall during the BUST period. It declined from 2563.90 in 2014 to 2396.31 in 2018.

Part 3 of the figure depicts the trend of rate of employment in agriculture during 1998 to 2018. The data represent the percentage of employment in agriculture to the total employment. It can be seen from the figure that employment in agriculture follows the inverse pattern to that of GDP during BOOM and stable periods. In fact, the employment ratio has been declining during the entire study period.

Poverty analysis is presented in part 4 of the figure. GDP per capita has implications on poverty reduction also. Unlike GDP data, poverty data are available on a decadal basis. The poverty gap at $1.90 a day (2011 PPP) (%) was 31.1%, 21.9%, and 21.8% in 1996, 2003, and 2009, respectively. The poverty gap remained almost unchanged (21.9 in 2003 to 21.8 in 2009) though it declined from 1996 (31.1%). Poverty headcount followed a similar trend. It declined from 63.5% in 1996 to 53.5% in 2003 and did not change subsequently. The association between GDP and poverty gap during BOOM and stable periods is understandable as value added (VA) and GDP increased during this period. Consequently, poverty gap reduced, though marginally. Increase in GDP, however, did not affect poverty headcount during the same period. The poverty data analysis also suggests that productivity improvement is one of the ways to reduce poverty in Nigeria.

It appears that GDP and VA go hand in hand during BOOM and BUST periods. During the BOOM period, VA increased from 3.94% in 1998 to 6.27% in 2008 and GDP increased from 1,577.09 in 1998 to 2,072.27 in 2008. During the stable period, VA declined to 5.88% in 2009 and to 2.94% in 2013. However, GDP continued to increase in the stable period and reached to 2,476.86 in 2013.

In the BUST period, growth of VA declined from 4.27% in 2014 to 2.12% in 2018. GDP followed the trend and declined from 2,563.9 in 2014 to 2,396.31 in 2018. The VA and GDP follow a similar trend to that of oil prices in international markets in BOOM and BUST periods. It is crystal clear from the analysis that international oil prices drove the VA and GDP in Nigeria in BOOM and BUST periods.

The declining trend of employment in agriculture in the entire study period suggests that the workforce is moving away from agriculture. This could be due to no opportunities in the sector. One of the possible reasons for this phenomenon could be that a small number of entrepreneurs are engaged in exports of primary products that do not necessitate a large workforce. Agriculture has a declining employment rate. One of the reasons could be that the labor force is moving away from agriculture to other industries. The poverty headcount remains unchanged since they have not moved to industry or to any other sectors. Hence it may be inferred from the findings that the Nigerian government needs to focus on the exporting of processed agri-products which would further increase the national income resulting in economic stability, and reduction of poverty and unemployment.

3.5 Analysis of Angola

The analysis of Angola is presented in four parts in Appendix 3.2 Figure 3.8. Part 1 of the figure presents growth of value added in agriculture during 1998 to 2018. The data for 1998 to 2002 are not available. It can be seen from the figure that growth of value added (agriculture, forestry, and fishing) has been highly volatile. This could be because of volatility of commodity prices in international markets. The overall trend of value added suggests that it has been parabolic during the study period.

Part 2 of Figure 3.8 presents the trend of GDP per capita during the study period. Data considered in the analysis are in USD constant at 2010. It can be seen from the figure that GDP has increased in the initial period (1998 to 2008) and remained stable during 2008 to 2014. The figure also shows that it has been declining since then.

Part 3 of the figure depicts the trend of rate of employment in agriculture during 1998 to 2018. The data represent the percentage of employment in agriculture to the total employment. It can be seen from the figure that employment in agriculture follows the similar pattern to that of GDP. During the BOOM period it increased from 37.79% in 1998 to 44.42% in 2008 and continued to increase and reaches 50.99% in 2013. It witnessed a marginal decline in the BUST period. It changed from 50.77% in 2014 to 50.52% in 2018. The results indicate the employment in agriculture is influenced by VA. During the BOOM period employment increased as the VA experienced a positive growth rate and declined in the BUST period when VA collapsed. The findings suggest that volatility in VA growth influenced the employment in the agriculture sector. It may be inferred that Angolan agriculture export is predominantly in primary products.

Poverty analysis is presented in part 4 of the figure. GDP per capita has implications on poverty reduction also. Unlike GDP data poverty data are available on a decadal basis. The poverty gap at $1.90 a day (2011 PPP) (%) was 14.6, 9.6, and 21.4 in 2000, 2008, and 2018 respectively. The poverty gap reduced from 14.6% to 9.6% during the BOOM period and increased during the BUST period from 9.6% to 21.4%. The poverty headcount ratio at $1.90 a day (2011 PPP) (% of population) follows a similar trend to that of the poverty gap which is very much on expected lines. It deceased from 32.3% to 30.1% during the BOOM period and increased to 47.6% in the BUST period. The poverty data analysis also suggests that productivity improvement is one of the ways to reduce poverty in Angola.

It appears that GDP and VA go hand in hand during the study period. During the BOOM period VA increased from 8.023% in 2003 to 16.303% in 2006 and GDP increased from 2,423.29 to 3,102.65 during the same period. VA declined substantially after 2006 and remained almost unchanged (between 4.01% and 5.55%) during 2007 and 2013. The period is regarded as a stable period. GDP also marginally increased (changed from 3,409.50 to 3,796.88) during this period. In the BUST period, growth of VA suddenly jumped to 17.32% in 2014 and declined subsequently to reach 0.47% in 2017. GDP follows a similar trend during the BUST period. It declined from 3843.19 in 2014 to 3229.62 in 2018.

The fluctuating trend of VA growth and employment rate suggests that Angola's agriculture exports are predominantly in primary products and are highly volatile which is reflected in GDP per capita trend. GDP might have been influenced by exports of commodities other than agriculture as well. It may be inferred from the findings that Angola needs to focus on exports of processed agri-products which would not only add to the national income but also contribute to poverty reduction and economic stability of the country.

3.6 Analysis of Algeria

The analysis of Algeria is presented in three parts in Appendix 3.2 Figure 3.9. Part 1 presents growth of value added in agriculture during 1998 to 2018. It can be seen from the figure that growth of agriculture, forestry, and fishing value added has been highly volatile. This could be because of volatility of commodity prices in international markets. The overall trend of VA suggests that it has been following a parabolic trend during the study period.

Part 2 of Figure 3.9 presents the trend of GDP per capita constant at USD 2010 (GDP) during the study period. It can be seen from the figure that GDP has continuously increased from 3,414.51 in 1998 during the BOOM and stable period to 4,702.09 in 2014. The figure also shows that it marginally declined during the BUST period (from 4,777.35 in 2015 to 4,764.38 in 2018).

Part 3 of the figure depicts the trend of rate of employment in agriculture during 1998 to 2018. The data represent the percentage of employment in agriculture to the total employment. It can be seen from the figure that employment in agriculture follows the inverse pattern to that of GDP during BOOM and stable periods. There is hardly any change from the declining trend except in the BUST period where the rate of decline has been much slower than the other two periods. During the BOOM period it declined from 22.69% in 1998 to 14.31% in 2008 while it changed from 13.01% in 2009 to 10.62% in 2013 during the stable period. The BUST period witnessed a very slow decline of employment rate (changed from 10.50% in 2014 to 10.02% in 2018). The Algerian case is different from many countries in the region in terms of magnitude of employment. It is comparatively very low varying just from 22.70& to 10.02% during the study period.

Poverty analysis cannot be done in the case of Algeria as the data are available only for 2011. The poverty gap at $1.90 a day (2011 PPP) (%) was 0.20 while the poverty headcount ratio at $1.90 a day (2011 PPP) (% of population) was just 0.50%.

It appears that GDP and VA go hand in hand during the study period. VA increased (changed from -4.6% in 2000 to 2.5% in 2007) with lot of fluctuations in between during the BOOM period while GDP also increased from 3414.51 in 1998 to 4409.74 in 2008. During the stable period, VA increased from -3.8% in 2008 to 8.2% in 2013. GDP followed a similar trend and increased from 4403.8 in 2009 to 4,702.09 in 2014. During the BUST period GDP and VA also moved in the same direction. The VA and GDP follow a similar trend to that of oil prices in international markets in the study period. It is crystal clear from the analysis that international oil prices drove the VA and GDP in Algeria.

The increasing trend of GDP and declining trend of employment in agriculture suggest that the workforce is moving away from agriculture. This could be due to no opportunities in the sector. Highly volatile VA in Algeria suggests a small number of entrepreneurs are engaged in exports of primary products that do not necessitate a large workforce. Hence it may be inferred from the findings that the Algerian government needs to focus on exporting processed agri-products which would further increase national income resulting in better socio-economic development of the country.

3.7 Analysis of Democratic Republic of the Congo

The analysis of the Congo is presented in four parts in Appendix 3.2 Figure 3.10. Part 1 presents growth of value added in agriculture during 1998 to 2018. It can be seen from the figure that the growth of agriculture, forestry, and fishing value added has been highly volatile. This could be because of volatility of commodity prices in international markets. The overall trend of value added suggests that it has been increasing during the study period.

Part 2 of Figure 3.10 presents the trend of GDP per capita constant at USD 2010 (GDP) during the study period. It can be seen from the figure that GDP declined from 341.78 in 1998 to 276.06 in 2002 and witnessed a positive trend thereafter. The figure also shows that it marginally declined during 2015 to 2017 (from 411.02 to 408.92) and reached 418.74 in 2018.

Part 3 of the figure depicts the trend of rate of employment in agriculture during 1998 to 2018. The data represent the percentage of employment in agriculture to the total employment. It can be seen from the figure that employment in agriculture follows the inverse pattern to that of GDP during entire study period.

There is hardly any change from a declining trend except in the beginning of the BOOM period (1998 to 2001). The employment rate registered a positive change from 72.64% in 1998 to 73.29% in 2001. It declined very steeply for the rest of the study period. The Congolese case is different in terms of magnitude of employment. It is very high and varies from 73.29% to 65.79% during the study period.

Poverty analysis is presented in part 4 of the figure. GDP per capita has implications on poverty reduction also. Unlike GDP data, poverty data are available on a decadal basis. The poverty gap at $1.90 a day (2011 PPP) (%) was 63.6 and 38.6 in 2004 and 2012 respectively. The poverty gap reduced from 63.6% to 38.6% from the BOOM to the stable period. This is very much understandable as VA and GDP increased during this period. The poverty headcount ratio at $1.90 a day (2011 PPP) (% of population) follows a similar trend to that of poverty gap which is very much on the expected lines. It decreased from 94.1% in 2004 to 76.6% in 2012. The poverty data analysis also suggests that productivity improvement is one of the ways to reduce poverty in the Congo.

It appears that GDP and VA go hand in hand during the study period. During the BOOM period, VA increased from -1.45% in 1998 to 5.64% in 2006 and GDP increased from 276.06 in 2003 to 324.04 in 2008. During the stable period, VA declined to 2.76% in 2007 and increased to 4.74% in 2014. GDP also increased (changed from 315.26 in 2007 to 397.34 in 2014) during this period. In the BUST period growth of VA declined from 4.74% in 2014 to 1.46% in 2018. GDP fluctuated during the BUST period (from 497.34 in 2014 to 418.74 in 2018). The VA and GDP fluctuations follow a similar trend to that of oil prices in international markets. It is crystal clear from the analysis that international oil prices drove the VA and GDP in Congo.

The case of Congo is slightly different than other African oil-exporting nations. During the BUST period the decline of VA is very marginal. Moreover, the overall trend of VA is positive which is reflected in the positive trend of GDP. However, the major concern for the DRC (Democratic Republic of the Congo) economy is the poverty gap and poverty headcount.

The increasing trend of GDP and the declining trend of employment in agriculture suggests that the workforce is moving away from agriculture. This could be due to no opportunities in the sector. One of the possible reasons for this phenomenon could be that a small number of entrepreneurs are engaged in exports of primary products that do not necessitate a large workforce. The possibility of going way the surplus workforce in other sectors is very remote as the poverty headcount is very large. Hence it may be inferred from the findings that the Congolese government needs to focus on the exporting of processed agri-products which would further increase the national income resulting in economic stability, reduction of poverty, and unemployment.

3.8 Analysis of Brazzaville

The analysis of Brazzaville is presented in four parts in Appendix 3.2 Figure 3.11. Part 1 of the figure presents growth of value added in agriculture during 1998 to 2018. It can be seen from the figure that growth of agriculture, forestry, and fishing value added has been highly volatile. This could be because of volatility of commodity prices in international markets. The overall trend of value added suggests that it has been increasing during the study period.

Part 2 of the figure presents the trend of GDP per capita constant at USD 2010 (GDP) during the study period. It can be seen from the figure that GDP has been fluctuating during the entire period. It witnessed a positive trend during the BOOM and stable periods while it drastically declined during the BUST period.

Part 3 of the figure depicts the trend of rate of employment in agriculture during 1998 to 2018. The data represent the percentage of employment in agriculture to the total employment. It can be seen from the figure that employment in agriculture follows the inverse pattern to that of GDP during BOOM and stable periods while in the BUST period the association of rate of employment followed a similar trend to that of GDP. There is hardly any change from the declining trend throughout the study period. It declined from 42.23% in 1998 to 34.60% in 2018.

Part 4 of the figure presents analysis of poverty. GDP has implications on poverty reduction also. Unlike GDP data, poverty data are available on a decadal basis. The poverty gap at $1.90 a day (2011 PPP) (%) was 21.1% and 14.9% in 2005 and 2011 respectively. The poverty gap reduced from 21.1% to 14.9% from the BOOM to the stable period. This is very much understandable as GDP increased during this period. The poverty headcount ratio at $1.90 a day (2011 PPP) (% of population) follows a similar trend to that of the poverty gap which is very much on the expected lines. It decreased from 53.4% to 37.0% from 2005 to 2011. The poverty data analysis suggests that productivity improvement is one of the ways to reduce poverty in Brazzaville.

It appears that GDP and VA go hand in hand during the study period. During the BOOM period, VA increased from 1.68% in 1998 to 5.58% in 2008 observing high volatility with a peak at 8.58% in 2002. GDP also changed from 2,465.87 in 1998 to 2,561.19 in 2008 with little volatility and having a peak at 2,640.32 in 2006. During the stable period, VA drastically dropped to -3.19% in 2009 and reached 7.99% in 2013 with a peak at 8.39% in 2011. GDP also increased from 2,663.58 in 2009 to 2,884.44 in 2013 during this period. In the BUST period VA declined from 8.07% in 2014 to -1.65% in 2018. GDP followed a similar trend and declined from 3,005.74 in 2014 to 2,651.70 in 2018. The VA and GDP fluctuations follow a similar trend to that of oil prices in international markets. It is crystal clear from the analysis that international oil prices drove the VA and GDP in Brazzaville.

The case of Brazzaville is different than the Congo in terms of magnitude of all the economic indicators. GDP is almost ten times higher than Congo and the rate of employment in agriculture is much lower. Higher GDP and lower employment in agriculture are expected to result in lower levels of poverty which is very much the case in Brazzaville. The analysis presented above shows that poverty gap and headcounts are much lower in Brazzaville than Congo.

The increasing trend of GDP and the declining trend of employment in agriculture suggests that the workforce is moving away from agriculture. This could be due to no opportunities in the sector. One of the possible reasons for this phenomenon could be that a small number of entrepreneurs are engaged in exports of primary products that do not necessitate a large workforce. The possibility of going way the surplus workforce in other sectors is very remote as the poverty headcount is still large. Hence it may be inferred from the findings that the Congolese government needs to focus on the exporting of processed agri-products which would further increase the national income resulting in economic stability, and the reduction of poverty and unemployment.

3.9 Analysis of Sudan

The analysis of Sudan is presented in four parts in Appendix 3.2 Figure 3.12. Part 1 presents growth of value added in agriculture during 1998 to 2018. It can be seen from the figure that growth of agriculture, forestry, and fishing value added has been highly volatile. This could be because of volatility of commodity prices in international markets. The overall trend of VA suggests that it has been following a parabolic trend during the study period.

Part 2 of the figure presents the trend of GDP per capita constant at USD 2010 (GDP) during the study period. It can be seen from the figure that GDP has been following an increasing trend with minor fluctuations during the study period. It witnessed continuous increase during the BOOM and stable period but declined during the BUST period.

Part 3 of the figure depicts the trend of rate of employment in agriculture during 1998 to 2018. The data represent the percentage of employment in agriculture to the total employment. It can be seen from the figure that employment in agriculture follows the inverse pattern to that of GDP during the entire study period. There is hardly any change from the declining trend. The employment rate declined from 52.24% in 1998 to 40.11% in 2018. The Sudanese case is different in terms of magnitude of employment from several countries in the region. It is very high.

Poverty analysis is presented in Part 4 of the figure. GDP per capita has implications on poverty reduction also. Unlike GDP data, poverty data are available on a decadal basis. The poverty gap at $1.90 a day (2011 PPP) (%) was 4.4 and 2.9 in 2009 and 2014 respectively. The poverty gap reduced from 4.4% to 2.9% from the BOOM to the stable period. This is very much understandable as VA and GDP increased during this period. The poverty headcount ratio at $1.90 a day (2011 PPP) (% of population) follows a similar trend to that of the poverty gap which is very much on the expected lines. It decreased from 16.2% to 12.7% from 2009 to 2014. The poverty data analysis also suggests that productivity improvement is one of the ways to reduce poverty in Sudan.

The analysis shows that GDP and VA go hand in hand during the study period. During the BOOM period, VA increased from 3.30% in 1998 to 8.68% in 2006 and GDP increased from 980.43 in 1998 to 1291.57 in 2006 during the same period. During the stable period, VA increased from -1.37% in 2007 to 4.0% in

2013. In the BUST period growth of VA declined from 2.78% in 2015 to -1.5% in 2018. GDP followed a similar trend and declined from 1869.55 to 1855.63 during the BUST period. The VA and GDP fluctuations follow a similar trend to that of oil prices in international markets. It is crystal clear from the analysis that international oil prices drove the VA and GDP in Sudan.

The increasing trend of GDP and the declining trend of employment in agriculture suggest that the workforce is moving away from agriculture. This could be due to no opportunities in the sector. One of the possible reasons for this phenomenon could be that a small number of entrepreneurs are engaged in exports of primary products that do not necessitate a large workforce. The possibility of going way the surplus workforce in other sectors is very remote as the poverty headcount is fairly large. Hence it may be inferred from the findings that the Sudanese government needs to focus on exporting processed agri-products which would further increase national income resulting in economic stability, and reduction of poverty and unemployment.

Summing up

More countries experienced higher growth rates before the crises than after. From the figure 3.4, there were just two countries with less than -1.00% growth rate before the 1973 crisis, the number of countries with similar growth increased to eight and 30 before falling to 17 before the 2020 crisis. When we compare the first three periods the number of countries experiencing decline of income gradually increased. The number of countries recording above 6% growth fell. Evidently, more and more countries record declining income due to oil crises and more significantly it gets harder to recover from the shocks.

The number of countries with high growth (more than 6%) decreased from 14 before the 1973 crisis to just five before the 2020 crisis. The decrease in number suggests that relatively high-growth developing countries that experienced loss of income growth due to external shocks have the propensity to migrate into the category of lower-income growing countries without taking remedial actions.

The simple average rate of growth of all the countries BEFORE the crises was (73:3.27%, 79:2.80%, 90:2.25%, 2008:2.01%) and dropped to (73:1.45%, 79:1.44%, 90:1.51%, 2008:1.37%) after the crises.

On the other hand, the average growth rate of major oil-producing countries before the crises was (73:3.30%, 79:3.01%, 90:1.96%, 2008:2.09%) and dropped to (73:1.50%, 79:1.40%, 90:1.70%, 2008:0.68%) after the crises. It is clear that oil shocks lead to greater income disparities between oil and non-oil producing countries.

Negative/low growth tends to experience path-dependency: in order to answer the question as to who loses and by what extent, we examine the movement of growth rates within each category band. In-depth analysis suggests that it is not only that the number of countries in the less than -1% growth category increased from the 1973 crisis to the 2020 crisis, but their growth rates also declined. The findings show that the impact of oil crises on low-growing countries is more severe than for high-growth countries.

4 Export Market Diversification in Asia and Africa

4.1 Introduction

In the 1970s, China's global exports were less than 1%. Prior to the 1980s, China was going through a period of social upheaval, poverty, and dictatorship under Mao Zedong. In 1979, for example, Shenzhen, one of the most dynamic manufacturing hubs today, was a town with around 30,000 inhabitants. China (excluding Taiwan and Hong Kong) had no place in the top ten of global exporters until the early 2000 when it hit a 3.3% share of global exports.[1]

Over time, China has become the *factory of the world* and, more impressively, *a trade giant* and manufacturing juggernaut. Only the US and Germany come close to its share of global exports, sitting at 8.1% and 7.8% respectively. China has achieved an incredible trading feat in terms of export product sophistication. Its biggest export partners in 2020 were the US (US$46.5 billion), Hong Kong (US$34.3 billion), Japan (US$13.4 billion), Vietnam (US$13 billion), and South Korea (US$11.7 billion). Beyond China's largest trade partners, however, it is rapidly increasing exports to several other countries across the world.

Twenty-years after the Vietnam War ended in 1975, Vietnam's economy was *one of the poorest in the world*. By the mid-1980s, per capita GDP (Gross Domestic Product) was around US$200 and $300. Subsequently, through a series of economic and political reforms, the country adopted what it termed a "socialist-oriented market economy". Up until the 1980s, Vietnamese industries depended on aid from the Soviet Union. After 1985, the industrial weaknesses were recognised and more autonomy was introduced to enhance efficiency, which resulted in a market-oriented economy called "Doi-Moi". In this strategy, indicative planning, i.e., coordination of private and public investment and a macroeconomic management system, was implemented. In this industrial policy, the shift was majorly towards small industries and exports rather than heavy industries. Today, Vietnam is one of the high-performing actors of the emerging markets universe. Its economic growth of 6–7% rivals China, and it exports are worth as much as the total value of its GDP. It manufactures anything from Nike sportswear to Samsung. China, Vietnam, and India became the most dynamic traders among all Asian economies. The development of regional value chains in office and telecom equipment highly

DOI: 10.4324/9781003245322-4

contributed to the pace of growth of economies such as Vietnam. Vietnamese exports of office and telecom equipment have grown considerably, accounting for 23% of Vietnamese exports in 2018, up from 1% in 2008.[2]

Notably, Vietnam has imitated successful Asian countries such as ROK (Republic of Korea) by pushing into relatively more complex product categories at its income level while also mastering horizontal diversification through processing agricultural commodities for export. It therefore expanded its export basket and made a move into higher value crops. Exports of processed agriculture products expanded driven by rice, cashew, coffee, fisheries, and vegetables and fruits. Importantly, Vietnam continues to diversify its agricultural exports to higher value crops, including vegetables and fruits, which surged to 42% in 2017 and 29% in 2018. The export value of vegetables and fruits has now surpassed export earnings from traditional commodities, such as crude oil, rice, and black pepper. Progressively, oil exports declined despite rising oil prices. While oil prices are up by 26.3% (annually), a substantial decline in volumes caused oil export earnings to contract by 27% in the first four months of 2018.[3]

Unlike Asia, raw materials remain the bulk of exports from African countries, although there is considerable variation by subregion: Southern and East Africa have more diversified export baskets than West and Central Africa. In terms of destinations, a number of African countries have diversified their trade partners. China and India recently overtook the United States as Africa's largest bilateral trade partners.

In a similar fashion, like Vietnam in 1991, Zambia embarked on a radical reform that reshaped the country's economy from a centrally planned to a market economy.[4] The reform involved massive privatisation of around an 80% share of public activity as well as wide liberalisation of commodity prices, among others. However, unlike Vietnam, Zambia did not succeed in diversifying the country's export base away from its persistent heavy dependency on copper. The country's dependence on foreign assistance remained as did poverty. This country remains a Least Developed Country (LDC).

Zambia's considerable endowment with mineral resources has been the main source of the country's foreign earnings from the export of minerals. For over 70 years the mining industry, consisting mainly of copper, and to a lesser extent, zinc, silver, gold, and cobalt, has fuelled its growth but this has been insufficient to take the citizens out of poverty. Due to volatile and decreasing world prices in copper, weak institutions, and harsh global investment, environment copper production has declined and its contribution to the sector of GDP has progressively diminished, from 19% in 1992 to around 4% since 1999.

Consider the Democratic Republic of the Congo's main exports in 2019. These are copper (56%), cobalt (21%), and gold (13%), all worth US$10 billion. Congo's most important export partners are China (24% of total exports), followed by South Africa (22%) and the European Union (4%). In the period of 2010 to 2012 the country's export composition remained essentially the same: gold, diamonds, copper, cobalt, coltan, zinc, tin, tungsten, crude oil, wood products, and coffee. At an estimated $8.8 billion, the country has been trading with the same partners: China 53.4% Zambia 24.5% Belgium 5.6% United Kingdom 4.4% (2012 est.).[5]

For several decades, Thailand was a mono-product economy, with traditional subsistence agricultural economy engaging about 70% of the population in rice cultivation. The year 1855 marked the opening up of the once closed economy when a trade agreement with Great Britain initiated the rice export trade. During the period 1855–1950, rice accounted for about 70% of all exports. As a consequence of its mono-product dependence, economic growth prior to 1950s was stagnant without structural changes However, during the period 1950–1961, the agricultural sector became diversified to include cultivation of other crops like cassava, corn, cotton, peanuts, soybeans, and tobacco, amongst others.

By 2020, Thailand had become a major exporter into the most sophisticated markets, its most prominent destination for exports are the United States ($32.2B), China ($29.1B), Japan ($23.8B), Vietnam ($11.8B), and Hong Kong ($11.1B). Significantly, the top ten export items were not raw agricultural and petroleum products but industrial machinery including computers: $40.2 billion (16.4% of total exports), electrical machinery, equipment: $33.9 billion (13.8%), vehicles: $28.9 billion (11.8%), gems, precious metals: $15.7 billion (6.4%), rubber, rubber articles: $15.3 billion (6.3%), plastics, plastic articles: $13.3 billion (5.4%).

The rapid growth experienced by Thailand in the 1980s was accompanied by structural diversification as the share of agriculture's contribution to GDP declined from 50.1% in 1950 to about 24.9% in 1980 and in 1988 saw a further decrease to an estimated 18%. The share of manufacturing in GDP rose from 10.3% in 1951 to 20.7% in 1980 and in 1988 a further increase to 23%; however, rice remained the dominant crop, but the total cultivated area for rice had fallen to around 62% by 1988. The export sector witnessed changes as the exports of manufactured goods exceeded those of agricultural goods for the first time in 1986. Further horizontal diversification proceeded and the top ten resource-based export items such as textiles, rice, tapioca products, gems and jewellery, integrated circuits, canned seafood, shoes, sugar, and frozen shrimp had more manufactured products with the value of textile exports doubling that of rice.

Amidst upheavals of the economic cycle, Thailand successfully transformed its economy from agriculture to export-oriented manufacturing, while integrating key manufacturing production into regional value chains, particularly in automobiles and electronics. While diversifying its economic base into tourism, health care, and other services, Thailand also established a regional hub for key transport and logistics with its world-class airport.

A once mono-product economy, it is now a leading producer of high-tech products, automobiles, and electronics, and ranked as the 12th largest automobile producer in the world. As a major exporter of high-value goods, its exports account for two-thirds of its GDP. In addition to the structural diversification strategies employed, Thailand's government has a system of innovation through science parks, provision of research grants, and establishment of public research institutions, among others.

Countries	Export Values (Billion USD)		Markets
China	1989	52.54	China, Hong Kong SAR, Japan, USA, Fmr USSR, Singapore
	2020	2590.60	USA, China, Hong Kong SAR, Japan, Vietnam, Rep. of Korea
South Korea	1980	18.11	USA, Japan, Saudi Arabia. Fmr Fed. Rep. of Germany, China, Hong Kong SAR
	2020	512.71	China, USA, Vietnam, China, Hong Kong SAR, Japan
Vietnam	1997	9.18	Japan, Singapore, Other Asia, China, China, Hong Kong SAR
	2020	281.44	USA, China, Japan, Rep. of Korea, Hong Kong SAR
Nigeria	1998	6.87	USA, Spain, France, Italy, Brazil
	2019	53.62	India, Spain, Netherlands, Ghana, France
South Africa	2000	26.30	Area, nes, USA, United Kingdom, Germany, Japan
	2020	80.85	China, USA, Areas, nes, Germany, United Kingdom

Figure 4.1 Export market diversification. Source: Authors.

The export market diversification of five sample countries is depicted in Figure 4.1, while product and market diversifications of all sample countries are presented in Appendix 4.1.

In this chapter, we focus on the dynamics and determinants of export market diversification. This dimension of economic diversification is concerned with a country and its major trade sectors and partners; how well a country succeeds in diversifying its basket of exports and its share of export to the largest trading partners are used to measure export diversification.

Export market diversification is part of economic development through a process of structural transformation whereby countries compete to transit from producing "poor-country goods" to "rich-country goods". Export diversification leads to increased diversity in the range, quality, and number of countries to which the country exports goods and services. For developing commodity-based economies, the aspiration is to move from the export of one or a few primary commodities such as oil and primary agriculture to a broader and higher quality set of manufactured goods and services. The destination of export is particularly critical, as success will be determined by a wide range of factors such as the country's overall system of skills to produce to the stringent standards set by rich countries.[6] The rise in the number of exported goods and in the diversity of trading partners point to the ability of exporters in breaking into and participating in regional and global value chains.

Industrialisation and capabilities acquired for product innovation drive export market diversification, another description of vertical diversification. These capabilities, both technological and institutional, are required for developing countries advance to a higher stage of development, by producing for markets that are more complex. This dynamic of structural change in the direction of manufacturing and export diversification in turn drives economic growth (Hesse, 2008). Poor developing countries that rely on easy export income from oil forgo several benefits. First, the drive towards entering new sophisticated markets through the export diversification process compels learning-by-doing to manufacture new products, new processes, and new markets in the Schumpeterian sense. The path of value addition, be it in old or new product modification, tends to engender higher productivity through knowledge spillovers. Second, export market diversification targeting new trade partners may involve breaking into new sectors or following other industrial trajectories, enhancing economic growth by promoting fostering backward and forward linkages. Third, findings from literature provide evidence that countries that manufacture complex products tend to grow more sustainably in the long-term and grow faster.[7]

In contrasting regional perspective, the past decade has seen Asia's share of world exports rising from 28% in 2008 to 34% in 2018.[8] In contrast, Africa's share in world exports declined from 3.5% to 2.5% – the lowest regional share. Africa's oil exporters continued to perform well until the pandemic struck; in 2018, it accounted for 38% of total exports. In other words, export growth of Africa and the Middle East over the past ten years has been clearly linked to fuel price developments. Even among the Least Developed Countries, Asian countries, notably, Cambodia is primarily an exporter of manufactured goods; apparel and clothing continues to be its top export. The comparator African economies are primarily commodity exporters comprising Burkina Faso and Ghana, which are large exporters of gold, and Guinea, primary exporter of aluminium ores and concentrates (bauxite). Guinea has the world's largest reserves of bauxite, the primary ore of aluminium. Its growth in bauxite exports has been driven by demand from China, the world's largest producer and consumer of aluminium.

The remainder of the chapter is organised as follows: Section 2 presents methodology and data sources while Section 3 contains conceptual framework and hypotheses. An analytical model and statistical findings are presented and discussed in Section 4. Finally, Section 5 summarises findings of the chapter.

4.2 Methodology and data

Economic diversification is broadly categorised into domestic product diversification and trade diversification. Domestic product diversification results from a shift of domestic output across sectors, industries, and firms. It requires resource reallocation across and/or within industries, from low productivity activities to industries that have higher productivity, thereby ensuring diversified production of goods and services in an economy. The capabilities for domestic product diversification prepare a country for breaking into global export markets although the extent of the market would depend on the country size (measured by national population) and market accessibility.

Trade diversification can occur in three main ways: first, via introduction of new products to the export portfolio; second, via changes in the export mix of existing products to new markets; and third, via a qualitative upgrading of exported or imported products (World Bank Group, 2019). Trade diversification often pertains to exportation; therefore, we can relate it to export diversification. Export diversification in itself is an objective for every country in order to reduce its vulnerability of exposure to adverse terms of trade shocks, to stabilise export revenues, as well as boost output diversification. In low-income countries, export diversification is associated with less output volatility and more rapid sectoral reallocation (World Bank Group, 2019). Nevertheless, for export diversification to occur in an economy, it needs to upgrade its products, so they fit competitively into the more sophisticated export basket.

For resource-dependent countries, such as Nigeria, it is more difficult to undergo export diversification as the process entails a shift in the production base from the primary sector to the secondary sector (manufacturing and industries). This process can be broadly termed as industrialisation. In economic diversification terms, industrialisation centres on the twin strategies of import substitution and export-led industrialisation. While the former seeks the promotion of domestic-focused industries in order to replace foreign-made goods with locally made goods, the latter is a drastic process aimed at opening domestic markets to foreign competition by supporting export industries. (Dennis and Shepherd, 2011; Songwe, 2019; World Bank Group, 2019)

Export market diversification focuses on expansion of exports, which can be achieved in two ways. First, a country can increase the exports by expanding the markets for the same products suggesting that it sought newer markets for the same product. There are several ways to achieve it. One of the possible ways is the production of goods in the home country and exported to the new markets. Alternatively, goods can be manufactured in new locations and marketed locally with regional ambitions, if found to be economically viable.

Another way is to augment exports is the creation of new, modified products, or market-specific products. Product innovation is central to this approach of export expansion; this is known as export product diversification. Several models are available for this approach of export diversification. New products are manufactured in the home country and exporting them to host countries and secondly production is also shifted to host countries. The choice of a particular model depends on the type of product innovation and financial and other resources needed in the process. Capital and skill-intensive new products are usually manufactured in the home country and shipped to export markets if it is economically viable to manufacture such products in the host countries.

In the event of export diversification whether it is derived by export market or export product diversification, the home country is likely to reap the benefit of diversification. In case of market diversification and if the new products are manufactured in the home country, it is likely to create substantial employment resulting in various economic gains. In the case that the additional demand is met by manufacturing in the host location, the home country would benefit economically as product costs are likely to be less resulting in higher profit.

In the event of export product diversification, the return would depend on the production model adopted by the exporting country. If the new product is manufactured in the home country, it is likely to create more employment resulting in other economic benefits. Establishing manufacturing facilities in host countries is expected to create more economic benefits in addition to employment generation. In the event of the second model, employment is likely to be created at managerial level and for highly skilled workers who would be responsible for offshore production.

The present study investigates the impact of export market and export product diversification on economic development. This chapter analyses export market diversification while Chapter 5 investigates the impact of technological capabilities on economic and product diversification.

The chapter uses the Herfindahl–Hirschman (HHI) market diversification index as a measure of export market diversification. The general definition of the HHI index is:

$$H = \sum_{i=1}^{N} S_i^2 \tag{1}$$

where,

S_i Market share of firm i in the market
N Number of firms

In the present situation

S_i Exports share of a particular country in export destination i
N Number of export destination of a particular country in a particular year

In this framework, there is an inverse relationship between number of export markets and HHI. For instance, if a country exports 20%, 30%, 40%, and 10% to four countries in a particular year, the HHI would be $(0.20)^2 + (0.30)^2 + (0.40)^2 + (0.10)^2 = 0.30$. On the other hand if there are two export destinations with 70% and 30% of exports for the country, HHI would be $(0.7)^2 + (0.3)^2 = 0.58$. Hence, we may infer that the higher the market diversification, the smaller the value of HHI. Based on the definition of HHI presented in EQ1, we estimate and present export market diversification indices for sample countries in Table 4.1.

It can be seen from the table that Export Market Diversification Index (EMDI) for Nigeria in 1998 was 0.204, which witnessed a declining trend and finally reached 0.066 in 2019. We conclude that export market diversification did take place in Nigeria during 1998 to 2019 although on closer examination the country continued to export the same set of petroleum products.[9] In the case of Ghana, diversification of exports markets has not been systematic. In fact, the country witnessed export market concentration from 1998 to 2010 and diversification during 2012 to 2015.

The EMDI scenario in Kenya and South Africa is similar to that of Nigeria. All the sample countries, except South Korea, in the Asian continent witnessed export market diversification. In the case of South Korea, market concentration has taken place. It is quite possible that South Korea might have focused on product diversification rather than market diversification.

In an important empirical study, Imbs and Wacziarg (2003) demonstrate that as income increases, economies become more diversified, and this process continues until the level of per capita income reaches about $9,000. Afterwards, countries start the specialisation process, which is shaped by endowments and various development policies. There is a U-shaped relationship between per capita income and sectoral concentration of the production. The authors show that this pattern holds true within a country over time. This implies that most developing countries are actually in the diversification stage and specialisation comes at a later stage of their development journey.

Product diversification might have resulted in concentrating on a select export destination. It is substantiated by Jinsoo Lee and Bok-keun Yu (2019).

In the next step, it is intended to identify factors that affect export market diversification. Before doing so, it is considered vital to analyse the consequence of export diversification on economic development. GDP per capita has been used as a proxy of economic development. South Korea has been excluded from subsequent analysis as there is no evidence of export market diversification in the country during the study period. The association between EMDI and economic development is depicted in Figure 4.2.

It can be seen from the figure that the association between the two is significant. The figure shows that the GDP per capita is much lower in countries with lower levels of diversification. This is evident in Ghana, Kenya, and India. The income levels of moderately diversified countries are higher than those of low diversified countries. Nigeria may be levelled as a moderately diversified country. The highly diversified countries are China, Indonesia, Malaysia, and South Africa. The income levels of these countries are much higher than the countries of the other two groups.

Table 4.1 Herfindahl–Hirschman market diversification index

Year	Nigeria	Ghana	Kenya	South Africa	China	India	Indonesia	Malaysia	South Korea
1998	0.204	0.090	0.074		0.120	0.070	0.083	0.100	0.059
1999	0.166	0.093	0.077		0.117	0.075	0.091	0.102	0.077
2000	0.218	0.115	0.071	0.053	0.111	0.070	0.098	0.105	0.086
2001	0.196	0.102	0.065	0.058	0.109	0.058	0.096	0.101	0.081
2002	0.134		0.087	0.047	0.108	0.062	0.087	0.098	0.083
2003	0.176	0.132	0.064	0.052	0.102	0.058	0.089	0.092	0.085
2004		0.159	0.068	0.053	0.098	0.054	0.089	0.086	0.086
2005		0.111	0.063	0.051	0.094	0.054	0.087	0.090	0.086
2006	0.230	0.110	0.055	0.053	0.088	0.050	0.087	0.085	0.081
2007	0.242	0.168	0.055	0.052	0.077	0.047	0.082	0.075	0.079
2008	0.204	0.218	0.055	0.048	0.067	0.042	0.081	0.071	0.074
2009	0.107	0.241	0.058	0.044	0.070	0.049	0.070	0.070	0.082
2010	0.145	0.300	0.054	0.043	0.068	0.045	0.072	0.068	0.088
2011	0.088	0.119		0.048	0.066	0.046	0.074	0.068	0.085
2012	0.071	0.123		0.044	0.070	0.047	0.072	0.071	0.088
2013	0.066	0.099	0.049	0.045	0.072	0.041	0.071	0.071	0.095
2014	0.065	0.063		0.040	0.067	0.043	0.063	0.069	0.188
2015	0.072	0.069	0.047	0.040	0.067	0.049	0.061	0.069	0.100
2016	0.077	0.089	0.047	0.040	0.067	0.052	0.061	0.069	0.097
2017	0.080	0.093	0.050	0.040	0.066	0.048	0.065	0.069	0.096
2018	0.071	0.096	0.048	0.040	0.066	0.048	0.068	0.070	0.106
2019	0.066	0.191	0.050	0.044	0.056	0.050	0.070	0.070	0.101

Source: compiled from COMTRADE data

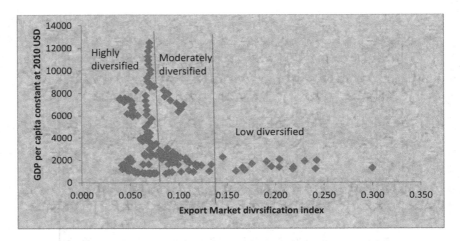

Figure 4.2 Export market diversification and economic development. Source: Authors.

4.3 Conceptual framework and hypotheses

In the third step, we intend to identify the factors that play a catalytic role in export market diversification. Several studies (Imbs and Wacziarg, 2003; Klinger and Lederman, 2006; Cadot et al., 2011) have examined the diversification and its association with economic factors. The study by Imbs and Wacziarg (2003) focusing on economic diversification finds a U-shaped relationship between specialisation and income. The study reports that low levels of income countries diversify as their income rises and start concentrating once they reach a threshold level of income. Focusing exclusively on export product diversification, the study by Klinger and Lederman (2006) substantiated earlier findings. Earlier studies find that factors that contribute to diversification vary from firm-specific to national policy initiatives. For instance, Callen et al. (2014) finds that incentive structure for workers is key to diversification in the Gulf countries while Cherif et al. (2016) reports the importance of industrial policy to develop and diversify the economy.

This being a cross-country study, it is hypothesised that country-specific factors are likely to play a pivotal role in influencing export diversification. These factors could be broadly categorised into four groups, i.e., financial resources, international investment, technological competence, and innovation capacity. All the variables used in multivariate analysis are grouped in these four categories. The variables encompassing these groups are discussed in detail in the following subsection. Infrastructure also plays a pivotal role in all industrial activities. Hence its role has also been discussed in the subsection.

4.3.1 *Financial resource*

Among many impediments in expansion of global markets, financial resources are the major ones. Financial resources are needed to set up a marketing base in foreign countries. It could be in the form of collaboration with local firms or setting up own marketing/manufacturing base. Financial resources are needed for effective logistics support as well. The main source of finance comes from national income which is proxied by GDP. National income in a given year can provide a financial base to be used in the following years for investment in a foreign country. Hence it is hypothesised that GDP with one year lag could affect market diversification. The role of financial resources in influencing export diversification has been investigated by Giri et al. (2019). The study concludes that a strong financial sector helps to increase export diversification.

Trade finance plays an indispensable role in export market diversification especially in low-income countries with significant levels of real or perceived risks. Exporters in these countries tend to lack the knowledge of the global players and intricacies of markets. Additionally, the smaller actors depend on short-term loan facilities from commercial banks and these exporters need to be paid as soon as goods are shipped. Financing takes on added importance due to the considerable time it takes for cargos to be transported from Europe to Asia which may take up to 80 days.[10] The trade finance market is therefore sizable as the vast majority of the US$23 trillion worth of goods requires a loan, payment guarantee, or credit insurance to cross borders.

Exporters and importers from Least Developed Countries tend to pay very high fees, which increase their costs of trade while traders from developed countries benefit from low interest rates and fees provided by international banks. According to the Bank for International Settlements,[11] trade finance markets have been relatively concentrated with around 30 to 40 international banks operating global networks of distribution that allow them to supply trade finance almost anywhere around the world.

The large gap that now exists between supply and demand for trade finance is affecting poorer countries and smaller companies in particular, according to an annual survey of the African Development Bank (AfDB).[12]

There is a need for intensified trade financing to reenergise Africa's trade in the wake of the Covid-19 pandemic.[13,14] According to the report, only 40% of Africa's trade is bank-intermediated – a far lower share than the global average of 80%. The trade finance gap also remains unacceptably high at $81 billion in 2019. The report found that these are some of the structural challenges that hinder banks' ability to effectively intermediate Africa's trade with the world. It also highlighted the critical role of development finance institutions in supporting the industry.[15]

In many developing countries and most of the poorest countries, alternatives to bank financing are scarce. When financing requests are rejected by banks, trade transactions are abandoned, the ADB study says, with 60% of trade finance requests by small and medium-sized enterprises (SMEs) being rejected. This persistent trade finance gap represents a significant barrier to trade and for the global integration of developing countries through trade. According to the World

Economic Forum, lack of trade finance represents one of the top three obstacles for exporters for half of the countries in the world.

4.3.2 Infrastructure

Economic diversification requires investment in infrastructure. Africa's infrastructure investment needs have increased over time, reaching US$130–170 billion a year by 2018, with a financing gap of US$68–108 billion (AfDB, 2018). Clearly, one of the most significant barriers to industrialisation, value addition, and competitiveness of firms is poor infrastructure. According to a recent *Financial Times* (FT)[16] report on Nigeria:

> The congestion at the port in Lagos has become so bad that it can cost more than $4,000 to truck a container 20km to the Nigerian mainland these days, almost as much as it costs to ship one 12,000 nautical miles from China. The estimated loss in economic activities is $55 million per day.

Industrial development depends on a wide variety of hard, soft, and advanced infrastructure. Electric power, water/sanitation, roads, railways, ports, and airports propel all modern production structures such as factories and agricultural value chains. The success of global productive agricultural and manufacturing economies works with extensive logistics support including ports and airports, among others. The world's most productive service economies rely on top-tier computer technology, transport equipment, and, in some instances, mechanised warehouses.

4.3.3 International investment

Inward and outward investments could help in export diversification. Inward investment helps in understanding technical competence of firms which in turn might encourage the investing country to promote the products in the home country. The process might put both the countries in a virtuous circle of expansion of the market in the home country and attraction of more inward investment in the host country. The outward investment is also expected to contribute to export diversification. The outward investment could be in the form of setting up manufacturing plant in the foreign country aiming at the local market. The foreign investment is made either to capture the local market or for export promotion in the regional market. In either of the situations, outward investment is likely to help in export diversification. Having no prior knowledge of the association between international investment and market diversification, it is hypothesised that inward and outward investments are likely to help market diversification.

4.3.4 Technological competence

Technological factors are the most crucial ones to have influenced export market diversification. In fact, they are the driving force behind any economic progress. Several variables could encompass the technological competence such as manufacturing value added as a percentage of GDP, share of employment in industry as a percentage of total employment, share of high-tech production as a percentage of total industrial output, and variables related to skill of workforce, etc. The data are permitted to use only two variables, namely; manufacturing value added as a percentage of GDP and share of employment in industry as a percentage of total employment in the analysis. The first variable indicates the manufacturing capability of the country while the second represents the suitability of the workforce for industrial production. Several studies (UNCTAD, 2018b; Abass and Ibrahim, 2018) find positive association between export diversification and value addition. The findings of the study by UNCTAD (2018b) are based on commodity exports while the focus of Abass and Ibrahim (2018) is on the agriculture sector. Since both these factors are crucial for manufacturing of globally competitive products, we hypothesise that technological competence fosters export diversification.

4.3.5 *Innovation capacity*

Innovation capability is central to the manufacture of diversified and function and market-specific products; it is the accumulation of innovation capacity that helps in economic diversification. Several proxies such as number of patents filed, number of commercialised patents, scientists working in R&D (Research and Development) labs, and government expenditure on R&D, etc. can be used to measure innovation capabilities. The present study uses percentage of government expenditure on R&D to GDP as a measure of innovation capability. We preferred R&D expenditure due to availability of data. In the case of other indicators, data were very sparse. There have been a few studies (Cirera et al., 2015; Rodríguez-Duarte et al., 2007) that examine the association between export diversification and innovation capabilities. The firm-level study of Brazilian industry by Cirere et al. (2015) finds that innovation efforts and strategic positioning of firms are important in explaining diversification. Based on the existing literature it is hypothesised that innovation capability is expected to contribute in the augmentation of export market diversification.

4.4 Analytical model and statistical analysis

Based on the hypothesis formulated above, the following econometric model is used to identify factors that influence export market diversification.

$$EMDI_{c,i} = f\left(LGDP_{c,i}[-1], OFDI_{c,i}[-1], IFDI_{c,i}[-1], \\ EMPIND_{c,i}, MVA_{c,i}, R\&D_{c,i}\right) \tag{2}$$

where,

c,i Represent country and year

$EMDI_{c,i}$ Export Market Diversification Index

LGDP$_{c,i}$[-1] One year lag of log of GDP in USD constant at 2010
OFDI$_{c,i}$[-1] One year lag of outward FDI
IFDI$_{c,i}$[-1] One year lag of inward FDI
EMPIND Share of employment in industry to the total employment
MVA$_{c,i}$ Manufacturing value added as % of GDP
R&D$_{c,i}$ Government expenditure on R&D as % of GDP

As indicated earlier, the analysis is based on South Africa, Nigeria, Kenya, Ghana, China, Indonesia, Malaysia, and India for 1998 to 2019. The unbalanced panel data was subjected to generalised least square estimation. The parameter estimates along with other statistics are presented in Table 4.2.

It can be seen from Table 4.2 that three different specifications have been used. This was primarily to get rid of the multicollinearity problem. In the first specification all the explanatory variables are used while in the second specification LGDP, OFDI, and EMPIND are dropped. This was necessary as the correlation between income and manufacturing value added and R&D expenditure are 0.622 and 0.590 respectively. Therefore, LGDP is dropped in the second specification. On similar grounds OFDI and EMPIND are dropped. In the third specification R&D was dropped because of high correlation between R&D and manufacturing value added. Moreover dropping of R&D in the third specification provided more degree of freedom to identify association between market diversification and manufacturing value added.

Before interpreting the results, it is worth mentioning that the negative sign of the coefficient of the explanatory variables represents the increasing trend of the variable with diversification. This is because diversification and the value of diversification index go in opposite directions. The results presented in Table 4.2 show that GDP and OFDI emerged significant at the 5% level. The results are according to our expectation. As argued earlier, financial resources provide ample opportunities for countries to explore the possibility of market expansion. The results substantiate findings of earlier studies. The significant emergence of outward FDI brings out new phenomenon in the export diversification process. The findings suggest that investing in a foreign country helps in expanding the market in that country. To some extent it is obvious because setting up manufacturing plants or providing manufacturing technology helps the host country to manufacture market-specific products. The strategy not only helps in marketing but also results in reduction in production cost.

A surprising finding of the study – the inverse relationship of export market diversification with inflow of FDI – suggests that the higher the extent of diversification the lower is the inward FDI. One of the interpretations of the finding could be that inward FDI has been reducing over time and market diversification has been taking place due to other factors. An increase in market diversification would result in a lower value of index leading to positive association between index and FDI inflows.

Results show that the employment share of industry has also emerged as significant with the highest level of significance (1%). The finding is according to

Table 4.2 Multivariate analysis results

Explanatory variables	Model I			Model II			Model III		
	Coeff.	Z	Sig.	Coeff.	Z	Sig.	Coeff.	Z	Sig.
Cons	0.312	3.58	0.000	0.062	5.50	0.000	0.100	11.93	0.000
LGDP[-1]	-0.009	-2.48**	0.013						
OFDI[-1]	-0.006	-2.25**	0.024						
IFDI[-1]	0.013	6.02	0.000	0.012	5.14***	0.000			
EMPIND	-0.002	-2.89***	0.004						
MVA	0.002	3.03	0.002	0.0005	0.74	0.460	-0.001	-2.34**	0.019
R&D	-0.010	-1.09	0.277	-0.031	-3.40***	0.001			
Log likelihood	164.230		0.000	154.212		0.000	275.199		0.019
Observations	77			77			162		

Note: *** and ** significant at 1% and 5% level; data source: World Development Indicators.

our expectation and suggests that countries where employment share in industry is higher witness more diversification. It may also be interpreted that countries that succeed in diversification create more employment in industry leading to a higher employment share in industry. The finding captures the issue of employability of workforce. The ability of industry to absorb more workforce reflects the technical competence of workers. This has something to do with proper learning and skill development opportunities in the country. Hence it may be inferred that countries that have proper human resource development infrastructure are likely to witness more diversification.

The other two factors that emerged as significant in influencing market diversification are share of manufacturing value added to GDP and ratio of expenditure on R&D to GDP. R&D is significant at 1% while manufacturing value added is at a 5% level. Both these variables represent technological and innovation capability. The higher share of manufacturing value added leads to more diversification and suggests that technically competent countries succeed in market diversification. Similarly higher investment of R&D may result in better innovation capacities that are helpful in creating new/efficient products and production processes. This in turn influences market expansion and diversification. Hence, it may be inferred that technological competence and innovation capabilities influence market diversification.

4.5 Summary and conclusions

The chapter investigates and identifies the factors that influence export market diversification. The findings are based on representative countries in Africa and Asia. Africa is represented by Ghana, Kenya, Nigeria, and South Africa while Asian economies included in the study are China, India, Indonesia, and Malaysia. The findings reveal that several macroeconomic factors influence export market diversification. These factors can be broadly grouped into four categories, namely; financial resource, international investment, technological competence, and innovation capabilities. Financial resource is represented by income while international investment encompasses inward and outward FDI. Share of manufacturing value added to GDP and share of employment in industry to the total represent technological competence while R&D expenditure as a percentage of GDP represent innovation capabilities. The results substantiate findings of several earlier studies (Giri et al., 2019; Cirera et al., 2015).

Financial resources are crucial for any economic activity, more so to develop new products based on the latest technologies. Therefore, the emergence of national income as one of the factors of market diversification is to some extent obvious. Having financial resources alone is not a sufficient condition for diversification but it is a necessary condition. Financial resources and technological progress mutually reinforce each other and put a country into a virtuous circle. The countries with higher income are in a better position to invest more in R&D activities. And higher investment in R&D coupled with a knowledge base of a scientific community lead to innovations resulting in new and energy-efficient products. Such products are better poised for market diversification.

The significant emergence of inward and outward FDI suggests that global integration of an economy is pivotal to diversification. Inward FDI is catalytic to the acquisition of the latest technology which is essential for production of new and market-specific products while outward FDI plays a critical role in understanding the global market preferences. And supply of market-specific products is expected to contribute in market diversification. In absence of global integration, it is virtually impossible to have the latest technology and consequently difficult to capture new markets and even the sustainability of existing markets might be difficult.

The findings suggest that manufacturing value added is a significant factor in influencing market diversification. The crux of the diversification is the manufacture of products with varying features. This is possible with higher skills of the workforce and the use of up-to-date manufacturing technology, a proxy of technological competence. Hence MVA (Manufacturing Value Added) of countries that have a highly skilled workforce is likely to be higher than the rest, which in turn is expected to result in the manufacture of market-specific products leading to more diversification. The findings substantiate the argument and suggest that there exists a positive association between MVA and market diversification. More manufacturing activities provide higher employment opportunities. And this is what has also been captured by the statistical analysis presented in the chapter.

The findings may be summarised as the global integration of an economy contributes to market diversification. The financial resources coupled with innovation capacity also influence market diversification. And the association between employment creation and market diversification is positive and significant.

Notes

1 www.worldstopexports.com/chinas-top-import-partners/.
2 www.worldstopexports.com/vietnams-top-10-exports/.
3 www.worldstopexports.com/vietnams-top-10-exports/.
4 Derive from: www.oecd.org/countries/zambia/2497663.pdf; accessed August 4, 2021.
5 www.google.com/search?q=drc+top+exports&rlz=1C1GCEB_enDE819DE819&oq=DRC%2C+top+&aqs=chrome.1.69i57j0i512j0i22i30l4j0i22i30i457j0i2 2i30l3.14016j0j7&sourceid=chrome&ie=UTF-8.
6 Hausmann, Hwang, and Rodrik, 'What You Export Matters'; Heiko Hesse, 'Export Diversification and Growth', Working Paper 21, World Bank Growth Commission (2008); Cadot et al. 'Export Diversification'.
7 Hausman, Hwang, and Rodrik (2007).
8 WTO, World Trade Statistics Report (2019).
9 Mineral fuels, lubricants, and related materials; petroleum, petroleum products and related materials, crude petroleum and oils obtained from bituminous minerals, , gas and manufactured.
10 www.afdb.org/en/documents/trade-finance-africa-trends-over-past-decade-and -opportunities-ahead; accessed August 7, 2021.

11 African Development Bank (2017), Trade Finance in Africa: Overcoming Challenges.
12 African Development Bank (2017), Trade Finance in Africa: Overcoming Challenges.
13 This is according to the latest trade finance report released jointly by the African Development Bank and the African Export–Import Bank.
14 African Development Bank (2020), Trade Finance Survey Report.
15 The report, titled 'Trade finance in Africa: Trends over the past decade and opportunities ahead', builds on two previous studies released in 2014 and 2017. It is based on a survey of over 600 unique commercial banks in 49 countries across Africa for 2011 to 2019.
16 https://www.ft.com/content/a807f714-7542-4464-b359-b9bb35bdda10, accessed October 2021.

5 Technological Capability and Export Diversification

5.1 Introduction

Central to the successful diversification and industrialisation efforts of Asia is equally their successful mastery of a wide range of technologies over the last five decades. At the heart of industrial manufacturing capability is a wide array of disciplines including mechanical engineering, chemical engineering processes, and notably, and most pervasive, Information and Communication Technologies (ICTs). These technologies, at different levels of complexities, are indispensable to the operation of the core routines of industrial organisations.[1] In many different ways, new technologies have deepened the systemic complexity of all industries and made high-level skills a key prerequisite for successful structural transformation in the 21st century. The acquisition of these technologies has significant implications for the capacity for processing scale, speed, flexibility of production, and the inclusion of products requiring high precision. Although many of these advances originated in advanced industrial economies, Asian countries took advantage of these new technologies by building up industrial capabilities through explicit learning.

Through sustained and diligent pursuit of technological learning, the manufacturing sector in Asia has been transformed into the largest in the world; China and South Korea, and other newly industrialising Asian countries before them, became dominant global exporters of manufactures. In the last fifty plus years, the Asian region recorded faster industrial growth far above global average during that period. The cases of South Korea and China are not outliers; Malaysia, Singapore, Thailand, and, more recently, Vietnam, transformed from natural resource and agricultural commodities exporters into machinery and electronics.

With little context-specific variations, most developing countries started from agrarian beginnings, they earned foreign exchanges through exports of basic agricultural primary commodities, minerals, or low-technology manufactures. Over time, economies are unable to sustain the living standards of their citizens by this trade regime as the competitiveness of basic raw materials deteriorates. Again, as urbanisation intensifies, citizens' demand for more sophisticated goods that require more complex technologies intensifies (Palma 2005). Two avenues open for low-income countries to address their trade deficit: the diversification

DOI: 10.4324/9781003245322-5

of production structure, which can move in two directions, namely, "horizontal" and "vertical" diversification. The former involves an expansion of other primary commodities or basic manufacturing goods; but far more demanding is "vertical" diversification, that requires a country or firm to master new technological capabilities. By this, diversification is accompanied by movement towards medium and high-technology intensive industries, Appendix 5.1. The countries in our sample fall roughly into three groups of technological capabilities.

The technological capability of a country is a function of several factors such as capabilities of researchers and scientific manpower, density of scientific community, R&D (Research and Development) infrastructure, and global integration of the economy, etc. Some of these factors are not measurable directly but their output is quantifiable. For instance, capabilities of researchers cannot be estimated directly but research output in terms of patents is quantifiable. The number of commercially viable patents could result in enhanced manufacturing value addition. Although information about commercially viable patents is not available in public domain, performance of the manufacturing sector can be used as a proxy of scientific achievements. In what follows, technological competence by means of manufacturing value added as percentage of GDP (Gross Domestic Product), researchers' density, R&D expenditure as percentage of GDP, and patent applications filed are used. Averages of all the indicators for the period of 1960 to 2020 are depicted in Figures 5.1 and 5.2.

The data used in these figures is presented in Appendix 5.2. The first part of Figure 5.1 shows that the Chinese manufacturing sector recorded the highest contribution (30.28%) to the GDP which is followed by the Republic of Korea (22.81%). The MVA (Manufacturing Value Added) contributions for Indonesia and Malaysia are very much similar to that of Korea (Republic of Korea). On the other hand, share of manufacturing among sample countries is lowest in Ghana

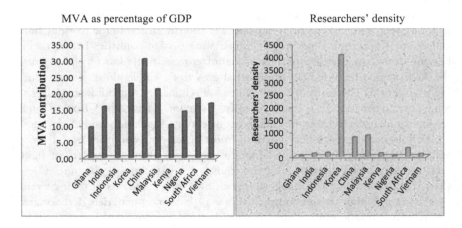

Figure 5.1 Manufacturing valued added as percentage of GDP and researchers' density. Source: Authors from WDI database.

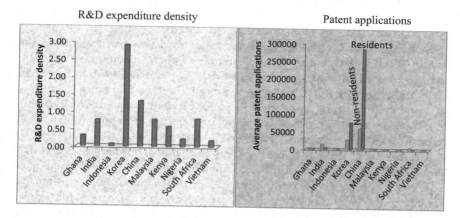

Figure 5.2 R&D expenditure density and patent applications. Source: Authors from WDI database.

(9.48%). In general, the contribution of manufacturing to GDP is less than 15% in African countries except for South Africa in which the sector contributes 18.23%, while in Asian sample countries it is more than 15%. It clearly establishes that a low manufacturing base exists in Africa.

The second part of Figure 5.1 depicts researchers' density which is measured as number of researchers per one million people. The figure shows that highest researchers' density (4,047) belongs to Korea followed by Malaysia (860) and China (785). In terms of research density also, Ghana is at the bottom with a density of just 28 persons. In general, the density in Asian countries is more than their African counterparts except for South Africa with researchers' density of 353 persons. It may be inferred that there exists a positive association between researchers' density and manufacturing base which is reflected in its contribution to GDP.

In Figure 5.2, we present R&D expenditure intensity and patent applications filed. It can be seen from part 1 of the figure that Korea stands first with R&D intensity of 2.89%, followed by China 1.29%. In other countries it is less than 1%. As far as patent application is concerned, China comes first followed by Korea. Although patent application may not be treated as patent granted, it indicates that a lot of innovation activities are being carried out in the country. A large number of patent applications and high R&D expenditure density could be treated as a reflection of a strong industrial and manufacturing base which is substantiated by part 1 of Figure 5.1.

The analysis presents the patent application filed by residents and non-residents separately. A noticeable fact is that in the cases of China and Korea, the numbers of patent applications filed by residents are several times higher than those filed by non-residents. On the other hand the situation is reversed in the other countries. It may be inferred from these findings that innovation activities by MNCs (Multinational Corporations) are done more than by domestic firms and researchers in other countries while in the case of China and Korea domestic firms and researchers are more innovative than MNCs.

Another proxy of technological competence used is the Global Innovation Index (GII). Its score range between 0 and 100. Depending on this score, countries are grouped into four categories, namely; highly advanced, advanced, catching up, and lagging behind. These categories are based on four equal intervals of the score in 2020 which range from 13.56 for Yemen to 66.08 for Switzerland. The countries along with their GII score are depicted in Figures 5.3 and 5.4. Data related to these figures are presented in Appendix 5.3.

The first group consists of the Newly Industrialising Economies (NIEs) that have successfully acquired advanced technologies; including high technologies (see Appendix 5.1). These countries have made the transition from copying and learning to the innovation phase. These are most notably, Japan, South Korea, and China, who combine to spend US$613 billion on R&D in 2018, taking three out of the top five global spots, along with the US (No. 1) and Germany (No. 4). The private sector plays the primary role, making up approximately 78% of total R&D spending. China's total public and private science and technology expenditures in 2019 rose 12.5% over the previous year to ($322 billion), according to the National Bureau of Statistics.[2] Spending on basic research accounted for 6% of the total; applied research, 11.3%; and development, 82.7%.

The second group includes middle-income economies, namely Thailand and Malaysia. They have had significant but varying levels of success in accumulating and adopting imported technologies. They have graduated from low to medium technology regimes shown in our schema. The third group consists of low-income economies in Asia, namely, Indonesia, the Philippines, Thailand, and Bangladesh which are still at the level of mastering low technologies such as garments, leather, and basic agro-industrial foods. In these countries two other strategies, industrialisation and diversification, especially the capability to transit into medium to high-technology regimes, follow the well-known learning pathways.

First, these countries made sustained investment in human capital. This is the sum total of the skills level of a country's entire workforce, which includes managers and administrators; it is strongly related to the potential real income per capita of a country and it is a function of the productivity of its labour. East Asian experience demonstrates that human capital is very important as a source of economic growth. The sources of competitive advantage in advanced technologies derive largely from superior education, training, and skills developed through "learning-by-using", "learning-by-doing", and "doing-by-innovation". Diversification has been achieved through consistent and explicit technological learning in order to climb the industrial technological ladder from low-technology to high-technology regimes. This has been made possible by long-term investment in knowledge and skills upgrading required to master new technologies.

Additionally, the Asian countries especially in group one have been investing heavily in research and development (R&D) as discussed earlier. In China, central to the country's rapid and publicly stated ambition is the 2015 strategic plan "Made

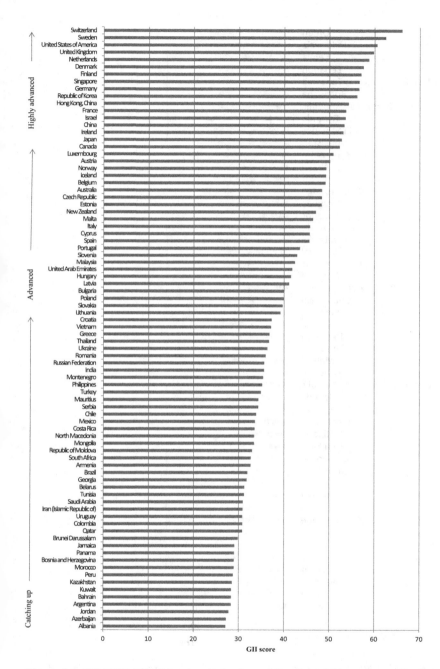

Figure 5.3 GII 2020 of highly advanced, advanced, and catching up countries. Source: https://www.wipo.int/edocs/pubdocs/en/wipo_pub_gii_2020.pdf

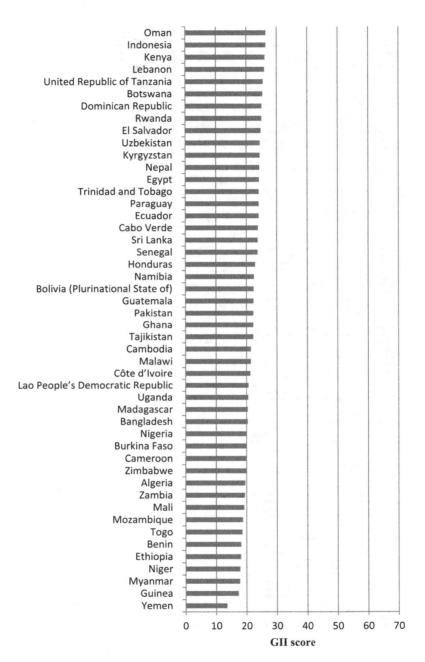

Figure 5.4 GII 2020 of laggard countries. Source: https://www.wipo.int/edocs/
pubdocs/en/wipo_pub_gii_2020.pdf

in China 2025", with a focus on innovation road maps that target next-generation information technology, robotics, aerospace and defence, maritime technology, advanced rail transportation, new energy vehicles, power equipment, agriculture technology, advanced materials, and pharmaceutical and medical devices.

Industrial manufacturing and innovation are the core of its strategy. Technologies like robotics and 3D printing are key areas of focus for domestic expertise as the country continues to intensify its capacity building in advanced technologies. Information technology ranks high, with China being a global leader in establishing a digital economy. The country has been very public with its ambitions of becoming the global leader in artificial intelligence in the next decade and is already a trailblazer in 5G technologies. Overall, Korea, Singapore, and China now devote 2% or more of GDP to R&D, comparable to the level in developed countries. China has seen a rapid intensification of R&D spending that has surpassed its official target of 1.5% of GDP; Newly Industrialised Economies (NIEs) such as Korea, Singapore, and Taiwan (China) now devote 2% or more of GDP to R&D, comparable to the level in developed countries. China has seen a rapid intensification of R&D spending that has seen its spending surpass its official target of 1.5% of GDP; at 2.23% of GDP in 2019.

The last group, on the other hand, consisting of middle-income economies such as Indonesia Thailand, spend a small proportion ranging from 0.1% to 0.2% of GDP on R&D. Again, patenting per capita in the high-income East Asian nations has grown at a speed pace four times that in the developed world and is now approaching average developed-country levels; on the other hand, patenting in most middle and low-income economies of the region remains negligible.[3] Additionally, patenting per capita in the NIEs has grown at a pace four times that in the developed world and is now approaching average developed-country levels; on the other hand, patenting in most middle and low-income economies of the region remains negligible.

Contrast the African experience with Asia by comparing two countries, Nigeria and South Korea, that were at the same level of per capita income in the 1960s. On the one hand, Korea, a non-resource based economy has performed incredibly strongly through export diversification and growth since the 1960s. It devoted considerable energy to the accumulation of industrial manufacturing technology and innovation that propelled its remarkable growth. The country is now ranked the "most innovative country on earth" followed by Germany, Finland, Switzerland, and Israel. In 1953 when the Korean War ended, the nominal GDP of Korea was $1.3 billion, it grew rapidly for the last six to seven decades; its GDP was $1.01 trillion in 2010 and $1.65 trillion in 2019. The well-being of a country measured by GDP/capita rose to $32,000 from a mere $158 in 1960.

In contrast, Nigeria, as with other oil economies, hardly diversified. These countries got locked in into petroleum export for export earnings to the detriment of value added agriculture and manufactures. The result is poor contribution of the manufacturing subsector, which fluctuates between 5% to 8%, to aggregate output in Nigeria compared with its peers in Asia (Korea about 30% in the 1990s), which is staggering. Due to a weak industrial base, the relatively high contribution of the oil sector to the industrial sector contribution is driven largely by crude production and not by value added products' components like refined oil, plastics, fertiliser, and petrochemicals.

The outcome is a Nigeria economy, and relatedly most African economies, characterised by structural dualism. The agricultural and informal sectors consist of peasants and poor low-skilled traders with an admixture of subsistence and modern farming, co-existing with an evolving industrial sector that is largely labour intensive. Nigeria's GDP/capita was $93 in 1960 and $2,222 in 2019. Oil export as percentage of GDP was 57% in 1970, this rose to 96% by 1985.

In contrast, Korea's per capita is just shy of that of Italy, a shout away from the status of a *rich advanced industrial nation*. Nigeria is stuck at low-medium income with a large proportion of very poor. Korea pursued diversification with great urgency. Korea's export composition changed practically every decade as it mastered relevant technologies and diversified into new markets and products. Before 1970, its major exports were ore mining and agricultural products as it was with Nigeria. At the early stage of industrialisation, Korea exported textile goods and other labour-intensive products. From the mid-1970s, Korea produced and exported electronic goods and ships; manufactured goods became more sophisticated.

In the 1980s, Korea exported products based on labour-intensive technologies which occupied its top ten exporting goods, namely: footwear, ocean vessels, man-made filament fabrics, articles of rubber. This pattern continued even in the 1990s when garments/clothes were the largest exporting goods; in addition to semiconductors which became the second largest exported good. By the 2000s, its exports were dominated by semiconductors, computers, automobiles, and ocean vessels, among other complex manufactures.

This chapter demonstrates the critical role of learning and technological investment in economic diversification and in achieving rapid economic growth. Sector success and performance had been associated with learning and accumulation of capabilities. From Appendix 5.1, we observe the progressive shift from low-technology sectors such as garment and leather, beverages, textiles and wearing apparel to plastics, chemicals and chemical products, pharmaceuticals, weapons and ammunition, computer, electronic, and optical products, and electrical equipment machinery and equipment, among others.

Figure 5.5 shows the relationship between technological competence or capability and progressive diversification.

The remainder of the chapter is organised as follows. Section 2 presents a selected and partial survey of literature. Section 3 encompasses theoretical framework and data, while hypotheses are formulated in section 4. Statistical results are presented and discussed in section 5 whereas section 6 presents summary and conclusions.

5.2 Technological capabilities and diversification

Technological capability or technical competence is the ability of a firm to learn, master, and execute its pertinent technical functions, including the ability to

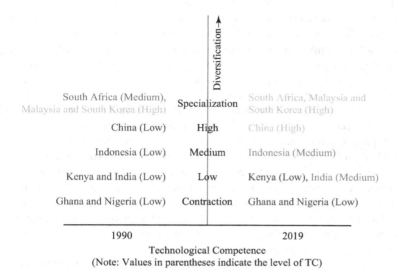

Figure 5.5 Technological competence and level of diversification. Source: Authors.

develop new products and processes; this is dependent on the accumulation of relevant technological knowledge and skills leading to higher levels of organisational efficiency (Patel and Pavitt, 1997). These types of competencies are closely aligned with the knowledge and skills, or "know-how" needed for successful performance (HRSG, 2015). The concept of technical competence could be applied at individual, firm, sector, and national levels. At the individual level, it is traditionally measured by the knowledge and skill of an individual. Technological capability could be tacit or codified. Educational background and experience are used to measure technical competence. However, many unmeasurable characteristics of an individual also constitute competencies. In literature these are regarded as behavioural competencies (Martone, 2003; Walsha and Lintonc, 2001). Characteristics such as sincerity, commitment, and interpersonal skills come under behavioural competencies.

At the firm level, they go beyond individual competencies. Individual competencies are necessary but not sufficient to make up for the overall firm-level competencies. Firms need to provide opportunities for effective use of individual competencies. For instance, a firm needs to have in place an appropriate technological base so that individual competencies can be utilised for better performance of the firm. Institutional competencies also include individual competencies of the management team towards goals and visions of the firm. Hence it is necessary to distinguish between individual competencies of the workforce and management team. Workforce competencies should be more related to the job while managerial competencies need to focus on managerial functions. For assessment of technical competency, it may be useful to evaluate it at various levels such as workers, supervisors, managers, and management team.

Individual and firm-level competencies alone cannot guarantee sectoral competencies, i.e., a few competent individuals cannot make a firm technically competent. Similarly, a few competent firms cannot represent a competent sector. For a sector to be competent, vertically and horizontally integrated firms needs to be technically competent. Sectoral competencies necessitate competent backward–forward linkages. It may require a different kind of industrial structure, such as development of a sector-specific cluster for a sector to be more vibrant.

The development of national-level technical competencies is much more than simply individual and firm-level competencies. This is where the role of governments comes in. Individual competencies may be acquired by acquiring better education beyond the boundaries of a country. However, competencies based on tacit knowledge are dependent on socio-economic and inherent factors. These may not be derived from education. Technically competent firms usually include equally competent individuals; these tend to require minimal government support is their quest to be competitive. However, for development of competencies at sectoral and national level, government support is usually needed through education, training, and subsidies for learning.

National technological capability is fostered in large part by soft and physical social infrastructure. Investment in roads, and reliable and cost-efficient electricity supply and telecommunications, among others, underpin firm-level and national-level ICT (Information and Communication Technologies).

Among the social institutions, a good quality education system is centre to the development of competencies. It is not only the educational system, but also a dynamic industrial development system that needs to be in place to develop 'sector-specific and national level competencies. The development of social infrastructure and industrial development systems is a long-drawn process. Hence development of sectoral and national competencies is sometimes regarded as path dependent (Patel and Pavitt, 1997). However, sectoral competencies might break path-dependencies in the case of paradigm shifts in technological progress. Emergence of new technologies may alter path-dependencies. It may also be argued that development of social infrastructure and competencies is mutually reinforcing. The high competencies generate more wealth which in turn can be used to develop/improve social infrastructure.

A crucial aspect of technological competencies is their measurement. Two sets of indicators can be used to quantify it. One set represents factors related to input to the competencies. These are educational background of individuals, skill intensity of workforce, and investment in R&D at firm level. The other set represents consequences of technological competencies, i.e., output factors. These factors include performance of firms in general, manufacturing value added, and share of high-tech exports, etc. The use of input or output factors in quantifying competencies is constrained by availability of relevant data (Huang, 2011; Patel and Pavitt, 1997, and others). There is an advantage of using output factors rather than input. As discussed earlier behavioural competencies that are part of technical competencies are unmeasurable and their contributions are included if the measurement is based on output factors. The present study uses a mix of input and output factors to assess the impact of technical competencies.

The chapter provides a classification and analysis in terms of typology of countries into manufacturing and non-manufacturing categories and how the composition of their exports have differentially influenced their earnings and volatility. The question can be framed thus: what differentiates the export portfolios of countries that predominantly comprise manufactured and non-manufactured products? We have a typology of two groups of economies (i.e., countries), namely: those which rely on exports of fossil fuel and extractive minerals or agricultural raw materials (typically classified as natural resource-based products) and countries that are manufactures dependent, see export composition analysis in Appendix 5.4 Tables 5.1–5.9.

From Appendix 5.4 Table 5.1 (Table 5.1 subsequently), it is clear that the top ten export products in 1992 from Ghana were predominantly natural resources based such as gold with an export share of 42.55% and agri-products such as coffee, tea, and cocoa, etc. (25.27% export share). After three decades from then the export profile remained dominated by gold (36.97% export share), petroleum products (31.70%), and agri-products (16.15%). It is noticeable that the economy is still heavily dependent on export of natural resources and agri-products.

The top ten export items from Kenya in 1990 are predominantly agri-products and items based on natural resources such as petroleum and petroleum products (Table 5.2). The export profile of the country did not change much during the next 30 years and topmost export products remained more or less the same except for articles of apparel and clothing accessories and low-level manufacturing products, which got a place in the export profile of Kenya in 2019. It may be inferred that very little effort was made to export products based on high technology. The story of Nigeria is not very different (Table 5.3). The export earning of the country in 1991 from petroleum and petroleum products was as high as 96.63% and in 2019 the economy remained heavily dependent on exports of oil and related products (86.88%). Even after the three decades from 1991, the country did not succeed in exporting high-tech products though it has started exporting manufactured products based on metal, a low-level manufacturing.

On the other hand, South Africa has been exporting manufactured products such as road vehicles for a long time (Table 5.4). Its exports share was just 6.91% in 2000 being the fourth topmost export item. With consistent efforts of the country on manufacturing the export of road vehicles reached the second slot in 2019 in the export profile with 12.84% share. The country has been exporting general industrial machinery and equipment and non-metallic mineral manufactured products. The differences in the export profile may be attributed to the technological competence of the countries. The technological competence of Ghana, Nigeria, and Kenya was low in the early 1990s and it remained low in 2019 (see Figure 5.5) leading to very little diversification. On the other hand, Asian countries graduated from medium-level competence to high in the two decades from 2000 resulting in more diversification compared to other sample African countries.

The analysis of Asian economies suggests an evolutionary transformation of the export profile of China, Malaysia, and South Korea from low-tech and natural

Table 5.1 Herfindahl–Hirschman product diversification index

Year	Nigeria	Ghana	Kenya	South Africa	China	India	Indonesia	Malaysia	Korea
1990			0.091		0.012	0.061	0.087	0.037	0.019
1991	0.053		0.102		0.013	0.049	0.072	0.030	0.018
1992		0.510	0.152		0.008	0.054	0.053	0.026	0.016
1993			0.090		0.009	0.063	0.043	0.024	0.015
1994			0.108		0.008	0.054	0.037	0.020	0.017
1995			0.100		0.007	0.052	0.035	0.019	0.018
1996	0.254	0.409	0.089		0.007	0.041	0.035	0.019	0.021
1997	0.709	0.400	0.105		0.008	0.042	0.044	0.018	0.021
1998	0.136	0.161	0.084		0.008	0.049	0.034	0.015	0.019
1999	0.079	0.112	0.079		0.008	0.063	0.030	0.015	0.014
2000	0.357	0.432	0.087	0.019	0.007	0.055	0.038	0.021	0.012
2001	0.708	0.438	0.074	0.037	0.007	0.043	0.036	0.021	0.014
2002	0.216		0.069	0.017	0.008	0.050	0.036	0.020	0.016
2003	0.315	0.108	0.059	0.029	0.008	0.051	0.040	0.021	0.017
2004		0.118	0.074	0.034	0.008	0.039	0.043	0.021	0.018
2005		0.325	0.050	0.029	0.008	0.041	0.045	0.023	0.022
2006	0.215	0.307	0.046	0.034	0.008	0.029	0.047	0.023	0.028
2007	0.077	0.458	0.043	0.036	0.007	0.032	0.039	0.025	0.029
2008	0.148	0.495	0.050	0.037	0.007	0.029	0.047	0.063	0.033
2009	0.267	0.704	0.057	0.034	0.008	0.042	0.033	0.033	0.042
2010	0.140	0.702	0.048	0.029	0.008	0.043	0.040	0.034	0.035
2011	0.296	0.290		0.051	0.007	0.049	0.052	0.043	0.028
2012	0.286	0.654		0.042	0.007	0.037	0.042	0.048	0.025
2013	0.144	0.613	0.048	0.037	0.007	0.033	0.035	0.051	0.022
2014	0.308	0.426		0.036	0.008	0.063	0.030	0.052	0.022

2015	0.324	0.445	0.046	0.030	0.007	0.029	0.024	0.031	0.023
2016	0.702	0.463	0.050	0.032	0.007	0.033	0.021	0.021	0.019
2017	0.642	0.549	0.053	0.040	0.010	0.046	0.031	0.029	0.027
2018	0.511	0.601	0.052	0.039	0.009	0.046	0.029	0.027	0.019
2019	0.383	0.610	0.078	0.040	0.009	0.042	0.025	0.028	0.018

Source: compiled from COMTRADE data

resource-derived products to being predominantly based on manufactured products. The manufacturing activities in 1990 in China were limited to low-tech manufacturing such as articles of apparel and clothing accessories, etc. in 1990 but shifted to high tech such as electric machinery, and appliances and telecommunications equipment in 2019 (Table 5.5). The technological competence of China in 1990 was relatively modest but was continually increased through sustained efforts that resulted in a high level of competence culminating in exports of high-tech products in 2019. The technological capacity acquired resulted in rapid diversification of the Chinese economy. In other words, both China and Malaysia have achieved horizontal and vertical diversification that achieved substantial agribusiness as well as manufacturing despite having a substantial endowment of natural resources.

The situations of South Korea (Table 5.9) and Malaysia (Table 5.8) are very similar. The two countries have made explicit efforts in developing their manufacturing capabilities despite Malaysia having a lot of natural resources. Consequently, both countries are highly competent technologically resulting in both product specialisation and diversification. The case of India (Table 5.6) is somewhat different than the other sample Asia countries. Its manufacturing activities were limited to non-metallic mineral manufactures and articles of apparel and clothing accessories in the early 1990s but with a sustained acquisition of manufacturing capability, it now produces and exports a wide range of medicines, pharmaceutical products, and road vehicles. Its technological competence changed from low to medium in three decades. Although technological competence has improved, it falls in the low-level category of diversification. The case of Indonesia (Table 5.7) is very much similar to that of India, but its diversification level has been far more than that of India.

Evidently, the capability of a country to achieve specialisation and diversification is directly associated with the technological competence of the country. Another noticeable fact is that highly advanced economies have preferred specialisation rather than product diversification.

5.3 Methodology and data

The chapter uses the Herfindahl–Hirschman (HHI) product diversification index as a measure of export product diversification. The index (HHI) is a commonly accepted measure of market concentration. It is calculated by squaring the market share of each firm competing in a market and then summing the resulting numbers. It can range from close to zero to 10,000. The definition of the HH product diversification index is presented in EQ1

$$EPDI = \sum_{i=1}^{N} S_i^2 \qquad (1)$$

where,

S_i Export share of product i in total exports from a particular country
N Number of products being exported from the country in a particular year

The index estimation uses UN-COMTRADE annual data at the 5-digit level of the SITC Revision 2 classification; there would be an inverse relationship between number of products being exported and HHI. For instance, if a country exports four products with respective share of 20%, 30%, 40%, and 10% in a particular year, the HHI would be $(0.20)^2 + (0.30)^2 + (0.40)^2 + (0.10)^2 = 0.30$. On the other hand, if there are two products being exported with a share of 70% and 30%, HHI would be $(0.7)^2 + (0.3)^2 = 0.58$. Hence, the higher the incidence of product diversification, the lower the value of HHI. Based on the definition of HHI presented in EQ1, Export Product Diversification Indices (EPDI) for sample African countries are estimated and presented in Table 5.1 in this chapter.

It can be seen from the table that all the sample countries except Kenya witnessed product specialisation or contraction rather than diversification. In the case of Nigeria, the index changed from 0.053 in 1991 to 0.383 in 2019 while for Ghana it changed from 0.510 in 1992 to 0.610 in 2019. Similarly South Africa registered a change of index from 0.019 in 2000 to 0.040 in 2019. The increases in index values in these countries clearly depicts poor diversification trajectory over time consistent with their lack of manufacturing dynamism. In the case of product specialisation manufacturing output should either increase or remain stagnant, in a situation of contraction the manufacturing would witness a declining trend. This is the phenomena witnessed across these countries. Manufacturing output measured as manufacturing value added as a percentage of GDP has witnessed a negative trend suggesting that these countries did not achieve meaningful product export specialisation, rather product contraction has taken place in these countries.

Table 5.1 also shows that there is no uniform trend of EPDI in Kenya. The country witnessed product contraction until the mid-nineties followed by a trend of diversification until 2015 and then reverted to product contraction thereafter. On the other hand there is a uniform trend of EPDI in three of the Asian countries, namely: China, India, and Indonesia. The trend of EPDI is sinusoidal in nature in Malaysia and South Korea.

The trend of EPDI in African sample countries is depicted in Figure 5.6. The figure shows that the trend of EPDI has an overall positive trend in Nigeria, Ghana, and South Africa. Moreover the index is discrete in nature. Discreteness may be attributed to non-availability of data. The positive slope of trend lines suggests that export product contraction has taken place in these countries. Although the slope of the EPDI trend is negative in the case of Kenya, the trend is highly volatile.

The EPDI trends of Asian countries are depicted in Figure 5.7; from the figure, China, India, and Indonesia experienced a sustained negative trend of EPDI. It may be inferred that these countries have achieved a sustained evolution of export product diversification during the study period. Although China which was highly diversified in the beginning of the last decade of the 20th century witnessed much less diversification compared to the other two countries. On the other hand, the slope of the trend of EPDI in Malaysia and South Korea is positive suggesting that while the latter maintained progress on product specialisation,

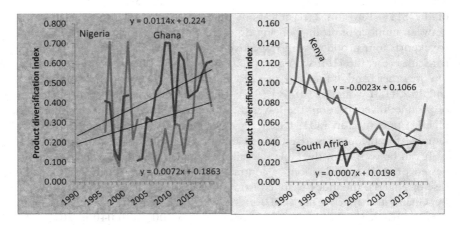

Figure 5.6 Trends in product diversification-contraction in Africa. Source: Authors.

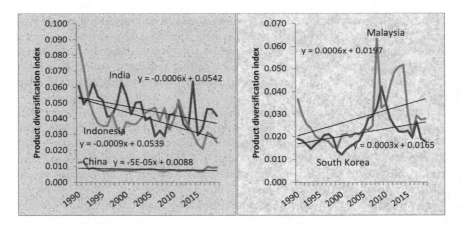

Figure 5.7 Trends in product diversification in Asia. Source: Authors.

the former experienced product contraction. The MVA of these countries suggests that Malaysia experienced product contraction while South Korea focused on specialisation.

The findings confirm much of the literature findings especially that very few resource-rich countries achieve diversified economic structures as they tend to be locked-in into a regime of raw materials export common to the extractive sector. The performance of countries like Chile, Indonesia, and Malaysia are exceptions to this broad pattern. From 1970 to 2008, the share of mining products in total Chilean exports declined from 85.5% to 58.7%, while the share of manufactured goods in total exports increased from 11.6% to 35.3%. In Malaysia, the share of agriculture in GDP fell from 26.7% in 1970 to 7% in 2005, whereas manufacturing's share increased from 12.2% to 35.8%.

5.3.1 Estimation of technological competence

Technological Competence (TC) consists of several indicators including those proxied by education, technological progress, innovation outputs, manufacturing and exports of technology intensive products, and technically skilled human resources, among others. The inclusion of indicators in the study is constrained by availability of data. Hence four indicators, i.e., manufacturing value added as a percentage of GDP, share of employment in industry as a percentage of total employment, percentage of high-tech exports to the total manufactured exports, and electric power consumption per capita are included in this study. The indicators such as share of high-tech production as a percentage of total industrial output, investment in higher education, and secured internet servers per million population could have provided more robustness to technological competence. However, sparseness of data related to these indicators did not allow us to include these indicators in the study.

Before formulation of hypotheses, we depict the trend of different components of TC. Figure 5.8 depicts the trends of MVA and employment in industry while trends of high-tech exports and electricity consumption are presented in Figure 5.9.

The first part of Figure 5.8 shows that manufacturing value added as a percentage of GDP is highest in all Asian countries compared to the African sample countries. Among Asian countries, China is on the top while India is right at the bottom. Among African countries, as expected, MVA in South Africa is highest followed by Ghana, Nigeria, and Kenya. The trend of Ghana and Kenya are very

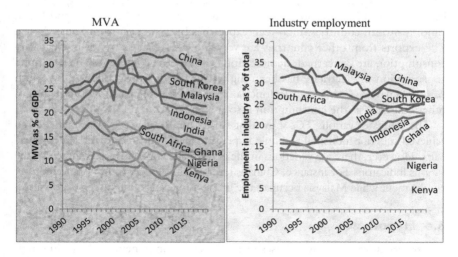

Figure 5.8 Trends in MVA and industry employment. Source: Authors.

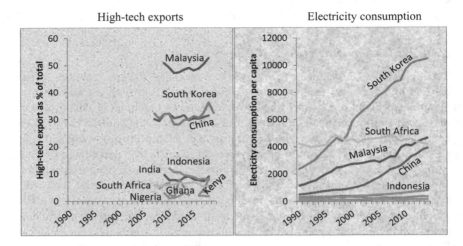

Figure 5.9 Trends in high-tech exports and electricity consumption. Source: Authors.

unique. MVA in Ghana until 2011 had been the lowest but picked up after that to occupy second position after South Africa. Similarly, the Kenyan trend shows that it had been holding the second position until 2012 before MVA began declining and it reached the lowest position in 2019.

Trends of high-tech exports and electricity consumption depicted in Figure 5.9 show that it follows a similar trend to that of MVA. High-tech exports as a percentage of total exports from Asian countries is higher than their African counterparts. The figure also shows that data for high-tech exports is missing for all the countries for several years. Among Asian countries, high-tech exports have been highest in Malaysia followed by South Korea, China, Indonesia, and India. Among African countries, high-tech export has been highest from South Africa. The exports from other countries are very similar. As far as trends in electricity consumption are concerned, demarcation is not by the continent. The per capita consumption of electricity has been highest in South Korea followed by South Africa, Malaysia, China, and Indonesia. It is not possible to show the names of other countries as the consumption is so similar.

The trends of various TCs show that Asian countries have over several decades achieved superior industrial technology performance compared to African counterparts. However, there are variations in the performance of countries as shown by the various indicators. For instance, China is leading with respect to MVA and industry employment while Malaysia occupies the first slot in terms of high-tech exports.

5.4 Hypotheses

The section formulates hypotheses related to each component of the technological component, i.e., manufacturing value added (MVA) as a percentage of GDP, share of employment in industry as a percentage of total employment (EMPIND), percentage export of high-tech products to the total exports (HITECH_EXP), and electric power consumption per capita (ELEC_CON).

5.4.1 Manufacturing value added

Manufacturing value added rises through a combination of horizontal and vertical diversification, where horizontal diversification entails the policies that promote increasing the production of an existing export commodity while vertical diversification involves adding value to the existing product or production of new products. The latter entails higher-level technological skills to innovate and manufacture products new to the domestic and international markets. The goal of product diversification could be realised by producing new products or modifying existing products with new features, including new processes. To innovate and upgrade product, process, or service demands continuous accumulation of firm-level technological competence that facilitates new products resulting in high value addition. Higher value addition could result in the gain of higher volumes to existing markets or entering new markets through competitive capabilities. An earlier study by Kaulich finds a positive association between MVA and the Herfindahl–Hirschman diversification index. New products innovation capability is required to usher in new and existing markets, it is therefore hypothesised that technological competence proxied by MVA is likely to help product diversification in export markets.

5.4.2 Employment share in industry

A larger share of employment in the manufacturing sector is an indication of a context of structural change and, as well, higher technological competence in an economy. With low levels of technological competence, it is difficult to manufacture products new to the local or global markets. Technological competence comes from various sources such as better education system, policies of the government, existence of manufacturing base, and export orientation of the economy.

The academic scholarship shows a strong link between the poor state of export diversification and the dismal nature of employment creation in developing countries, especially in Africa (FAO, 2004 and Osakwe, 2015). Creating meaningful and stable employment usually requires relatively high and stable growth, which in turn is dependent on exports diversification that allows a country to spread its risks over a broader number of countries and commodities, and to hedge against real and potential terms of trade shocks emanating from commodity prices (Acemoglu and Zilibotti, 1997). Indeed, it is widely believed that the considerable progress in the structural transformation of a number of Asian countries has been the result of the shift towards export diversification, that is, from primary to labour-intensive manufactured exports, and further to more resource-intensive manufactures (World Bank, 1993; Sarel, 1996).

In general TC is path dependent, but deliberate policy-induced shifts of technological progress may lead to emergence of competence in new technical areas leading to discontinuity. Innovation and technical competencies enable the set-up of new manufacturing facilities leading to higher employment in the industrial sector. The production of such goods would lead to creation of employment in manufacturing. The economies capable of manufacturing new products are likely to engage in product diversification. Hence it may be argued that product diversification and manufacturing employment are likely to be positively associated.

5.4.3 *High-tech exports*

The share of high-technology exports to the total exports is considered a component of technology competence because such products cannot be produced without an appropriate level of technological knowledge. High technology, in this context, is referred to as to be globally advanced. Higher export share of such products suggests that the country is technically very competent. And exports of such products could contribute in product export diversification. Therefore, it is hypothesised that product diversification is highly associated with export share of high-technology products.

5.4.4 *Electric power consumption per capita*

The consumption of electricity per capita is directly related to the industrial base of an economy. More and more industrial activities would necessitate a higher consumption of electricity. Higher consumption of electricity would also depend on electric gadgets used at the household level which is governed by availability and affordability of such gadgets. Availability could be ensured by importing such products but affordability depends on income. And high income is usually achieved by production and export of high-value products. Therefore, it may be argued that high levels of electricity consumption may reflect prosperity of the people. This prosperity could be due to export market or product diversification. Hence it is hypothesised that higher levels of electric power consumption reflect technological competence and that in turn is associated with export diversification.

5.5 Multivariate analysis

Subsequently data were subjected to multivariate analysis. Data for both the continents were analysed separately as countries in Africa witnessed product contraction while several countries in Asia experienced product diversification. In multivariate analysis the dynamic nature of unbalanced panel data has been taken into consideration. This is achieved by using the Generalized Method of Moments (GMM) method of estimation.

5.5.1 Analytical model

Based on the hypothesis formulated above, the following econometric model is used to identify factors that influence export market diversification.

$$EPDI_{c,i} = f\left(MVA_{c,i}, EMPIND_{c,i}, HITECH\_EXP_{c,i}, ELEC\_CON_{c,i}\right) \quad (2)$$

where,

c,i Represent country and year
$EPDI_{c,i}$ Export Product Diversification Index
$MVA_{c,i}$ Manufacturing value added as % of GDP
$EMPIND_{c,i}$ Share of employment in industry to the total employment
$HITECH\_EXP_{c,i}$ Percentage export of high-tech products to the total exports
$ELEC\_CON_{c,i}$ Electric power consumption per capita

As discussed in the methodology section, African sample countries have witnessed product contraction rather than diversification while most of sample countries in Asia experienced production diversification. Therefore, it was not considered appropriate to analyse the pooled data. Consequently, data for both the continents are analysed separately. Tables 5.2 and 5.3 in this chapter present the results of Asian and African sample counties.

It can be seen from Table 5.2 that the initial value of the diversification emerged significant in determining the future growth of the diversification. This brings out the path-dependency aspect of the technological progress. The finding is consistent with the literature and our assumption.

The share of employment in industry to the total employment, a proxy of technological competence, emerged significant in influencing the diversification index. The results may be interpreted with care as the variable is positively associated with product as well as export market diversification. As far as the association of employment in industry with product diversification is concerned, the finding is on the expected lines. This is because new products are first developed and manufactured in the home country resulting in creation of employment in home country. And this is what has been captured by the econometric analysis. The production base may be shifted to host countries particularly when market diversification takes place. Therefore, it may be concluded that technological competence not only influences product diversification but has set the path for future diversification activity. The findings of the study are substantiated by a firm-level study of Guillou and Treibich (2019).

Although MVA, another measure of technological competence, has not emerged as significant, the direction of influence is according to our expectation. The negative sign of association between MVA and the product diversification index suggests that product diversification and MVA are positively associated. A similar argument could be extended to the next proxy of TC, i.e., electric power consumption per capita.

Table 5.2 Multivariate analysis results of Asian sample

Explanatory variables	Model I			Model II			Model III		
	Coeff.	Z	Sig.	Coeff.	Z	Sig.	Coeff.	Z	Sig.
Cons	0.156	1.36	0.175	.0263941	3.73	0.00	0.018	2.31	0.021
Initial value of EPDI	0.116	0.67	0.503	.477375	6.83	0.00***	0.545	8.01	0.00***
MVA	-0.004	-1.53	0.126				-0.0002	-0.60	0.546
EMPIND	-0.0012	-0.79	0.428	-0.0005	-2.03	0.042**			
HITECH_EXP	0.0002	0.21	0.834						
ELEC_CON	1.83e-07	0.06	0.949						
Chi-Sqr	4.79		0.44	80.90		0.00	68.51		0.00
Observations	28			140			127		

Source: WDI and UN-COMTRADE
Note: *** and ** significant at 1% and 5% level.

Table 5.3 Multivariate analysis results of African sample

Explanatory variables	Model I		
	Coeff.	*Z*	*Sig.*
Cons	0.472	0.75	0.453
Initial value of EPDI	−0.386	0.90	0.369
MVA	0.0201	0.84	0.400
EMPIND	−0.030	−0.57	0.572
HITECH_EXP	0.007	0.23	0.815
ELEC_CON	0.00002	0.08	0.936
Chi-Sqr	3.05		0.692
Observations	17		

Source: WDI and UN-COMTRADE

The findings of the African sample countries are presented in Table 5.3. As expected, none of the variables representing technological competence emerged as significant in influencing product contraction.

The results presented in Table 5.3 offer a very important message. Although, none of the proxies of TC emerged significant in explaining product contraction, the direction of association between product contraction and TC confirms our hypothesis on employment. It may be inferred from the negative sign of association between share of employment in industry to the total employment and product contraction index that contraction leads to a reduction in share of employment in industry. The sample countries in Africa have not achieved requisite diversification exemplified by product contraction over time. We conclude that the lack of export technological capability, the pattern of non-manufacturing export, and the absence of the required infrastructure historically handicapped these countries, making it difficult to match the severe competition from other countries which has led to the export product contraction.

5.5.2 Typology of countries

In the analyses presented in this chapter, non-resource endowed countries focused on the acquisition of capabilities that enabled them to make faster technological progress while oil and mineral producers relied on exports of raw materials and over time fell behind in terms of industrial capacities.

Appendix 5.4 Tables 5.1–5.9 displays the change in products exported from 1990 to 2019. The purpose of these tables is to understand the dominance of industrial association of exports in each sample country. Based on the exported products, export typology is prepared which is presented in Table 5.4 in this chapter.

On the one hand, from Appendix 5.4, African countries in our sample are engaged in the export of products dominated by agri-products, low-technology

Table 5.4 Export typology of sample countries

Country	Export typology
Ghana	Natural resource and agri-products
Kenya	Agri-products and low-tech industry
Nigeria	Natural resource and agri-products
South Africa	Natural resource and low-tech industry
China	High and low-tech industry
India	Low-tech Industry
Indonesia	Low-tech industry
Malaysia	Low and high-tech industry
South Korea	High and low-tech industry

Source: authors

goods, and mineral and oil resources. There is an inverse relationship between product diversification indexes based on such products and technological competence parameters included in the analysis; this is equally captured by econometric analysis. On the other hand, our export typology shows that Asian countries are predominantly industrial manufacturing dependent and the diversification index based on such products is closely associated with the technological competence considered in the study. The multivariate analysis substantiates this point.

The analyses show that while some African countries started at the same level of per capita income several decades ago, these countries on account of their reliance on natural resources are different from the Asian countries adoption of economic and export diversification and they tended to have fallen far behind in development. Clearly, the metrics of TC are significantly lower in resource-rich countries compared with advanced economies and emerging markets of Asia. Another key finding of this study is that in resource-dependent countries natural resources tend to have slowed economic growth. In our sample, only a few notable resource-rich nations (Chile, Indonesia, and Malaysia) succeeded in diversifying their economies from the extractive sector into non-resource sectors. The recent global pandemic and the attendant economic downturn, particularly the experience of resource-dependent countries, show clearly that the failure to pursue economic and export diversification by these economies exposes them to high vulnerability to various external shocks.

5.6 Summary and conclusions

The chapter analyses the association between technological competence and export product diversification in sample countries. The Asian and African countries possess varying levels of technological capabilities and, as well, policy and institutional capacities to make and implement industrial policy. We classified them into highly advanced to "laggard" categories and these knowledge levels correlate with the intensities of diversification. We conclude that weak capabilities explain to a large extent the difficulties the poorer nations face in transforming knowledge-through-learning activities to technological capabilities and innovative performance (Oyelaran-Oyeyinka and Lal, 2006).

Export product diversification is measured by the Herfindahl–Hirschman product diversification index. It is found that three out of four African sample countries did not experience product diversification during 1990 to 2019, rather they witnessed export product contraction leading to an increase in the diversification index. On the other hand, three out of five Asian countries experienced product diversification. This behaviour of sample countries motivated us to analyse data for both the continents separately.

As far as technological competence is concerned, it encompasses four indicators, namely; manufacturing value added as a percentage of GDP, share of employment in industry as a percentage of total employment, percentage export of high-tech products to the total exports, and electric power consumption per capita. The findings of Asian countries suggest that technological competence is positively associated with export diversification. On the other hand, analysis of African countries suggests that there does not exist any significant association between export product contraction and technological competence.

One of the major limitations of the study is the indicators used as a proxy of technological competence. The indicators such as the Global Innovation Index, expenditure of human resource development, and quality of governance by institutions, etc. could have been more appropriate. We could not use the Global Innovation Index as the data for the indicator is available from 2007 onwards while our sample include data from 1990. Other variables could not be included in the analysis due to sparseness of data. The role of institutions in promoting export diversification is delineated in the next chapter.

Notes

1 Oyelaran-Oyeyinka and Lal (2006).
2 www.xinhuanet.com/english/2020-08/27/c_139322217.htm.
3 https://openknowledge.worldbank.org/bitstream/handle/10986/4438/wbro _25_2_177.pdf?sequence=1&isAllowed=y.

6 Export Diversification, Governance Institution and Policies

6.1 Introduction

According to Acemoglu: "The most common reason why nations fail today is because they have extractive institutions ... Nations fail today because their extractive economic institutions do not create the incentives needed for people to save, invest, and innovate."[1]

The quality of institutions and governance are essential to economic diversification.

The divergence observed in the growth paths of successful resource-rich countries and unsuccessful resource-rich countries is explained in large part by the differences in governance and institutional quality because these factors affect countries' ability to circumvent the resource curse (Gelb, 2010). The lessons from our various country and analytical reviews are that irrespective of the political context as well as the administrative management types, any country whose fate is subject to the whims and caprices of the *strong man* rather than *strong institutions* that provide the bounds for human behaviour is likely to fail or fall.

As Acemoglu and Robinson (2012) again puts it: "Extractive political institutions support these economic institutions by cementing the power of those who benefit from the extraction. Extractive economic and political institutions, though their details vary under different circumstances, are always at the root of this failure."[2]

The rules and regulations available as checks and balances on the powerful restrain despotic tendencies and provide rail guards for accountability and transparency; it seems even more imperative in countries that rely almost exclusively on revenues from natural resource rents. In most cases, it is in countries where institutional quality is low that resource rent negatively impacts growth,[3] According to a World Bank (2018, p.40) assessment, the governance system in the DRC (Democratic Republic of the Congo) has evolved essentially into a patrimony in nature and has been the root of persistent lack of progress towards poverty reduction and shared prosperity. This governance model is channelled through political patronage and cronyism: and therefore, "key positions in the administration are also allocated on the basis of cronyism and patronage politics rather than on merit".

Consider another oil-dependent African country. Resource-dependence and the consequent Dutch disease effect has been attributed to the slow and often

DOI: 10.4324/9781003245322-6

stagnating pace of industrialisation and diversification in a country with such abundant human and material potentials like Nigeria. However, it is difficult to ascribe the country's befuddling unravelling simply to volatility and over-valued exchange rate. According to van der Ploeg (2011), "[i]t is hard to maintain that the standard Dutch disease story of worsening competitiveness of the non-oil-export sector fully explains [Nigeria's] miserable economic performance". Other studies connect this to the debilitating impact of natural resources on the quality of institutions, and through that channel natural resources harm economic development, even in the absence of Dutch-disease effects (Sala-i-Martin and Subramanian, 2003). Deeply entrenched dysfunctional institutions shaped by resource-abundance are often in control of stakes that fight anticorruption efforts.

Export diversification has remained a desirable and stated objective of successive governments of Nigeria since political independence due to the unbalanced nature of its export structure, principally characterised by oil dominance over all other exports. The government has over the years attempted to implement economic policies such as export promotion strategy; trade liberalisation policy; establishment of the Nigerian Export-Import Bank (NEXIM), among others, with the sole aims of diversifying the country's export structure and improving access to international trade as has been implemented in other emerging economies. Strongly entrenched interests diametrically opposed to industrialisation have jeopardised all these policies.

Additionally, several academic studies equally supported and recommended the pursuit of economic diversification through large-scale industrialisation based on the non-oil (manufacturing) sector, that lead to a deepening of trade and investment in technologies and improvement in agriculture. Some studies premised their recommendation on the effect of economic diversification in stabilising and enhancing economic growth in Nigeria. Lack of diversification led to the neglect of agriculture and the fall in Gross Domestic Product (GDP).[4]

Clearly, oil dependence did little to promote economic growth and development. Therefore, the key issue with the failure to diversify the Nigerian economic might not be structural but institutional which clearly showed that economic diversification may not achieve the necessary results without appropriate economic institutional reform.

The natural resource (NR) sector is a natural space for conflicts related to public procurement in the extractive industries. Evidently, the greater the contribution of natural resource rents the stronger the negative impact on economic growth and the benefits to the citizens in the country.

Clearly, the structure of both formal and informal rules and the character of their enforcement are what define the incentives and wealth-maximising opportunities of individuals and organisations; this includes political organisations, economic organisations, and educational organisations. North (1990) asserts that low-income countries such as the DRC are poor because the institutional constraints define a set of pay-offs to political economic activity that do not encourage productive activities. Such rules affect both economic and social organisations. Therefore, the institutional framework affects growth because it is related to the amount spent on both the costs of the transactions and the cost of transformation in the production process. Transaction costs, for example, are far higher when property rights or the rule of law is not reliable such as observed in situations where patrimony and cronyism rule. Again, when elites devote public resources to achieving private political influence, these social costs, along with rent-seeking behaviour, translate to an unproductive use of inputs and may jeopardise investments in the productive and manufacturing sector thereby negatively impacting economic growth.

We organise the rest of the chapter as follows. In the next section we review selectively what the literature says about the role of institutions on industrialisation and economic diversification. Sections 3 and 4 articulate the key hypotheses and data analysis. Section 5 provides a summing up of key findings.

6.2 Review of diversification, governance, and institutions

Poor governance is closely tied to the lack of strong institutions and weak policies especially in resource-dependent nations where considerable energy is exerted on short-term gains rather than on long-term development objectives. Effective governance is critical to all aspects of economic development including the process of diversification. For example, the quality of institutions tends to influence the behaviour of investors and the openness to domestic financial sector development and consequently foreign direct investment (FDI) (Calderon et al., 2019).

Again, institutions and governance quality transmit into how risks from violent conflicts impact economic growth, (Collier et al., 2003; Miguel et al., 2004). The academic literature shows that growth that depends on increasing resource-abundance could trigger conflicts in countries combining weak institutions and a corrupt elite structure. When countries' development trajectory and output structure depend on oil and other minerals alone, the propensity to violent conflict intensifies (Collier et al., 2003).

Institutions contribute to successful economic diversification through their effects on productivity levels. These include a wide variety of knowledge institutions including learning organisations such as universities, research and development (R&D) organisations, and libraries; and social ones such as the press that collect information from which knowledge is disseminated. These all generate knowledge and disseminate information to the public according to some form of disciplinary criteria. These knowledge organisations are constrained by institutions that determine their rules, such as a country's constitution. Knowledge institutions may also be strengthened or weakened by legal regimes enacted by the legislature or regulators, or developed by courts.

Since good institutions spur a high level of productivity, they also exert a positive influence on the average standard of living in a country as measured by income per capita. Manufacturing sectors are usually more transactions-intensive, unlike extractive oil and traditional agricultural sectors, therefore they tend to be more responsive to institutional factors such as established systems of contract enforcement, rule of law, and favourable business environments. As a result, resource-rich countries with absent, stagnating, or deteriorating institutional frameworks also experience a setback in the evolution of the structure of the economy from manufacturing intensive activities to resource-intensive and subsistence agricultural production (Gelb, 2010; Acemoglu et al., 2003). On the other hand, countries with better regulatory environments and state capacity tend to experience better growth and progress in diversification than countries with lower rankings in institutional quality on the World Governance Indicators. North (1990) argues that institutions also play the role of reducing uncertainty by providing a structure to everyday life, and they are a guide to human interaction. In relating the institutional role to economic development, he adds that institutions have their effects upon the performance of the economy by their effect on the costs of exchange and production. In addition to the costs of technology utilised in the production process, institutions constitute the remaining part of total cost. Therefore, institutions play a key role in the costs of production, and hence the profitability and feasibility of engaging in economic activity. Furthermore, North argues that the most fundamental role of institutions in societies is that they are the underlying determinant of the long-run performance of economies.

In other words, there is an intertwined relationship between dimensions of transparency, good governance, strong institutions and economic diversification, infrastructural development, and demographic dividends as well as important variables in political economy. Compare Nigeria and Indonesia; the two countries share similar characteristics of historical antecedents (colonial rule and military rule), ethnic and religious diversity, and huge populations including Christians and Muslims, among other factors. However, they have progressively diverged in terms of economic performance as well as in levels of social performance. This is because unlike Nigeria, comparatively, Indonesia has utilised a more transparent system and progressive political economy strategies to enhance development, recorded less debt, and recorded higher scores on the United Nations' Human Development Indices, and above all, has a more diversified economy that thrives on oil, agriculture, the service sector, and Information and Communication Technology (ICT) (Fuady, 2015).

History matters to institutional evolution. For three decades, Nigeria passed through a chaotic governance experience with cycles of coups and counter-coups while Indonesia projected a more stable political order, which conduced economic development. This may partly account, for example, for the substantial foreign aid and investment partnership received by Indonesia compared to Nigeria in the former's journey to a developmental state. Hence, while Nigeria remains a fragile, close-to-failing state, Indonesia made the successful transition to an economic and social giant in the 1990s. It is not only that. In contrast to Nigeria's institutional lacuna featuring weakly performing, corrupt, and divided institutions, Indonesia managed to transform that problem and became a more capable state in the area of policy formulation, execution, and economic development generally. In other words, Nigeria was and continues to be slowed down by the politics of distribution, a feral political economy in which office holders contest and appropriate a substantial proportion of national revenue.

Political stability matters for institutional evolution. Indonesia grew under relative stability and enjoyed political longevity among office holders, while there had been a rapid flux of Nigerian office holders resulting in the frequent interruption of well-laid out policies with every government seeking to start afresh rather than continue the policies of its predecessors. Not surprisingly, Indonesia subsequently outpaced Nigeria not just in growth – contrast Indonesia's impressive GDP growth at 7% annually to Nigeria's 3% between 1970 and 1990 – but in the alleviation of poverty. Nigeria descended recently to the world's poverty capital while Indonesia decreased the proportion of citizens living below the poverty line from roughly 60% in the 1970s to less than 30% by the beginning of the 1990s. A final factor is that Indonesia has done much better than Nigeria in managing its population growth while Nigeria's continuously increasing population threatens to become a Malthusian nightmare and a demographic disaster.

These two countries started with similar initial conditions, but institutional factors differentiate those factors decades after. A government's ability and the discipline of its political class underpin its management of public revenues and allocation of resources. How effectively state capacity is deployed is conditioned by not only the nature and quality of inherited institution and development prior to extractives production, but also by the evolution of its economic and political institutions subsequently. Crucial to how the flow of extractives revenue are managed is the character the state–business elite relationship which influences the way governments manage rent capture; so common to resource-dependent countries (Lahn and Stevens, 2018). This is why governance capabilities that a state acquires are determinants of its success in implementing industrial strategies effectively (Khan, 2000). The literature on managing resource revenues has often featured a static view of the trade-off between the risks and benefits associated with the domestic investment of resource revenues.

Governance's close correlate with economic diversification is demonstrated by the World Bank's Worldwide Governance Indicators, which we will use for our analysis in this chapter. Consider Vietnam. The country succeeded in diversification from natural resources in part through building governance capacity. As rent seeking from natural resources rises in Vietnam during 1990 to 1992, foreign direct investment (FDI) inflow decreased. However, the net FDI inflow showed an increasing trend during 1994 to 1998 and 2015 to 2019. The overall FDI inflow indicates a positive trend while rent seeking on natural resources is declining. The control of corruption was an important factor. The rule of law is another economic parameter depicting creation of various laws and their enforcement for transparent economic management and improvement of living standards of citizens. The data on control of corruption and rule of law extracted from World Development Indicators (WDI) online indicates the association between governance and rent seeking on natural resources (Oh et al., 2020). It shows that while corruption was high in Vietnam during initial years, rent seeking on natural resources also was high. However, after 2005, various government policies promoted good governance and subsequently the institution of rule of law became stronger after 2016. Concomitantly, the GINI index of Vietnam decreased as rent seeking in natural resources decreased after 2008; the GINI index shows improvement. The association between natural resources and the GINI index shows a negative trend indicating the country moving towards equality.

We employ an instrument developed and maintained by the World Bank to measure the capacity of a country to support sustainable growth, poverty reduction, and the effective use of development assistance. The Country Policy and Institutional Assessment (CPIA), based on parameters within the control of individual countries, measures the quality of institutions and governance of the countries. The instrument is measured on a scale of 1 to 6 (1=low to 6=high); we present the CPIA score of a few African and Asian countries in Figure 6.1.

We observe from the figure that CPIA of all African sample countries, i.e., DRC, Kenya, and Nigeria have been improving with varying pace. For instance, in Nigeria it almost remained constant from 2005 to 2015. The value of CPIA score in the country in 2005 was 3.08 and remained the same in 2015 with some improvement in between. The highest value it attained is 3.99 in 2007 to 2009, and in 2012. Whereas DRC witnessed comparatively more improvement in governance, the level of governance is lowest among the sample countries. The enhancement in governance is reflected by the change in CPIA score from 2005 to 2015. Although it was 2.83 in 2005 and dropped to 2.50 the next year, it has shown continuous improvement subsequently. CPIA was 3.34 in 2019. On the other hand, governance improvement in Kenya was better than Nigeria but less than DRC while level of governance has been better than both the countries. Its score changed from 3.88 in 2005 to 4.21 in 2015 with some variations in between. The country attained its highest score of 4.25 in 2013.

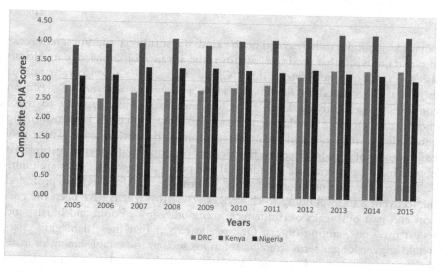

Figure 6.1 Composite CPIA scores for selected African and Asian countries Source: AfDB CPIA Website, 2020.

It may be inferred from the findings that African countries are moving in a very right direction in improving the quality of governance and institutions which would pay dividends in the long run. Although the direction of movement is appreciable, they need to enhance the pace of improvement.

In the next section, we examine the role of policy and institutions in the diversification trajectories of Asia and Africa. We employ North's definition of institutions as "the rules of the game", the rules take two forms: formal laws, such as a constitution that codifies the rules under which a society and an economy function; and informal codes of conduct and behaviour. A society, however, is also governed by other established codes of conduct and norms that shape behaviour in all interactions. While modern economies have functioned within the bounds of formal laws, they are in large part established by informal codes. For example, subsistence agricultural villages remain strong in Africa and have been so governed effectively for centuries without formal laws; yet they have always had definite standards of social conduct. These are socially enforced, largely by sanctions of an individual's own conscience but also by communal sanctions, such as ostracism.

> Arthur Lewis observes, anticipating the widespread innovation-driven and knowledge-based development that characterise advanced industrial nations, that: In every community there are some men whose natural bent is to experiment with new techniques, new products, or new economic forms, in defiance of established opinion or of vested interests. Some societies admire and encourage such people, while others regard them as buccaneers to be suppressed, but economic growth depends very largely on the extent to which the social atmosphere nourishes such people and gives them scope.
>
> (p.51)

What Lewis alludes to here could be the kind of institutional rigidities, rent seeking, and cronyism that tend to slow down the advance of knowledge in African society. The point he wrote is this: "Given [a] country's resources, its rate of growth is determined by *human behaviour and human institutions*".[5] African countries possess varying levels of policy and institutional capacity to make choices that promote development. Many still have difficulties in transforming knowledge to technological capabilities and industrial performance. These very basic constraints can be traced to the capacity of formal and informal institutions upon which the governance of industrial and policy processes in Africa are built.

Due to the aforementioned factors, institutions in Africa exhibit profound ineffectiveness in responding to challenges. The most recent have been the current and past outbreaks of pandemics, commodity price boom and bursts, and locust invasions, among others. One would expect that these damaging crises would trigger longer-term strategic solutions such as the establishment of institutions for scanning and responding to crises including production of medicines and vaccines. It is hard to find scientific organisations and institutions with comparable capacity as comparators outside the continent. When coupled with poorly functioning policy-making bureaucracies, Africa can be said to be characterised by lack of both broad and specific competencies in their coordination functions. For the most part, we have a situation in which policy coordination is largely politically driven in the absence of strong market coordination.

The persistence of sub-optimal institutions and subsequent underdevelopment is therefore a result of individuals and groups whose interests are not evidently served by new ways of doing things such as the adoption of new techniques. While some actors seek new forms of industrial change, groups whose material interests lie in the extant model will be reluctant to make changes even if they lead to a more productive economy. In societies with fragmented ethnic groups, what benefits the dominant group may all-too-frequently disadvantage the growth and economic performance of the country. For example, in many societies, rulers and their political organisations profit not through promoting economic growth but through giving rewards to key constituents who keep them in power. This applies to bureaucracies too. Powerful bureaucrats benefit not by supporting production but rather by taking control of resources and allocating such in ways that promote cronies and political allies.

Informal codes may therefore have a more powerful hold on behaviour than formal laws. In other words, while (formal) rules may be enacted by the state, informal institutions persist and usually change over time especially through incentives and strong penalties. From an institutional perspective, differences in development outcomes go beyond badly implemented economic policies as both markets and states function within broad institutional structures some of which have been in place for a long time and shaped by cultures and ideologies. The institutions therefore shape economic growth of nations positively or negatively over time; they affect transaction costs, the incentives that influence the behaviour of economic and non-economic agents and how they interact with and learn from one another (Oyelaran-Oyeyinka and Gehl-Sampath, 2010 authors are in reverse order in the list of references). Clearly, three key institutional structures are essential for economic and industrial progress: a conducive and business-friendly political order guaranteed by the state (Olson, 2000); an autonomous and competent state including the bureaucracy that formulates and execute policy; and regulatory regimes that exert checks and balances to constrain both the state and business in the pursuit of development goals (Chang and Cheema, 2002).

6.3 Hypotheses

The right institutional conditions are required for economic diversification although other drivers of change such as human capital and infrastructure, among others, are necessary. For this reason, only a few resource-rich developing countries have managed to successfully diversify economically. We identify about six such cases, most of which we analyse in this book: (Chile, Indonesia, Malaysia, Sri Lanka, Vietnam, and Thailand). Institutions contribute to successful economic diversification through their effects on productivity levels. Since institutions spur a high level of productivity, they also exert a positive influence on the average standard of living in a country as measured by income per capita. Manufacturing sectors are usually more transactions-intensive, unlike extractive oil and traditional agricultural sectors, therefore they tend to be more responsive to institutional factors such as established systems of contract enforcement, rule of law, and favourable business environments. As a result, resource-rich countries with deteriorating institutional frameworks also experience a retreat in the structure of the economy from manufacturing intensive activities to resource-intensive and subsistence agricultural production (Gelb, 2010; Acemoglu et al., 2003). On the other hand, countries with better regulatory environments and state capacity tend to experience better growth and progress in diversification than countries with lower rankings in institutional quality on the World Governance Indicators. (Gelb, 2010)

In addition, a resource-rich country's progress in diversification is determined by the use pattern of its resource earnings. Effective public investments in infrastructure, human capital development, and efficiency-enhancing institution building tend to bring a chain of gains such as increased efficiency, reduced cost of production, and increased inflow of foreign capital and investors who can transmit fresh information and capabilities to the domestic economy via demonstration effects. However, such public spending policies need to play a balancing act so that market incentives and stakes of the political elite are harnessed towards effective diversification. Such gains from diversification are apparent in the cases of Chile, Malaysia, and Indonesia. Though these resource-rich countries differ in comparative advantages as well as socio-economic and demographic characteristics, a string of factors contributed to their successful diversification experiences. They all set three long-term priorities: accelerating development, sustaining economic and social stability, and increasing the scope and intensity of exports. In addition, the country governments integrated and implemented their resource development strategies by leveraging stable, strong, and credible technocratic systems (Gelb, 2010).

Quality and governance of institutions are pivotal in the process of economic development in general. Their role becomes even more crucial in export performance, which requires interaction with institutions of other governments. Good governance necessitates production of visible outcomes from all kinds of institutions such as technology, financial, human resource development, and administrative. The governance and quality of institutions are judged by better economic performance such as rising share of manufactured exports or manufacturing value added to GDP for example. In recent times, the issue has drawn the attention of social scientists to investigate the association between institutions and economic performance in general and export performance.

One such study by Joseph et al., (2013) examined the relationship between export performance and quality of institutions. The authors hypothesised that institutional quality would be more important to increasing the export performance of new and small firms compared with their large established counterparts. The results, using the World Business Environment Survey, support their hypothesis. The study further finds that some institutional variables appear to be more important to export performance than others. Another study by Jama (2020) investigates the relevance of governance of institutions for the export performance of the Middle East and North African (MENA) countries. The findings reveal all institutional variables except "political stability and absence of violence" are insignificantly associated with export performance. The findings are based on panel data set over 2010 to 2017. The study concludes that out of several indicators of governance, only political stability and absence of violence emerged as significant determinants of export performance.

A study by Chand (2020) analyses the nexus between exports and indicators of governance in Fiji. The study finds the complementarity between exports and governance. The cooperation between the two contributed significantly in the economic growth of the country. The study concludes that the quality of Fijian institutions needs to be improved to further augment export performance. Another study by Nguyen and Wu (2020) focusing on export performance in Vietnam identified the factors that contributed positively to exports. The focus of the study is on bilateral-specific governance performance indicators during 1996–2014. The findings suggest that Vietnam's export efficiency is positively correlated with the bilateral governance indicators. The study also reveals that export efficiency is not uniform across all the sectors of the economy. The study concludes that higher efficiency could further be achieved by improving the governance of institutions.

In view of existing empirical evidence and theoretical arguments in favour of positive contributions of quality and governance of institutions, we hypothesise that good and strong institutions are likely to influence export performance. Although the earlier studies examined export performance in general, the present study would analyse export diversification, which is a metric of dynamic export performance.

6.3.1 Analytical framework

The analytical framework used in the study is presented in Figure 6.2. It is assumed that exports diversification is influenced by quality as well as governance of institutions. The institutions considered in each category are depicted separately. The unidirectional arrows show the direction of influence.

6.4 Data and econometric analysis

Good governance and strong institutions do create an enabling environment for economic diversification to occur. Diversification does thrive within a framework of an appropriate trade policy design and implementation. This enables the private sector to invest in innovation, and productivity-enhancing technical change that fosters economic diversification within the right regulatory framework. We employ the Country Policy and Institutional Assessment (CPIA) index (World Bank) to capture governance and institutional behaviour and quality based on an overall score.

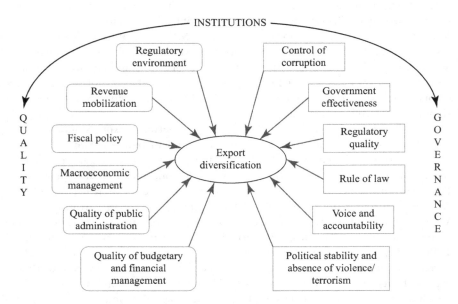

Figure 6.2 Analytical framework Source: Authors.

Quality of institutions (percentile rank): business regulatory environment, efficiency in revenue mobilisation, financial sector rating, fiscal policy rating, macroeconomic management rating, quality of budgetary and financial management rating, and quality of public administration.

Governance indicators (on a scale of 1–6): control of corruption, government effectiveness, political stability, and absence of violence/terrorism; regulatory quality, rule of law, voice and accountability

The index is such that a score of 1 is low and a score of 6 is high quality. Furthermore, the Worldwide Governance Indicator is used to measure the quality of governance. The results presented in Table 6.1 depict that the overall governance quality and a sub-component, regulatory quality, correlated in an insignificantly weak and negative manner with the export concentration index. Table 6.2? illustrates that the overall policy and institutional quality index also correlated in an insignificantly weak and negative manner with export diversification. However, a sub-component of the country policy and institutional assessment index, the trade rating that assesses how government policy framework fosters trade in goods, correlated with export diversification in a significantly strong and negative manner. This signals that trade institution may be a good predictor of export diversification such that as the trade framework improves, there is more exports diversity. Generally, the correlation results show that an improvement in governance and institutional quality can aid the process of export diversification. An appropriate regulatory framework should, therefore, be adopted while

Table 6.1 Export diversification and governance of institutions

Independent variables	Dependent variable: EMDI			Description of variables
	Coeff.	Z	Sig.	
One-year lag of EMDI	0.60922	10.46***	0.000	Exports market diversification index
Governance variable	–0.00049	–1.73*	0.084	Political stability and absence of violence/terrorism
Constant term	0.04603	4.54***	0.000	
Wald Chi2	116.07		0.000	
Observations	140			

Source: Authors estimation.
Note: *** and * significant at 1% and 10% level.

Table 6.2 Export diversification and quality of institutions

Independent variables	Model I			Model II		
	Coeff.	Z	Sig.	Coeff.	Z	Sig.
One-year lag of product diversification index	0.16127	1.15	1.15	0.31308	2.22**	0.027
Fiscal policy rating	–0.13094	–3.44***	0.001			
Macroeconomic management rating				–0.09278	–2.07**	0.038
Constant term	0.7002903	4.28	0.000	0.55667	2.79	0.005
Wald Chi2	32.24		0.000	21.09		0.000
Observations	43			43		

Source: Authors estimation.
Note: *** and ** significant at 1% and 5% level.

bottlenecks such as corrupt practices should be eliminated to allow the private sector to thrive and to attract foreign direct investment into Nigeria (World Trade Organization and OECD, 2019).

6.4.1 Data and analysis

Data for governance indicators come from Worldwide Governance Indicators while quality of institutions data come from Country Policy and Institutional Assessment. Both data sets are from World Development Indicators. The governance indicators are measured as a percentile rank ranging from 0 to 100. The highest rank is considered as best while 0 is considered the worst. Institutional quality data are measured on a scale of 1 to 6 with 1 as the lowest rating and 6 as the highest rating. The sample consists of countries of two continents, namely, Africa and Asia. African countries included are Ghana, Kenya, Nigeria, and South

Africa while Asia is represented by China, India, Indonesia, Malaysia, and South Korea.

In order to quantify the impact of quality and governance of institutions on export diversification, we apply the following econometric specification.

$$ED = f(QI, QG) \tag{1}$$

where,

ED Export diversification
QI Quality of institutions
QG Quality of governance

The econometric estimation uses Generalised Method of Moments (GMM). GMM is preferred over other techniques for various reasons such as (1) a small time period and large cases in a year, (2) independent variables are not strictly exogenous, (3) dependent variable is dynamic and is dependent on its own past, and many more. In the present study it is being used for the last two reasons.

The results related to association between export diversification and governance of institutions are presented in Table 6.1 while Table 6.2 displays the results related to export diversification and quality of institutions. Several variables indicating governance such as control of corruption, government effectiveness, political stability and absence of violence/terrorism, regulatory quality, rule of law, and voice and accountability were included in the analysis. However, it is found that these indicators are highly correlated to each other. Hence, findings related to only one indicator are presented in Table 6.1

On violent conflicts and terrorism, governments of resource-dependent countries for the most part are not able to provide basic security to their citizens, since natural resource wealth elicits violence driven by group interests and competing interests. In conflict-rife environments, three main factors put the environment in an unstable situation (World Bank, 2011) First, the lack of trust between elites and the mistrust of the state by citizens due to ethnicity and disillusionment that attends widespread poverty and inequality in poor countries. Second, the difficulty of respecting contracts and agreements since institutional change can increase the risks of violence in the short term, this is due to political backlash from the groups that lost power or economic benefits; and finally, institutional transformation can be quickly derailed from external security threats or economic shocks that derail progress. In short, fractionalisation, conflict both violent and non-violent, thus leads to over-dissipation of resource rents.

From the table, the initial value of the diversification emerged significant in determining the future growth of the diversification. The governance variable, which emerged significant at 10% in influencing export diversification, is political stability and absence of violence/terrorism. The results also show that the association is significant with a negative sign. The sign is negative because a lower value of diversification index represents a higher diversification level while the higher the value of the governance indicator indicates that there is a larger degree of political stability and absence of violence/terrorism in the country. We infer from the findings that countries that better manage political stability and ensure control of violence/terrorism witness more export diversification. Export market diversification is used as a proxy of export diversification because governance is likely to influence market diversification more than product diversification which is more likely to be influenced by quality of institutions.

The results are consistent with much of earlier findings. Clearly only a stable government can enact and guarantee sustainable economic, industrial policies, and the technological policies needed for diversification. Fragile governments are for the most part putting out fires of dissent rather than focusing on development; in other words, the absence of peace tends to dissipate the resources and energy of states. Similarly, it is only absence of violence and terrorism that enables government to devote its energy and resources to development activities. On the contrary, the prevalence of violent conflicts and terrorism diverts government's attention towards maintenance of peace again at the cost of socio-economic development. The high levels of political stability and absence of violence/terrorism are necessary but not sufficient conditions for export diversification; the quality of institutions, which we examine subsequently, is very vital.

In resource-dependent countries across Africa, persistent conflicts seem to be connected to the absence of, or weak, institutions that are unable to mediate and adjudicate conflicts and, as well, the historic grievances over natural resources, land, and the perceived greed of the elite appropriation of state resources. In the DRC, for example, political actors in alliance with ethnic leaders continue to fan the embers of ethnic and communal conflicts. In these countries, poverty, inequality, and, lately, disease tend to add fuel to the raging fires of decade-long resourced-induced conflicts. The nature of the relationship between these development indicators and conflict depends on the prevalence of the greed hypothesis or the grievances hypothesis (World Bank, 2018).

Table 6.2 presents the results of association between export production diversification and quality of institutions. The quality of institutions indicators encompass business regulatory environment, efficiency of revenue mobilisation, the financial sector, fiscal policy, macroeconomic management, quality of budgetary and financial management, and quality of public administration.

Two specifications have been used to capture the impact of quality of institutions on the export diversification due to high correlation among these indicators. The findings indicate the path-dependency of export diversification. It can be seen from the results that fiscal policy rating and macroeconomic management rating emerged significant in influencing export diversification. The results are according to our expectation as significant indicators play a pivotal role in resource allocation in R&D and various other innovation activities. And for export production diversification, such activities are crucial.

Appropriate fiscal policies enable development of social and technological infrastructure which is necessary for industrial development. It is the sufficiently developed industrial sector that could help in innovating new products or products with new

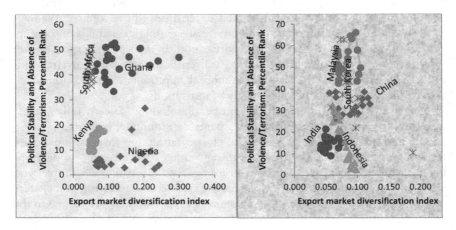

Figure 6.3 Export market diversification and governance of institutions Source: Authors.

feature. Path-dependency plays an important part in this process. The fiscal policies coupled with better macroeconomic management could result in the development and production of diversified products which are the basis of export diversification. And this is what has been captured by the econometric analysis.

The association of significant variables with export diversification is discussed in detail in the following subsections. The association of market and product diversification is presented and discussed separately. Figure 6.3 shows the association of the market diversification index with governance of indicators in sample countries.

We observe from the figures that political stability in South Africa (40.61)[6] is much better than Nigeria (6.78) and is associated with market diversification. The market diversification in South Africa (0.047)[7] is much higher than Nigeria (0.134). This establishes positive association between political stability and market diversification. This association does not hold true in the case of Ghana where political stability is high but market diversification is low.

6.4.2 *Export market diversification index and institutions*

The analysis of Asian sample countries suggests that the average market diversification of China (0.080) is very high while the political stability in the country is also ranked fairly high (52.60 percentile). On the other hand, the market diversification in South Korea is lowest (0.091) among the sample countries while the political stability rank is also low (39.34 percentile). It may be inferred from this kind of relationship that political stability contributes to market diversification. The case of India is an exception where market diversification is fairly high (0.053) and political stability ranking is very low (14.42).

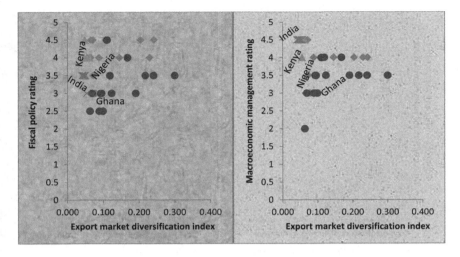

Figure 6.4 Export market diversification and quality of institutions Source: Authors.

The association between market diversification and quality of institutions is depicted in Figure 6.4. It is seen from the figure that market diversification in Kenya (0.060) is largest among the sample African countries while fiscal policy rating is also very high (3.97). On the other hand, the market diversification in Ghana is very low (0.132) and the rating of fiscal policy is the lowest (3.30). This establishes a positive relationship between market diversification and fiscal policy rating.

The association between market diversification and macroeconomic management follows a similar trend to that of fiscal policy. The market diversification in India (0.053) is largest while the macroeconomic management rating (4.50) is highest among the sample countries. On the other hand, Nigeria witnessed the least diversification (0.134) with a very low rating of macroeconomic management (3.80).

6.4.3 Export product diversification index and institutions

Figure 6.5 depicts the association between export product diversification and governance of institutions. It can be seen from the figure that the pattern of association is similar to that of market diversification. It can be seen from the figure that political stability in South Africa (40.61) is much better than Nigeria (6.78) and is associated with product diversification. The product diversification in South Africa (0.034) is much higher than Nigeria (0.313). This confirms positive association between political stability and product diversification. This association does not hold true in the case of Ghana where political stability is high, but product diversification is low.

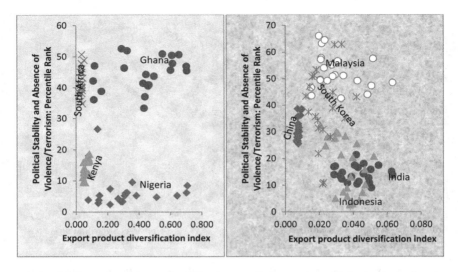

Figure 6.5 Export product diversification and governance of institutions Source: Authors.

The analysis of Asian sample countries suggests that the average product diversification of China (0.008) is very high while the political stability in the country is also ranked fairly high (31.09 percentile). On the other hand, product diversification in India is comparatively low (0.043) among the sample countries while the political stability rank is also low (14.42 percentile). We infer that political stability contributes to product diversification.

The association between product diversification and quality of institutions is depicted in Figure 6.6. It can be seen from the figure that product diversification in Kenya (0.060) is largest among the sample African countries while fiscal policy rating is also very high (3.97). On the other hand, product diversification in Ghana is the lowest (0.429) and the rating of fiscal policy is also the lowest (3.30). This shows a positive relationship between market diversification and fiscal policy rating.

The association between product diversification and macroeconomic management follows a similar trend to that of fiscal policy. The product diversification in India (0.043) is largest while the macroeconomic management rating (4.50) is highest among the sample countries. On the other hand, Ghana witnessed least diversification (0.429) with a very low rating of macroeconomic management (3.43).

In sum, poor governance and weak institutions emerged as significant constraints to diversification in African resource-dependent countries. On the contrary, the experience of East Asian countries shows that progressive improvements to economic governance and institution building lead to export market diversification and sustainable growth.

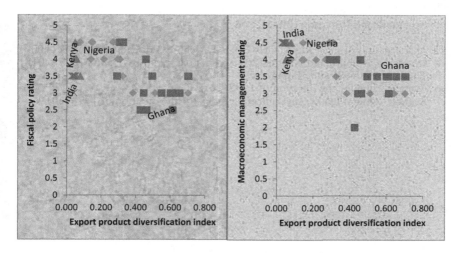

Figure 6.6 Export product diversification and quality of institutions Source: Authors.

6.5 Summing up

In this chapter, we examine the role on governance and institutions on diversification. Findings are based on a sample of African and Asian countries. The empirical findings suggest that a strong institution and governance rules are associated with higher GDP per capita growth rates. The effect of natural resources on socio-economic development therefore depends on the quality of institutions. The findings also show that African countries that are largely less diversified and highly dependent on natural resources tend to realise lower growth returns than Asian countries that have shifted from NR to manufactures. The latter depends comparably less on resource rents in GDP. Specifically, findings show that good macroeconomic management and fiscal policies are strongly related to export product diversification.

Our empirical analysis shows that diversification has a circular reference, that is, the level of diversification in the previous year significantly influences diversification in the present year. We find this to be true for the export market as well as product diversification. To some extent it sets the path-dependency in export diversification. Political stability and absence of violence/terrorism are also found to be significantly influencing the export market diversification.

The study also analyses an instrument called Country Policy and Institutional Assessment (CPIA), based on parameters within control of individual countries. It measures quality of institutions and governance of the countries. The instrument is measured on a scale of 1 to 6 (1=low to 6=high). The CPIA score in African sample countries witnessed a positive change. We surmise from the findings that African countries have been moving in the very right direction in improving the quality of governance and institutions that would pay dividends in long run.

Notes

1 Acemoglu and Robinson (2012), 368, 372).
2 Ibid
3 Aljarallah and Angus (2020); Gelb (2010); Mehlum, Moene, and Torvik (2006).
4 Onodugo, Amujiri, and Nwuba (2015); Ayobola, Ekundayo, and Muibi (2018).
5 These are authors' underlining.
6 Average value for the duration of 1998–2019.
7 Average value of market diversification index for the duration of 1998–2019.

7 Summary and conclusion

7.1 Introduction

This final chapter summarises the key findings of the comparative analysis of Asian and African countries; it synthesises lessons from the different chapters. The central thesis of this book is that Africa fell behind in development because for about five decades it relied on the low-growth pathway of commodity extraction and export while Asia made spectacular progress as it took the high road of learning and mastering of technologies that undergird industrialisation. The Covid-19 pandemic has clearly thrown African nations into unprecedented economic, food, and health crises. This particular crisis has resulted in cessation of economic activities that will lead to a significant decline in GDP (Gross Domestic Product), an unprecedented social disruption, and the loss of millions of jobs. It gave us the added motivation to revisit the challenge of economic diversification. According to estimates by the African Development Bank (AfDB), the region's economies contraction will cost sub-Saharan Africa between US$35 billion and $100 billion due to output decline and a steep fall in commodity prices, especially the crash of the oil price.

More fundamentally, the pandemic has unsparingly exposed the hollowness of African economies on two fronts: the fragility and weakness of Africa's economies and its lack of industrial capabilities. The two are complementary. In the absence of an industrial capacity, there will be no sustainable long-term change in the living standards of African citizens as happened in Asia.

The possession of Natural Resources (NR) has led to a pathology of resource-dependence resulting in what the literature terms as the thesis of "resources curse". Of the 15 least diversified countries in the world, eight are in Africa.[1] Clearly, little economic diversification appears to have taken place in Africa even among those with relatively higher income levels due largely to continuing and high dependence on natural resources of many middle-income African countries. At current estimation, natural resources account for more than one-fifth of GDP in five of the ten African countries with GDP per capita of more than $5,000.

We also conclude that Natural Resource abundance is not by itself a curse or a blessing. What determines the development trajectory and development outcome of NR-abundant countries are the nature of policies and the institutional context within which a country operates.

DOI: 10.4324/9781003245322-7

Several factors both broad and specific shape the development paths of countries. We categorise them into political stability, governance, quality of institution, and economic policies. Countries that have visions for long-term economic development transform natural resources assets into opportunities, while others see NR as everlasting resources and remain solely dependent on them. The entrenchment of rent-seeking policies results into resource curse while use of NR as a means for development leads to resource blessings.

We employed two broad sets of explanatory variables, the first are political factors focusing on the notion of resource curse (rentier state theories, rent seeking, conflict, corruption, among others.) The second set are economic variables (volatility of commodities cycles, Dutch disease, and exchange rate fluctuations, among others). What is becoming clear is that these factors do not point to the inevitability of bad outcomes resulting from resource-abundance.

This book examined Asia and Africa in comparative diversification perspectives. We traced the uneven growth in wealth between the two regions. Clearly, state and institutional capabilities underlying the generation and diffusion of knowledge in Asia distinguished it from Africa. We analyse factors that separate the sample countries that made rapid progress in "catching up" and those that tend to be stagnating and "falling behind".

Progress made by Asian countries over the last five decades was due in large part to their pursuit of industrialisation, technological acquisition underpinned by good governance, and policies in the right institutional contexts. There was not one grand development formula however; the strategy has consisted of industrial (vertical) diversification as well as (horizontal) diversification in agriculture. African countries on the contrary took the low road in exporting minerals and raw agricultural commodities with little value addition; in the process, Africa has experienced a *reversal of fortune*. The African condition is manifestly a reversal of fortune because in the 1950s they were ahead of, or equal to, Asia in per capita income as well as in other development metrics.

Reversal of Africa's fortune manifests in economic, social, technological, and industrial conditions. Compared with comparator Asian countries, by analysing the disparities in development metrics, particularly the levels and rates of growth of national incomes and HDI (Human Development Index), the differences are stark, see Figure 7.1.

We base the analysis in the figure on average value (1996–2019) of rent on natural resources as percentage of GDP and HDI. From the figure, HDI in South Korea, the most diversified in our sample, has the highest (0.87) with lowest value of rent (0.03%) while Chad has the lowest HDI and substantially higher resource rent (HDI 0.36 and rent 21.37%). There is a negative association between the two suggesting they are inversely related to each other. The negative correlation between the two (-0.59) also indicates the same type of association.

7.2 Growth trajectory of countries

While Asian countries – many without natural commodities – were forced to creatively innovate to maximise their competitive advantages, most African countries

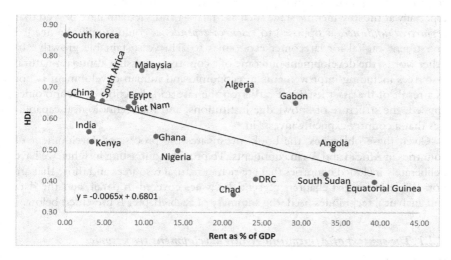

Figure 7.1 Association of HDI and resource rent. Source: Authors; data from HDI (UNDP); Rent (WDI).

have remained reliant on the easy money from resource exports. As fluctuating commodity prices have made volatility the norm of African countries unstable in the last decade, many have turned to their Asian counterparts for loans and aids to sustain economies that had fallen far behind. Asian nations assimilated manufacturing technologies and other aspects of the value chain that multiply the value of resources and create higher value jobs. The success of Asia proves that in less than three decades, focused leadership and sustained industrialisation can drag nations out of poverty.

The most prominent set of issues relate to resource boom and commodity super cycle; and how these phenomena induce volatility and appreciation of the real exchange rate. Other significant factors include the relationship between resource-dependence and rent-seeking behaviour; the triggering of civil conflict, ethnic fractionalisation particularly in the context of dysfunctional institutions, and prevalence of corruption. In this book, the most critical issue that we identified regarding long-term development are that resource-rich developing economies tend to forgo industrialisation and technological acquisition and consequently experience the least diversification and structural transformation.

Another key finding resonating in the literature and in this book on resource-abundance is the role of institutions in explaining resource blessing or curse. First, that within strong institutional contexts it is possible for policies to prevent the Dutch disease effect; however this has been very rare in the experience of developing countries and hardly so in the African experience except for Botswana.

The conventional wisdom on resource-abundance much earlier was that of a "blessing" not a "curse". Several scholars attributed economic development of earlier industrial nations to their mineral and commodities-abundance.[2] Latecomer countries that pursue technology-driven horizontal and vertical diversification especially at the low-income stage such as Malaysia and Vietnam have proved that *resource-abundance*, as opposed to *resource-dependence* could supply the needed investment capital for latecomer economies to achieve sustainable growth.[3] In other words, the development outcome of a country possessing abundant natural resources including improvements in economic and human development is not as a result of the asset itself but rather on the rate and direction of technologies applied, the structure of knowledge institutions, and the technological capabilities that a country explicitly invests in.

Given these objectives, the book investigates the process of development of countries in African and Asian continents. To provide contrasting insights, we have deliberately included countries that are rich in natural resources and those that are not. While individual chapters present the issues covered in detail, and the data and analytical techniques used, the summary of each chapter is presented below.

7.2.1 *The context of Africa and Asian development trajectories*

We identified the causes of reversal of Africa's fortune. We showed empirical evidence to show that four decades ago many "Asian Tigers" had income several times less than many African countries and by the second decade of the 21st century they converted themselves into global economic and industrial leaders with income several times higher than their African counterparts. For instance, Nigeria's per capita income in 1980 was six times that of China but the per capita income of China is almost three and half times to that of Nigeria in 2019. On comparing average per capita income of Asia with Africa, we found that Africa was ahead of Asia before the 1960s. Thereafter relative average per capita income in Asia has been increasing while in Africa it has been declining and the ever-increasing gap has been enormous in both the continents in recent times.

The analysis shows that the endowment of natural resources in Africa has proved to be a curse for the region while in large part a blessing for Asia. Improvement in these factors in Asia has put the region in a virtuous circle of prosperity and development. On the other hand, many countries in Africa have treated natural resource assets as everlasting resources and reaped the consequences of destructive rent-seeking activities. Consequently, the region has gone into a vicious cycle of poverty and underdevelopment.

7.2.2 *The nexus of export diversification and economic development*

The book systematically analysed the association between export diversification and economic development. The sample covers countries that are rich in natural resources and those that are not. The evidence presented suggests that export diversification is strongly associated with sustained economic performance resulting in improvements in higher living standards. On the other hand, the countries that could not diversify faced unstable income and widespread unemployment resulting in poor economic performance. In general, Asian countries have achieved greater economic diversification and, not surprisingly, higher living standards compared to their African counterparts.

Regarding the theoretical focus on specialisation versus diversification, there has been a significant theoretical shift over the years. The initial classical and neoclassical economic thought was that a country should specialise in producing and exporting a commodity in which it had a comparative advantage and, thus, use more of the factor in which it had a relatively large endowment. That meant that (African) developing countries would continue ad infinitum to produce and export largely primary products while importing manufactures. In contrast, recent theoretical understanding emphasises the need for export diversification into manufacturing in developing countries. Indeed, empirical evidence seems to be in concert with the latter theories, in that those countries pursuing export diversification have performed better in terms of sustained growth and development. Further, the theory of derived demand suggests that such growth would likely result in a relatively large demand for labour leading to higher employment, though the rate of increase would be dependent on the labour-intensive nature of the technology employed.

The manufacturing sector has witnessed more diversification compared to other sectors. Consequently, the export share of manufacturing in total exports from leading countries is around 80% in 2019 in Asia compared to less than 50% in Africa. The evidence presented in Chapter 2 of our book suggests a strong association between export diversification and employment creation. The chapter concludes that export diversification is one instrument that could be applied for better economic performance.

7.2.3 Economic diversification and structural stability

An important innovative approach to diversification focuses on the analysis of export of primary commodities and its consequences on structural stability and economic development in Asia and Africa. We analysed the countries in order to understand the devastating impact of external shocks including the recent pandemic (Covid-19) on oil-exporting countries compared to non-oil exporters. We provide empirical evidence showing that continuous concentration on commodities exports is strongly related to relative economic instabilities. For Africa as a whole, the dependency figures are significant and troubling as commodity exports on average account for 80% of total merchandise exports.

The chapter on structural stability presents evidence to support the argument that the GDP growth rate in oil-rich countries has been declining consistently with the impact of successive oil crises; however, the magnitude of decline in growth has been much less in non-oil exporters. The country case studies presented in the chapter suggest that during boom periods of oil export, oil-rich countries witness very high growth rates while in crisis period, the massive reduction in exports lead to high export income volatility. With such high volatility in income, country-level plans and implementation are completely destabilised resulting in poor socio-economic development. The chapter recommends that

African countries need to devote greater resources to master exports of processed products rather than primary products.

In both historical and contemporary terms, export diversification has been found to be a catalytic factor in socio-economic development. There are two dimensions of export diversification, namely, market diversification and product diversification. Both these aspects are analysed in the book. The respective chapter (4) investigates and identifies factors that influence export market diversification. The findings presented in the chapter reveal that several macroeconomic variables influence export market diversification. We group these factors into four broad categories, these are financial resources, international orientation, technological competence, and innovation capabilities. The findings point to the dynamics of global integration of an economy as a contributor to market diversification. The financial resources coupled with innovation capacity clearly influence market diversification while the association between employment creation and market diversification is positive and significant. Market diversification itself has a circular effect.

7.2.4 Diversification and technological capability acquisition

We tested the theoretical position that export diversification is dependent on the technological competence of a country. Drawing on this view, we analyse the association between technological competence and export product diversification in sample countries. The export product diversification is measured by the Herfindahl–Hirschman product diversification index. We found that the majority of the African sample countries did not experience product diversification during 1990 to 2019 rather they witnessed export product contraction leading to an increase in the diversification index. On the other hand, the majority of the Asian countries experienced product diversification.

We proxy technological competence with four indicators, namely; manufacturing value added as a percentage of GDP, share of employment in industry as a percentage of total employment, percentage export of high-tech products to the total exports, and electric power consumption per capita. The findings on Asian countries suggest that technological competence is positively associated with export diversification. Like market diversification, product diversification is also found to have a circular effect. On the other hand, the analysis of African countries suggests that there does not exist any significant association between export product contraction and technological competence.

Broadly, Asian countries made sustained investment in human capital. This is the sum total of the skills level of a country's entire workforce which includes managers and administrators; it is strongly related to the potential real income per capita of a country and it is a function of the productivity of its labour. East Asian experience demonstrates that human capital is very important as a source of economic growth. Their sources of competitive advantage in advanced technologies derive largely from superior education, training, and skills developed through "learning-by-using", "learning-by-doing", and "doing-by-innovation".

Diversification has been achieved through consistent and explicit technological learning in order to climb the industrial technological ladder from low technology to high-technology regimes. This has been made possible by long-term investment in knowledge and skills upgrading required to master new technologies.

In contrast, oil-dependent economies with weak technological capabilities hardly diversified. These countries are locked-in into petroleum export for export earnings to the detriment of value added agriculture and manufactures. The result is poor contribution of the manufacturing subsector which fluctuates between 5% and 10% to aggregate output in these countries compared with its peers in Asia (Korea about 30% in the 1990s), which is staggering. Due to a weak industrial base, the relatively high contribution of the oil sector to the industrial sector contribution is driven largely by crude production and not by value added products components like refined oil, plastics, fertilisers, and petrochemicals.

7.2.5 *Economic diversification governance and institutions*

Theoretically, we identify with the notion that quality of governance and institutions are critical to export diversification. The empirical findings suggest that a strong institution and governance rules are associated with higher GDP per capita growth rates. The effect of natural resources on socio-economic development therefore depends on the quality of institutions. The findings also show that weak institutional factors in African countries have resulted in less diversification and high dependence on natural resources, which tend to realise lower growth returns than for Asian countries that have shifted from dependence on natural resources to manufactures. The latter depends comparably less on resource rents in GDP. Specifically, our findings show that good macroeconomic management and fiscal policies are strongly related to diversification. Along with time-relevant industrial policies, political stability and absence of violence/terrorism are also found to be significantly influencing the export diversification.

Our analyses on institutions employed an instrument called Country Policy and Institutional Assessment (CPIA), which is based on parameters within the control of individual countries. It measures quality of institutions and governance of the countries. The instrument is measured on a scale of 1 to 6 (1=low to 6=high). The CPIA score of African sample countries witnessed a relatively positive change but not nearly enough to effect significant diversification. We infer that African countries are moving in a very right direction in improving the quality of governance and institutions which would pay dividends in the long run. Although the direction of movement is appreciable, they did not enhance the pace of improvement.

7.3 Lessons from case studies

In order to substantiate the empirical findings presented in earlier chapters, we carried out detailed case studies of a few countries and analysed the lessons that advanced the diversification dynamics of the successful countries. We examined case studies in Asia represented by South Korea, Malaysia, and Vietnam while in Africa we considered countries such as Nigeria and DRC (Democratic Republic of the Congo), among others. The case of South Korea is important as it is a highly advanced economy with its growth now dependent on manufacturing and services. On the other hand, Malaysia, despite being a natural resource-rich country has transformed itself into an advanced economy as a result of its concentration on industrial activities other than rent seeking. Vietnam has witnessed one of the highest GDP growths in the region for the last three decades.

The Asian countries followed relatively similar industrialisation policies albeit with contextual differences in timing, sequencing, and sectoral choices. The industrialisation strategy includes significant investment in creating spatial agglomerations in addition to giving incentives to firms that allows them to benefit from the process of clustering. The policies led to the creation of both product specific clusters and large sectoral clusters generating diversified products, particularly in the context of South Korea. With special policy initiatives, such clusters evolved into dynamic productive zones, cutting down transaction costs and making the agglomeration economies work significantly. Better matching of firms and workers does take place in such clusters. Besides, information sharing, innovation, and technological progress was faster in these clusters resulting in rapid gains in productivity.

South Korea focused on not only developing industrial clusters but also creating agro-Industrial Parks with sectoral focus on industrialising agriculture. The experiences of Malaysia and Vietnam show that creating high value added goods by processing high value agricultural products is an important route to prosperity. Secondly, the policy-induced clusters offer a wide range of benefits to both producers and consumers. The agglomeration economies operate with a concentration of industrial activities, significantly enhancing productivity growth, which is competitiveness enhancing in the international markets. Firms manufacturing different industrial goods and specialised products both benefit from concentration in the specially designated zones. With availability of rich infrastructure and reduced information cost and labour turnover cost returns to investment are much larger in the clustered spaces.

Malaysia's economic diversification is a typical example of a combination of horizontal and vertical diversification, where horizontal diversification entails the policies that promote increasing the production of an existing export commodity and vertical diversification involves adding value to the existing product or manufacture of new products. As a matter of strategy, Malaysia in spite of being rich in terms of primary products did not remain confined to those products in the raw form. For example, Malaysia is famous for rubber production but it made explicit efforts to process rubber and added value significantly: this includes manufactures and exports of rubber products like tyres and gloves, making it the biggest producer of rubber gloves, and diversifying into higher-end products of medical gloves for the health sector.

Malaysia's horizontal diversification is illustrated by the country's efforts in turning its oil palm sector into a successful multi-product strategy. The most significant example of vertical diversification is Malaysia's electronics. Along with other Asian

Tigers, Malaysia is able to manufacture and export a diverse range of electronic goods, which are exported worldwide. The cost advantages are reflected in the prices which attracted a number of customers from different countries.

Vietnam is also a country endowed with significant natural resources, but has made a successful transition of turning natural wealth into assets. It has done so with reform of macroeconomic policies, improved governance, building quality institutions, reduction in corruption, and paying due attention to human resource development, among others. The country experienced a major industrialisation shift due to the different policies promulgated over time. The various economic development initiatives were undertaken in the country through its five-year plans. The major shift in socio-economic development was achieved in Vietnam after 1985 as the industrial weaknesses were recognised and reforms were introduced in the system to enhance efficiency which resulted in a market-oriented economy called "Doi-Moi".

Apart from the policies encouraging industry-led growth, cluster-based industrialisation, infrastructure development, and human capital formation were key success drivers in its export-led growth strategy encouraged by the government since the beginning. Vietnam transited from the export of primary products into the manufacture of industrial goods; which subsequently underpinned the growth and development miracle of other Asian countries before it. The exports of high value products including technology and ICT (Information and Communication Technologies) could helped it earn foreign exchange, which is utilised for the import of inputs, ensuring the production of quality products.

The above policies and similar others led to rapid diversification in these successful countries. In South Korea, massive investment was made in education, which turned the country into a major international technological powerhouse. The country's national economy benefited from a highly skilled workforce. Korea regarded education as a high priority instrument for South Korean families. In 2015, the country spent 5.1% of its GDP on all levels of education: roughly 0.8 percentage points above the Organisation for Economic Co-operation and Development (OECD) average of 4.3%. A strong investment in education and an aggressive drive for success helped the resource-poor country grow its economy rapidly over the past 60 years after a long and painful war. The International Monetary Fund had in the past acknowledged the resilience of the South Korean economy in managing various economic crises, citing low state debt and high fiscal reserves that can be quickly mobilised to address financial emergencies.

South Korea equally invested heavily in infrastructure including in a technologically advanced transport network consisting of high-speed railways, highways, bus routes, ferry services, and air routes. Importantly, the industrialisation process in South Korea has supported technology-based corporations with a variety of incentives including export subsidies. As Lane (2021) argued, South Korea's industrial policy in the late 1970s played a critical role in building its modern economy. Analysts describe the success and effectiveness of South Korea's industrial strategy as unique in the modern history of industrialisation (Kim and Song, 2020). Within one generation, the country achieved rapid transformation from a poor agrarian society into a modern industrial power. From 1962, the South Korean government aggressively pursued an economic development strategy with a central focus on manufacturing sector growth driven by industrial complexes. As Kim and Song (2020) point out, more than 900 industrial clusters account for 62% of the country's manufacturing production and 80% of total exports. This unique feature of South Korea's policies includes designation of physical sites and facilitation of growth platforms that reinforce cooperation and coordination between industries, academia, and research. The path of industrial development in South Korea revolved around building industrial clusters scattered across the country, and it initiated the measures and policies that enabled such industrialisation. Agglomeration and cluster-based industrialisation reduce the transaction cost of operation, help reduce the problems associated with information asymmetry, and encourage efficient utilisation of the resources (Zheng and Aggarwal, 2020). Agglomeration economies resulting in rising productivity growth would imply higher competitiveness, which offers clear technological advantages in economic diversification and access to international markets.

The power of vision and long-term commitment to industrialisation are critical to diversification. In 1991, the Malaysian Prime Minister outlined his ideal in the country's Vision 2020, suggesting that Malaysia would become a self-sufficient industrialised nation by 2020. Malaysia planned to attain a developed country status much earlier than the actual target in 2020, with the help of two specific programmes: the Government Transformation Programme and the Economic Transformation Programme. The electronic equipment, petroleum, and liquefied natural gas production per capita were to be augmented significantly. Human capital formation was a key pillar. Malaysian life expectancy and the relatively high level of schooling evidently supported the rapid expansion of the economy. In Malaysia's growth history, the nation generated resources from horizontal and vertical diversification, which in turn improved various development indicators including education and health. Malaysia's economic diversification is a typical example of a combination of horizontal and vertical diversification, where horizontal diversification entails the policies that promote increasing the production of an existing export commodity and vertical diversification involves adding value to the existing product or production of new products. It is interesting to note that Malaysia in spite of being rich in terms of primary products did not remain confined to those products in the raw form. For example, Malaysia is famous for rubber production but when it comes to export Malaysia is seen to have added value significantly: it also manufactures and exports rubber products like tyres and gloves, making it the biggest producer of rubber gloves, and diversifying into higher-end products of medical gloves for the health sector.

In the 1970s, the predominantly mining and agricultural-based economy began a transition to a more multi-sector diversified economy. Since the 1980s, the industrial sector, with a high level of investment, led the country's growth. A relatively highly diversified economy enabled a fast recovery from the Asian financial crisis of the nineties. International trade and manufacturing were the key sectors: manufacturing has a large influence on the country's economy, although Malaysia's economic structure has been shifting away from this sector into services.

In an effort to diversify the economy, the government has also encouraged tourism in Malaysia. Knowledge-based services are expanding and privatisation is encouraged significantly with a view to initiate competitiveness and efficient utilisation of resources. Science policies in Malaysia are regulated by the Ministry of Science, Technology, and Innovation and the country is one of the world's largest exporters of semiconductor devices, electrical devices, and ITC products. The government's persistent drive to develop and upgrade its infrastructure has resulted in massive success and it has emerged as one of the newly industrial-ising countries of Asia with the most well-developed infrastructure with over 200 industrial parks. These include specialised parks such as Technology Park Malaysia and Kulim Hi-Tech Park. Malaysia's energy infrastructure sector and road and railway infrastructure are also highly developed.

The remarkable economic expansion was progressively led by manufacturing as a result of which the manufacturing sector's share in total GDP rose signifi-cantly from 13.3% in 1970 to about 30% by 1997 and export of manufactured goods increased from a mere 12% of total exports in 1970 to 81% by 1997. The macroeconomic conditions underpin the growth and structural transformation of an economy with a fairly liberal trade and investment regime; and as well, the extensive use of so-called functional and selective industrial policies.

In sum, apart from the policies encouraging industry-led growth, cluster-based industrialisation, infrastructure development, and human capital forma-tion, one of the fundamental reasons of the success of these countries lies with the export-led growth strategy encouraged by the government. Unlike the African counterparts that were content with short termism of primary products exports, Asian countries focused on advanced industrial goods which would explain the growth and development miracle of these countries. They invested in gathering intelligence to understand the requirement of international market regimes and therefrom developed their diversification strategy accordingly.

Exports of high value products including technology and ICT helped these countries earn foreign exchange, which could then be utilised for the import of inputs, ensuring the production of quality products. Diversification and exports have proceeded hand in hand, both being complementary to each other. Diversified industrialisation led to productivity growth, which improved com-petitiveness, offering an edge over other competitors in the international markets. Further, export potentiality and its realisation could offer opportunities for diver-sified economic growth to pick up and sustain itself in the end.

7.4 Impact of oil dependence and poor diversification on the Nigerian economy

Nigeria unlike Asian counterparts remains dependent largely on its oil sector which remains a major source of the revenue needed to finance infrastructures and govern-ment spending. Over the years, the dependence of the Nigerian economy on oil contributed positively in boosting its gross domestic product (GDP), raising revenue and employment and correcting balance of payment defects. For instance, the proportion of the total revenue of the Nigerian economy from oil rose from 62.4% to 79.8% from 1990 to 2004.[4] However, this earlier trend was due to the relatively high price of oil in the world market, the stable exchange rate, and the capacity of Nigeria to meet its share in crude oil market. The increase in government revenue was used to support government expenditures especially recurrent expenses which includes foreign and domestic interest payments and capital expenses such as foreign, domestic, and non-debts.

However, in the past decades, the over-dependence of the Nigerian economy on oil led to the poor performance of the non-oil sectors of the economy particularly in their contribution to value of exports as the exploration and export of oil have been the major source of government revenue. In addition, the over-dependence of the Nigerian economy on oil has caused great environmental hazards to the country and led to the decay of political, economic, and, as well, judicial institutions. For instance, the government, international oil companies, and host communities have been in continuous confrontations arising from petroleum exploration in the Niger Delta due to the effect of gas flaring and environmental degradation, which has deprived the inhabitants of the communities of their livelihood. In addition, systematic corruption has undermined key extractive institutions of the Nigerian oil and gas industry and made it impossible for successive governments to translate the good fortune of oil to build an efficient modem society.[5]

Although huge wealth has been generated from the oil sector, upon which Nigeria greatly depends, mismanagement and corruption of the ruling class either through squandering on questionable public investment or outright looting of the public treasury have denied the ordinary Nigerian citizens the benefits of the wealth, hence increasing the level of inequality, poverty, unemployment, inflation, and the low standard of living in the country. Nigeria's over-dependence on oil has had varied implications on her economic development as seen in the neglect of the agricultural sector as an alternative source of revenue to the government. Also, the influx of the petrol-dollar boom has been the cause of a persistent inflationary trend and commodity price volatility with attendant negative effects on the country's currency and value of the national currency, the naira.

Clearly, oil dependence led to a negative and significant effect on the economy and this effect is transmitted from the exchange rate to the balance of payment, down to the manufacturing sector. The manufacturing sector remains impeded because the government has been unable to sustain a single productive developmental strategy due to the high level of dependence on volatile oil prices, making diversification more challenging to implement

7.5 Comparative impact of natural resources rents on development

In this section we compare the impact on NR rents in four countries, the percentage contribution of natural resources to GDP is depicted in Figure 7.2. The

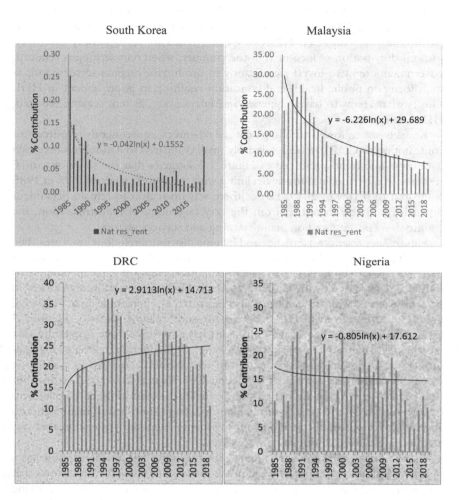

Figure 7.2 Contribution of natural resources. Source: Authors.

figure shows that the trend line of the contribution of NR to GDP for Malaysia, South Korea, and Nigeria has a negative slope suggesting that the contribution has been declining over the study period. Looking at details of the trend in Malaysia, we notice that it fluctuated until 1989 and declined subsequently until 2000. It follows a sinusoidal trend thereafter leading to just 6.26% in 2019. The highest contribution of 27.54% was in 1987. In general, the contribution has been declining at the annual rate of 3.67% during the study period. On the other hand, rent seeking in DRC is still increasing.

The impact of reduction in rent-seeking activities is evident on HDI in Malaysia. While the HDI had been improving for the last three decades, it changed from 1.76 in 1986 to 2.50 in 2019 with a peak of 8.76 in 1992. The improvement in HDI can be attributed to reduction in rent-seeking activities. As the literature suggests, NR rent seeking tends to be negatively associated with misdistribution of income. On the contrary, when rent seeking is reduced, governments tend to invest significantly in productive income sectors, and, as well, focus on public health and education resulting in improvement in HDI. This is what seems to have happened in Malaysia, i.e., as rent seeking reduced, HDI improved.

Korea is not endowed with huge natural resources, consequently resource rent contribution to GDP had been relatively small compared to natural resource-rich countries. The trend presented in Figure 7.2 suggests that the share of natural resources has been continuously declining with the highest share of 0.25 in 1985 compared to 0.10% in 2019. Hence there was no reason to remain dependent on such resources; therefore, from the very beginning of industrialisation, the country has concentrated on manufacturing and services sectors.

Figure 7.3 presents governance and income distribution in four countries. The figure depicts the changes in quality of governance and distribution of income in Malaysia. Governance consists of rule of law and corruption while income distribution is represented by the Gini index. The control of corruption is measured in percentile terms[6] while rule of law is also estimated as a percentile rank.[7] The Gini index data, taken from UNDP database, measure[8] income disparity. Figure 7.3 shows that the trend line of the Gini index has a negative slope suggesting that income disparity has been declining over time. The reduction in income inequality may be attributed to the reduction in rent-seeking activities. In a situation when the economy is dominated by income from natural resources, the distribution of income remains limited to a few individuals due to limited employment opportunities. On the other hand, when modern sectors such as manufacturing and services dominate the economy, plenty of employment opportunities are created leading towards more income equality.

It can also be seen from the figure that the trend line for corruption has a negative slope while that of the rule of law trend line is positive; this shows that corruption in the country declined over time and rule of law has been improving over time. This is consequent upon good governance. The analysis presented in the section suggests that the Malaysian government converted natural resources into blessings by focusing on developing manufacturing and services sectors rather than relying on natural resources. Consequently, the share of the latter to GDP has been declining. The country also improved governance which resulted in less corruption and greater equality in income distribution.

The figure depicts the prevailing situation of income disparity and governance in South Korea. As expected, the trend line of rule of law has a positive sign suggesting that the Korean government is continuously engaged in improvement of rule of law. Public perception of control of corruption in the country remains very high. It almost did not change during the study period. The negative slope of the Gini index suggests that the Korean government is still concentrating on policies towards more income equality. Good governance and high-income

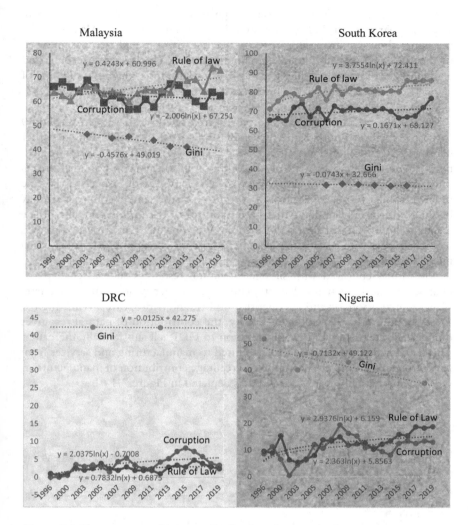

Figure 7.3 Governance and income distribution. Source: Authors.

equality are the consequences of the development model which Korea has followed over the years.

It can be seen from the figure that the trend of the Gini index has a negative slope in all the countries suggesting that income inequality is declining. Surprisingly it declined at a very high pace in Malaysia and Nigeria which is appreciable. The lowest levels of magnitude of Gini in South Korea show that income inequality is very low in the country. Additionally, although the slope of the trend lines of rule of law[9] is positive in all the countries, it improved at a comparatively higher pace in South Korea than others. Evidently, the evolution towards a more just system of rule of law is a positive sign towards an equally more inclusive society. As far as control of corruption, it has a declining trend in Malaysia only; the figure shows an increasing trend in Nigeria. with the highest rate. followed by the DRC. The corruption index in South Korea is almost static over time and is much better controlled. The figure also shows that the magnitude of rule of law and corruption in Malaysia and South Korea is much higher than in DRC and Nigeria.

The percentile rank of control of corruption in Malaysia varies from 56.80 to 68.69 while in South Korea it varies from 65.48 to 76.92. On the other hand, in DRC and Nigeria it varies from 0.51 to 8.17 and 0.51 to 19.42 respectively suggesting that the control of corruption in Malaysia and South Korea is much better than in DRC and Nigeria. The situation with respect to the rule of law is similar to that of control of corruption in the sample countries. It may be inferred from the findings that better control of corruption and rule of law results in improved distribution of income. We conclude that African countries have challenges with governance leading to systemic corruption and institutional inefficiencies.

Vietnam is endowed with significant natural resources such as coal, phosphates, rare earth elements, bauxite, chromate, copper, gold, iron, manganese, silver, zinc, offshore oil and gas deposits, timber, and hydropower. While high in the beginning of its development history, the contribution of natural resources diminished after 1980 and its contribution to GDP fell substantially thereafter. This happened as the country's focus shifted to manufacturing and services from agriculture and crude oil exports. The percentage contribution of manufacturing, services, and natural resources to GDP is depicted in Figure 7.4

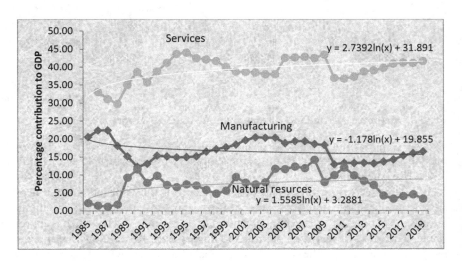

Figure 7.4 Contribution of manufacturing, services, and natural resources to GDP.
Source: Authors.

From Figure 7.4, government policies undertaken in the 1980s induced a structural shift of the country from natural resources to manufacturing and services sectors. This diversification resulted in substantial contribution of both sectors to GDP. However, the contribution to GDP by the services sector has been much higher than the manufacturing sector. As far as growth of contributions during 1985–2019 is concerned, the services sector increased its share while manufacturing sector growth is negative though it has witnessed a positive trend in the latter years. Its contribution changed from 12.95 in 2010 to 16.48% in 2019. The CAGR (Compound Annual Growth Rate) of services and manufacturing sectors during this period has been 0.41 and -0.42% respectively. The figure also shows a positive trend of contribution of natural resources. This is primarily due to high rent seeking until 2005. It has been steeply declining since then. It declined from 14.18% in 2008 to just 3.37% in 2019.

The Human Development Index summarises the average achievements in key human development. The parameters include health, education, and standard of living. The association between rent seeking on natural resources and HDI is depicted in Figure 7.5.

The figure shows that the slope of the trend line of natural resource is negative while that of HDI is positive suggesting that HDI and rent seeking go in opposite directions which is understandable as rent seeking prohibits socio-economic development. The figure also indicates that rent seeking on natural resources was high (11.52%) in 1990 whereas HDI was 0.48. In 2019 the rent on natural resources declined to 3.37% resulting in an increase of HDI to 0.70.

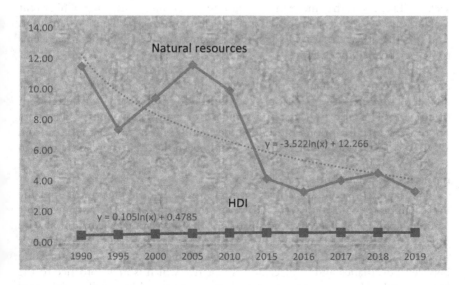

Figure 7.5 Association between natural resources rent and HDI. Source: Authors; data from WDI online and UNDP.

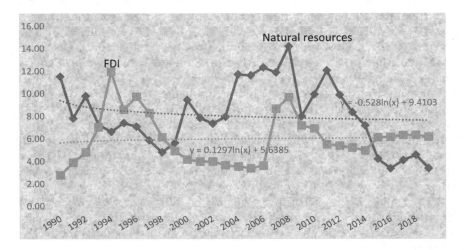

Figure 7.6 Association between FDI and natural resources rent. Source: Author.

The FDI (Foreign Direct Investment) inflow in a country depicts economic achievements and its ability to promote competition in the domestic market. The association between FDI inflow and rent seeking on natural resources is presented in Figure 7.6.

The figure suggests that there exists an association between FDI and rent seeking. Like HDI, they move in the opposite directions. At the time of high rent seeking, there is a lack of industrial activities leading to virtually no inward FDI. And it is the other way round when rent seeking is reduced. This is what seems to have happened in Vietnam.

The control of corruption is another parameter to identify the extent of control of government in a country. The rule of law is an economic parameter depicting creation of various laws and their enforcement for betterment of citizens. This also indicates the standard of living in a country. The data on control of corruption, the Gini index, and rule of law, extracted from WDI (World Development Indicators) online, indicates its percentile rank in a country. The association between governance and rent seeking on natural resources is depicted in Figure 7.7.

The figure above indicates that corruption was high in Vietnam during the initial sample years of the study. However, the trend over time remains static. Although the trend line has a positive sign, the association of corruption with time is very weak. The figure also shows that rule of law has been improving over time which is reflected by the positive slope of the trend line. The association between governance and rent seeking is negative which is in accordance to the literature related to governance.[10] The slope of the trend line of the Gini index has a negative sign suggesting that it has been declining over time. Decline in

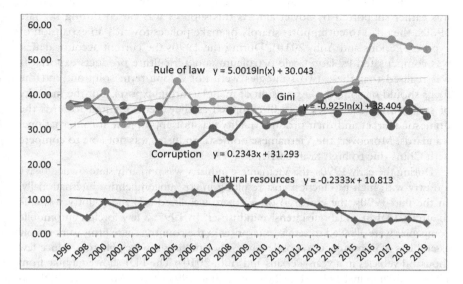

Figure 7.7 Association between governance and rent seeking of natural resources. Source: Author.

Gini means the income inequality is reducing as the World Bank definition of the Gini index is the measurement of income inequality between 0 and 100, where 0 means perfect equality and 100 means perfect inequality. It may be inferred from the findings that as rent seeking reduces the income inequality also reduces.

7.5.1 Vietnam industrial policies

The country witnessed its first reform period during the 1980s, which resulted in a shift from a highly centralised command economy to a mixed economy. A comprehensive industrial policy was put in place which ensured consistency in industrial inputs and outputs but the promotion of efficiency in the system was not focused. During this period, Vietnamese industries depended on aid from the Soviet Union. After 1985, the industrial weaknesses were recognised, and more autonomy was introduced to enhance efficiency which resulted in a market-oriented economy called "Doi-Moi". In this strategy, indicative planning, i.e., coordination of private and public investment, and a macroeconomic management system was implemented. In this industrial policy, the shift was majorly towards small industries and exports rather than heavy industries.

Many provincial states owned large enterprises which had to be closed while some had to deal with retrenching employees and production as they faced losses due to government policies. As a result, overall industrial output fell by 3.3% in 1989. Vietnam also had to face the challenge of limited funding from its exports and had to cut down on its imports due to the reason that its trade was earlier supported by Soviet aid. As this support was closed during the late 1980s, they had to cut imports sharply or make polices towards an expansion of exports (Perkins and Anh, 2010). During the 1990s the current account deficit was compensated by large-scale petroleum and agriculture products exports. It was realised that these two strategies were not a long-term solution, and the focus should be shifted to expansion of manufacturing exports. But the majority of state-owned industries were ill-equipped as they were oriented towards the domestic market and their product quality was not appropriate for international standards. Moreover, the Vietnamese domestic industry was not able to compete with China due to high tariff barriers.

During the early 1990s, the Vietnamese industry was primarily state-owned heavy industry with high production cost resulting in cost-uncompetitive internationally. In the mid-1990s, the embargo on Vietnam was lifted and the country was able to attract FDI in its labour-intensive industries. In 1997, a few foreign automobile companies were allowed to set up enterprises in the country, these firms were mainly assemblers of imported automobile parts. The enterprises were able to produce few thousand vehicles in a year (Perkins and Anh, 2010). The FDI showed a hike from US$575 million in 1992 to US$2,041 million in 1994 (ibid.). Most of the FDI was pushed into exports, particularly manufacturing exports.

After 2000, in order to expand the manufacturing base and export-oriented economy, many bilateral trade agreements were signed, such as the Vietnam–US trade agreement. They also joined the Asia-Pacific Economic Cooperation (APEC), and the WTO (World Trade Organization), etc. in this period. During 2001 to 2005, GDP growth was about 7.5%, and stabilisation of macro-economy was achieved as balance of economic parameters such as budget receipts and expenses, and consumption, etc. improved. The total investment capital also increased and major projects were undertaken. In this period, the Enterprise Law 2005 was instituted that increased the participation of private ownership in industry. So, with major industrial policy changes and complete removal of international trade barriers, manufacturing became competitive.

After 2005, the modern sectors, such as telecommunications and ICT, were strengthened. In these sectors, the country involved private enterprises in Internet Service Provider (ISP) business while the internet exchanges were state owned. FDI was also allowed in the telecom sector but with limited control. In order to further boost the economic development, two main types of economic zones have been established, near the land borders, coastal economic zones and border gate economic zones. More than 499 industrial parks were established by 2018 in which several foreign-invested enterprises (7,745) and domestically invested (6,992) enterprises are established (Oh et al., 2020). Some of these high-tech enterprises support scientific and technology research and training focusing in to building hi-tech industries, particularly robotics, software, informatics, and shipping, etc. Also, supplementary industries were encouraged in these zones for better supply chain management. Consequently, Vietnam has become major a exporter of phones, textiles, electronic goods, computers, and footwear.

Notes

1 International Monetary Fund's Export Diversification Index (2020).
2 Innis (1956).
3 Viner (1952), Lewis (1955).
4 Ishakq and Ogbanje (2017).
5 Ayoola (2005), Usman (2011).
6 Control of corruption captures perceptions of the extent to which public power is exercised for private gain, including both petty and grand forms of corruption, as well as "capture" of the state by elites and private interests. The percentile rank indicates the country's rank among all countries covered by the aggregate indicator, with 0 corresponding to the lowest rank, and 100 to the highest rank. Percentile ranks have been adjusted to correct for changes over time in the composition of the countries covered by the WGI (World Governance Indicators).
7 Rule of law captures perceptions of the extent to which agents have confidence in and abide by the rules of society, and in particular the quality of contract enforcement, property rights, the police, and the courts, as well as the likelihood of crime and violence. The percentile rank indicates the country's rank among all countries covered by the aggregate indicator, with 0 corresponding to the lowest rank, and 100 to the highest rank. Percentile ranks have been adjusted to correct for changes over time in the composition of the countries covered by the WGI.
8 Gini index measures the extent to which the distribution of income (or, in some cases, consumption expenditure) among individuals or households within an economy deviates from a perfectly equal distribution. A Lorenz curve plots the cumulative percentages of total income received against the cumulative number of recipients, starting with the poorest individual or household. The Gini index measures the area between the Lorenz curve and a hypothetical line of absolute equality, expressed as a percentage of the maximum area under the line. Thus a Gini index of 0 represents perfect equality, while an index of 100 implies perfect inequality.
9 It must be clarified that measurement of rule of law and corruption is based on percentile rank of control of these factors; this means that a higher value of rank suggests that the particular aspect is better controlled than a country with a low rank (not much controlled).
10 van der Ploeg (2011).

Appendix

Appendix 3.1 List of major oil-exporting countries in Asia and Africa

African	Asian
Algeria, Angola, Cameroon, Chad, Congo, Côte d'Ivoire, Democratic Republic of Congo, Egypt, Equatorial Guinea, Gabon, Ghana, Libya, Mauritania, Morocco, Niger, Nigeria, South Sudan, Tunisia	Indonesia, Iran, Iraq, Kazakhstan, Kuwait, Malaysia, Oman, Qatar, Russia

Appendix 3.2 Oil price fluctuations and their impact on sample economies

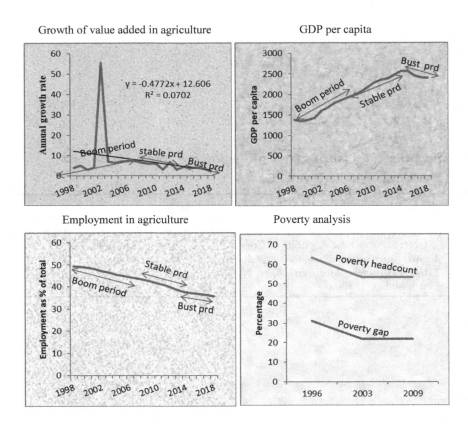

Figure 3.7 Analysis of Nigeria Source: WDI

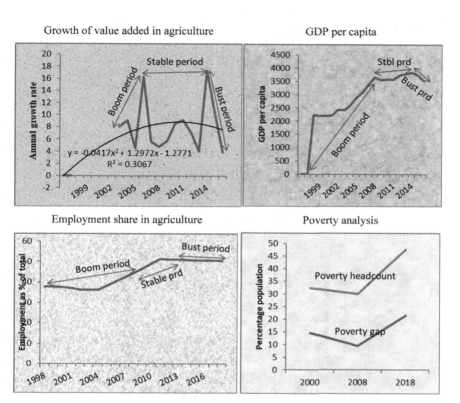

Figure 3.8 Analysis of Angola Source: WDI

Growth of value added in agriculture   GDP per capita

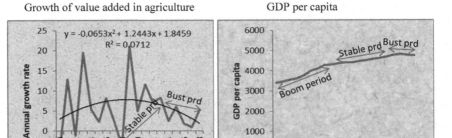

Employment in agriculture

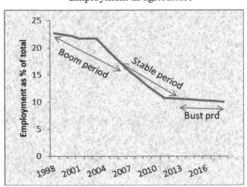

Figure 3.9 Analysis of Algeria Source: WDI

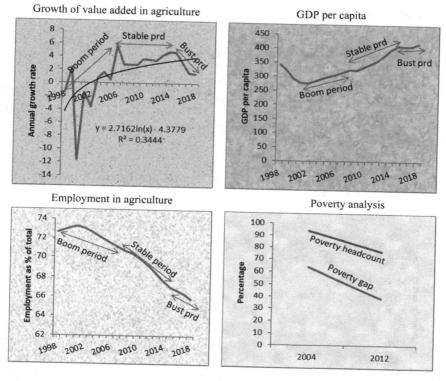

Figure 3.10 Analysis of Congo Source: WDI

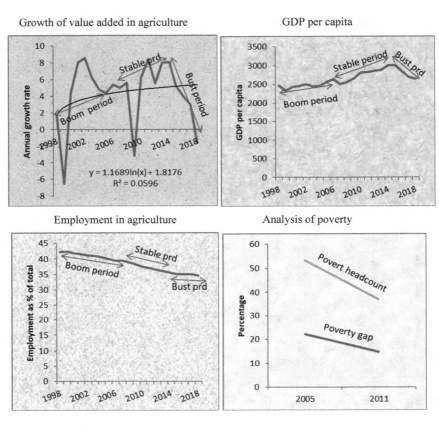

Figure 3.11 Analysis of Brazzaville Source: WDI

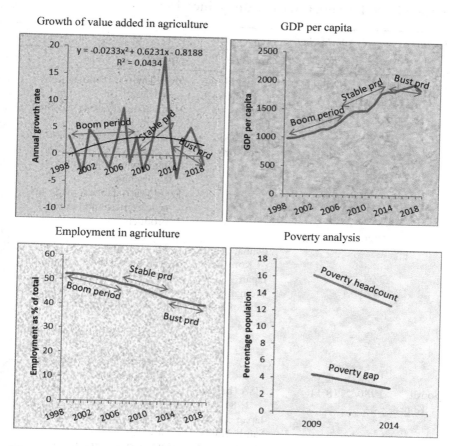

Figure 3.12 Analysis of Sudan Source: WDI

Appendix 4.1 Export market diversification

Country		Value in billion USD	Top 5 export	
			Markets	Products
China	1989	52.54	China, Hong Kong SAR	Miscellaneous manufactured articles
			Japan	Manufactured goods classified chiefly by materials
			USA	
			Fmr USSR	Articles of apparel and clothing accessories
			Singapore	
				Machinery and transport equipment
				Textile yarn, fabrics, made-up articles, nes, and related products
	2020	2590.60	USA	Machinery and transport equipment
			China, Hong Kong SAR	Special transactions, commodity not classified according to class
			Japan	
			Vietnam	
			Rep. of Korea	Miscellaneous manufactured articles
				Manufactured goods classified chiefly by materials
				Electric machinery, apparatus and appliances, and parts
South Korea	1980	18.11	USA (before 1981)	Manufactured goods classified chiefly by materials
			Japan	Miscellaneous manufactured articles
			Saudi Arabia	
			Fmr Fed. Rep. of Germany	Machinery and transport equipment
			China, Hong Kong SAR	Articles of apparel and clothing accessories
				Textile yarn, fabrics, made-up articles, and related products
	2020	512.71	China	Machinery and transport equipment
			USA	Special transactions, commodity not classified according to class
			Vietnam	
			China, Hong Kong SAR	
			Japan	Electric machinery, apparatus and appliances, and parts
				Thermionic, microcircuits, transistors, valves, etc.
				Chemicals and related products,

(*Continued*)

(Continued)

Country		Value in billion USD	Top 5 export	
			Markets	Products
India	1980	7.53	Fmr USSR USA (before 1981) Japan United Kingdom Fmr Fed. Rep. of Germany	Manufactured goods classified chiefly by materials Food and live animals chiefly for food Textile yarn, fabrics, made-up articles, and related products Crude materials, inedible, except fuels Miscellaneous manufactured articles
	2020	275.49	USA China United Arab Emirates China, Hong Kong SAR Singapore	Special transactions, commodity not classified according to class Manufactured goods classified chiefly by materials Chemicals and related products Machinery and transport equipment Miscellaneous manufactured articles
Malaysia	1980	12.94	Japan Singapore USA (before 1981) Netherlands Fmr Fed. Rep. of Germany	Crude materials, inedible, except fuels Mineral fuels, lubricants, and related materials Petroleum, petroleum products, and related materials Crude petroleum and oils obtained from bituminous minerals Crude petroleum and oils obtained from bituminous materials
	2020	233.93	China Singapore USA China, Hong Kong SAR Japan	Machinery and transport equipment Special transactions, commodity not classified according to class Electric machinery, apparatus and appliances, and parts Thermionic, microcircuits, transistors, valves, etc. Miscellaneous manufactured articles

(Continued)

(Continued)

Country		Value in billion USD	Top 5 export	
			Markets	*Products*
Vietnam	1997	9.18	Japan Singapore Other Asia, China China, Hong Kong SAR	Miscellaneous manufactured articles Food and live animals chiefly for food Mineral fuels, lubricants, and related materials Petroleum, petroleum products, and related materials Crude petroleum and oils obtained from bituminous minerals
	2020	281.44	USA China Japan Rep. of Korea China, Hong Kong SAR	Machinery and transport equipment Special transactions, commodity not classified according to class Miscellaneous manufactured articles Telecommunications, sound recording and reproducing equipment Telecommunication equipment; parts and accessories,
Nigeria	1998	6.87	USA Spain France Italy Brazil	Mineral fuels, lubricants, and related materials Petroleum, petroleum products, and related materials Crude petroleum and oils obtained from bituminous minerals Crude petroleum and oils obtained from bituminous materials Machinery and transport equipment
	2019	53.62	India Spain Netherlands Ghana France	Mineral fuels, lubricants, and related materials Petroleum, petroleum products, and related materials Crude petroleum and oils obtained from bituminous minerals Crude petroleum and oils obtained from bituminous materials Gas, natural and manufactured

(*Continued*)

(Continued)

Country		Value in billion USD	Top 5 export	
			Markets	Products
South Africa	2000	26.30	USA	Manufactured goods classified
			United Kingdom	chiefly by materials
			Germany	Special transactions, commodity
			Japan	not classified according to class
				Machinery and transport equipment
				Commodities and transactions not classified elsewhere in the SITC
				Special transactions, commodity not classified according to class
	2020	80.85	China	Manufactured goods classified
			USA	chiefly by materials
			Areas, NES	Machinery and transport
			Germany	equipment
			United Kingdom	Crude materials, inedible, except fuels
				Special transactions, commodity not classified according to class
				Non-ferrous metals
Ghana	1998	1.16	United Kingdom	Food and live animals chiefly for food
			Netherlands	Coffee, tea, cocoa, spices, and
			Germany	manufactures thereof
			Spain	Cocoa
			France	Cocoa beans, raw, roasted
				Crude materials, inedible, except fuels
	2019	16.77	China	Commodities and transactions
			Switzerland	not classified elsewhere in the
			India	SITC
			South Africa	Gold, non-monetary (excluding
			Netherlands	gold ores and concentrates)
				Gold, non-monetary (excluding gold ores and concentrates)
				Gold, non-monetary (excluding gold ores and concentrates)
				Gold, non-monetary, unwrought or semi-manufactured

(*Continued*)

(Continued)

Country		Value in billion USD	Top 5 export	
			Markets	Products
Côte d'Ivoire	1981	2.54	France Netherlands USA Italy Fmr Fed. Rep. of Germany	Food and live animals chiefly for food Coffee, tea, cocoa, spices, and manufactures thereof Cocoa Cocoa beans, raw, roasted Coffee and coffee substitutes
	2019	12.72	Netherlands USA France Malaysia Vietnam	Food and live animals chiefly for food Coffee, tea, cocoa, spices, and manufactures thereof Cocoa Cocoa beans, raw, roasted Mineral fuels, lubricants, and related materials

Appendix 5.1 Country classification of export products diversification

Manufacturing industries by technological intensity

Medium-High & High- Technology

- Chemicals and chemical products
- Pharmaceuticals
- Weapons and ammunition
- Computer, electronic and optical products
- Electrical equipment
- Machinery and equipment n.e.c.
- Motor vehicles, trailers and semi-trailers
- Other transport equipment except ships and boats

Medium Technology

- Rubber and plastics products
- Other non-metallic mineral products
- Basic metals
- Ships and boats
- Other manufacturing except medical and dental instruments
- Repair and installation of machinery and equipment

Low Technology

- Food products
- Beverages
- Tobacco products
- Textiles
- Wearing apparel
- Leather and related products
- Wood and products of wood and cork
- Paper and paper products
- Printing and reproduction of recorded media
- Coke and refined petroleum products
- Fabricated metal products except weapons and ammunition

- Furniture
- Tobacco products
- Textiles
- Wearing apparel
- Leather and related products
- Wood and products of wood and cork
- Paper and paper products
- Printing and reproduction of recorded media
- Coke and refined petroleum products
- Fabricated metal products except weapons and ammunition

Appendix 5.2 Average indicators during 1960 to 2020

Country	MVA as percentage of GDP	Researchers per million people	R&D expenditure as percentage of GDP	Patent applications by	
				Non-residents	Residents
Ghana	9.48	28	0.30	19	14
India	15.80	134	0.75	14,475	5,052
Indonesia	22.56	167	0.07	3,731	414
Korea	22.81	4,047	2.89	26,928	75,923
China	30.28	785	1.29	59,632	2,84,233
Malaysia	21.13	860	0.76	4,408	548
Kenya	10.22	144	0.57	73	79
Nigeria	14.31	39	0.22	440	60
South Africa	18.23	353	0.79	5,729	1,617
Vietnam	16.75	114	0.18	1976	202

Appendix 5.3 Countries and their level of advancement

Level of advancement	Countries	Rank	GII score in 2020
Highly advanced	Switzerland	1	66.08
	Sweden	2	62.47
	United States of America	3	60.56
	United Kingdom	4	59.78
	Netherlands	5	58.76
	Denmark	6	57.53
	Finland	7	57.02
	Singapore	8	56.61
	Germany	9	56.55
	Republic of Korea	10	56.11
	Hong Kong, China	11	54.24
	France	12	53.66
	Israel	13	53.55
	China	14	53.28
	Ireland	15	53.05
	Japan	16	52.70
Advanced	Canada	17	52.26
	Luxembourg	18	50.84
	Austria	19	50.13
	Norway	20	49.29
	Iceland	21	49.23
	Belgium	22	49.13
	Australia	23	48.35

(*Continued*)

(Continued)

Level of advancement	Countries	Rank	GII score in 2020
	Czech Republic	24	48.34
	Estonia	25	48.28
	New Zealand	26	47.01
	Malta	27	46.39
	Italy	28	45.74
	Cyprus	29	45.67
	Spain	30	45.60
	Portugal	31	43.51
	Slovenia	32	42.91
	Malaysia	33	42.42
	United Arab Emirates	34	41.79
	Hungary	35	41.53
	Latvia	36	41.11
	Bulgaria	37	39.98
	Poland	38	39.95
Catching up	Slovakia	39	39.70
	Lithuania	40	39.18
	Croatia	41	37.27
	Vietnam	42	37.12
	Greece	43	36.79
	Thailand	44	36.68
	Ukraine	45	36.32
	Romania	46	35.95
	Russian Federation	47	35.63
	India	48	35.59
	Montenegro	49	35.39
	Philippines	50	35.19
	Turkey	51	34.90
	Mauritius	52	34.35
	Serbia	53	34.33
	Chile	54	33.86
	Mexico	55	33.60
	Costa Rica	56	33.51
	North Macedonia	57	33.43
	Mongolia	58	33.41
	Republic of Moldova	59	32.98
	South Africa	60	32.67
	Armenia	61	32.64
	Brazil	62	31.94
	Georgia	63	31.78
	Belarus	64	31.27
	Tunisia	65	31.21
	Saudi Arabia	66	30.94
	Iran (Islamic Republic of)	67	30.89

(*Continued*)

(Continued)

Level of advancement	Countries	Rank	GII score in 2020
	Uruguay	69	30.84
	Colombia	68	30.84
	Qatar	70	30.81
	Brunei Darussalam	71	29.82
	Jamaica	72	29.10
	Panama	73	29.04
	Bosnia and Herzegovina	74	28.99
	Morocco	75	28.97
	Peru	76	28.79
	Kazakhstan	77	28.56
	Kuwait	78	28.40
	Bahrain	79	28.37
	Argentina	80	28.33
	Jordan	81	27.79
	Azerbaijan	82	27.23
	Albania	83	27.12
Lagging behind	Oman	84	26.50
	Indonesia	85	26.49
	Kenya	86	26.13
	Lebanon	87	26.02
	United Republic of Tanzania	88	25.57
	Botswana	89	25.43
	Dominican Republic	90	25.10
	Rwanda	91	25.06
	El Salvador	92	24.85
	Uzbekistan	93	24.54
	Kyrgyzstan	94	24.51
	Nepal	95	24.35
	Egypt	96	24.23
	Trinidad and Tobago	98	24.14
	Paraguay	97	24.14
	Ecuador	99	24.11
	Cabo Verde	100	23.86
	Sri Lanka	101	23.78
	Senegal	102	23.75
	Honduras	103	22.95
	Namibia	104	22.51
	Bolivia (Plurinational State of)	105	22.41
	Guatemala	106	22.35
	Pakistan	107	22.31
	Ghana	108	22.28
	Tajikistan	109	22.23
	Cambodia	110	21.46

(*Continued*)

(Continued)

Level of advancement	Countries	Rank	GII score in 2020
	Malawi	111	21.44
	Côte d'Ivoire	112	21.24
	Lao People's Democratic Republic	113	20.65
	Uganda	114	20.54
	Madagascar	115	20.40
	Bangladesh	116	20.39
	Nigeria	117	20.13
	Burkina Faso	118	20.00
	Cameroon	119	19.98
	Zimbabwe	120	19.97
	Algeria	121	19.48
	Zambia	122	19.39
	Mali	123	19.15
	Mozambique	124	18.70
	Togo	125	18.54
	Benin	126	18.13
	Ethiopia	127	18.06
	Niger	128	17.82
	Myanmar	129	17.74
	Guinea	130	17.32
	Yemen	131	13.56

Note: Countries marked are sample countries; level of advancement is estimated by dividing score into four equal intervals.
Source: www.wipo.int/edocs/pubdocs/en/wipo_pub_gii_2020.pdf

Appendix 5.4 Product diversification in sample countries

Table 5.1 Change in export products in Ghana during 1992–2019

2digit SITC code	Top 10 export products in 1992	Value in USD	% share
97	Gold, non-monetary (excluding gold ores and concentrates)	52,51,98,528	42.55
7	Coffee, tea, cocoa, spices, and manufactures thereof	31,18,83,680	25.27
24	Cork and wood	9,95,38,936	8.06
28	Metalliferous ores and metal scrap	5,26,29,856	4.26
68	Non-ferrous metals	4,51,36,180	3.66
35	Electric current	4,29,76,552	3.48
5	Vegetables and fruit	2,46,88,056	2
27	Crude fertilizer and crude minerals	2,42,74,976	1.97
33	Petroleum, petroleum products, and related materials	2,32,09,788	1.88
63	Cork and wood, cork manufactures	2,00,67,352	1.63
	Total export	1,23,44,25,926	

2digit SITC code	Top 10 export products in 2019	Value in USD	% share
97	Gold, non-monetary (excluding gold ores and concentrates)	6,19,88,65,169	36.97
33	Petroleum, petroleum products, and related materials	5,31,59,57,521	31.7
7	Coffee, tea, cocoa, spices, and manufactures thereof	2,70,82,10,873	16.15
28	Metalliferous ores and metal scrap	41,56,34,780	2.48
5	Vegetables and fruit	39,66,34,049	2.37
89	Miscellaneous manufactured articles, nes	23,85,88,310	1.42
3	Fish, crustacean and molluscs, and preparations thereof	19,95,59,261	1.19
52	Inorganic chemicals	12,31,36,532	0.73
42	Fixed vegetable oils and fats	11,09,51,227	0.66
24	Cork and wood	10,85,36,894	0.65
	Total export	6,76,82,75,151	

Table 5.2 Change in export products in Kenya during 1990–2019

2 digit SITC code	Top 10 export products in 1990	Value in USD	% share
7	Coffee, tea, cocoa, spices, and manufactures thereof	33,95,63,744	33.02
33	Petroleum, petroleum products, and related materials	13,46,44,256	13.09
5	Vegetables and fruit	7,90,41,904	7.69
78	Road vehicles	5,96,20,008	5.8
29	Crude animal and vegetable materials, nes	3,23,90,676	3.15
27	Crude fertilizer and crude minerals	2,50,73,436	2.44
4	Cereals and cereal preparations	2,32,43,406	2.26
26	Textile fibres (not wool tops) and their wastes (not in yarn)	2,31,39,564	2.25
65	Textile yarn, fabrics, made-up articles, nes, and related products	2,15,46,262	2.1
61	Leather, leather manufactures, nes, and dressed furskins	2,08,57,838	2.03
	Total export	1,02,83,88,528	

	Top 10 export products in 2019	Value in USD	% share
7	Coffee, tea, cocoa, spices, and manufactures thereof	1,34,45,43,231	23.05
29	Crude animal and vegetable materials, nes	68,37,76,023	11.72
5	Vegetables and fruit	45,30,71,504	7.77
33	Petroleum, petroleum products, and related materials	44,76,77,218	7.67
84	Articles of apparel and clothing accessories	34,16,92,128	5.86
28	Metalliferous ores and metal scrap	22,77,37,842	3.9
9	Miscellaneous edible products and preparations	17,28,23,078	2.96
89	Miscellaneous manufactured articles, nes	17,20,67,896	2.95
67	Iron and steel	15,21,88,579	2.61
55	Oils and perfume materials; toilet and cleansing preparations	13,69,97,720	2.35
	Total export	5,83,44,18,102	

Table 5.2A Details of code 29

Code 29 contains	Description
29111	Bone, horn-core, unworked, defatted, degelatinised, etc., and waste
29115	Coral, shells, unworked or simply prepared, and waste
29116	Ivory, tortoise-shell, etc., unworked or simply prepared, and waste
29193	Gut, bladders, and stomachs of animals (other than fish)
29194	Fish waste
29198	Ambergris, civet, musk, etc., used for pharmaceutical products
29199	Animal products, nes; dead animals unfit for human consumption
29261	Bulbs, tubers, corms, and others; dormant, in growth, or in flower
29269	Other live plants
29271	Cut flowers and flower buds, fresh, dried, bleached, etc.
29272	Cut foliage, fresh, dried, bleached, etc.
29291	Vegetable saps and extracts; agar-agar and other mucilages
29298	Vegetable materials and products, nes

Table 5.3 Change in export products in Nigeria during 1991–2019

SITC code	Top 10 export products in 1991	Value in USD	% share
33	Petroleum, petroleum products and related materials	12,39,56,63,360	96.63
7	Coffee, tea, cocoa, spices, and manufactures thereof	14,58,76,688	1.14
93	Special transactions, commodity not classified according to class	8,12,89,984	0.63
23	Crude rubber (including synthetic and reclaimed)	5,59,62,628	0.44
65	Textile yarn, fabrics, made-up articles, nes, and related products	2,63,85,784	0.21
56	Fertilizers, manufactured	2,47,64,730	0.19
3	Fish, crustacean and molluscs, and preparations thereof	2,21,53,674	0.17
61	Leather, leather manufactures, nes, and dressed furskins	89,02,785	0.07
8	Feeding stuff for animals (not including unmilled cereals)	72,87,951	0.06
21	Hides, skins and furskins, raw	66,81,267	0.05
	Total export	12,82,79,40,337	

SITC code	Top 10 export products in 2019	Value in USD	% share
33	Petroleum, petroleum products, and related materials	41,15,14,17,559	76.75
34	Gas, natural and manufactured	5,43,02,20,299	10.13
79	Other transport equipment	3,25,07,71,220	6.06
69	Manufactures of metals, nes	2,11,20,25,448	3.94
7	Coffee, tea, cocoa, spices, and manufactures thereof	31,78,17,084	0.59
22	Oil seeds and oleaginous fruit	29,53,27,342	0.55
56	Fertilizers, manufactured	15,19,03,957	0.28
68	Non-ferrous metals	13,09,60,875	0.24
5	Vegetables and fruit	11,61,81,699	0.22
12	Tobacco and tobacco manufactures	10,37,28,137	0.19
	Total export	53,61,73,79,970	

Table 5.4 Change in export products in South Africa during 2000–2019

SITC code	Top 10 export products in 2000	Value in USD	% share
93	Special transactions, commodity not classified according to class	3,53,71,59,808	13.45
67	Iron and steel	2,76,59,62,835	10.52
66	Non-metallic mineral manufactures, nes	1,95,16,69,715	7.42
78	Road vehicles	1,81,64,31,611	6.91
28	Metalliferous ores and metal scrap	1,38,28,00,314	5.26
32	Coal, coke, and briquettes	1,32,63,67,981	5.04
33	Petroleum, petroleum products, and related materials	1,32,48,48,251	5.04
68	Non-ferrous metals	1,20,89,85,873	4.6
74	General industrial machinery and equipment, nes, and parts of, nes	1,08,18,98,609	4.11
5	Vegetables and fruit	81,85,64,914	3.11
	Total export	26,29,79,51,893	

	Top 10 export products in 2019	Value in USD	% share
28	Metalliferous ores and metal scrap	13,23,53,33,242	14.81
78	Road vehicles	11,48,21,57,203	12.84
68	Non-ferrous metals	10,88,27,92,448	12.17
67	Iron and steel	5,52,33,03,241	6.18
32	Coal, coke, and briquettes	4,75,84,14,708	5.32
97	Gold, non-monetary (excluding gold ores and concentrates)	4,75,81,52,025	5.32
5	Vegetables and fruit	3,97,34,86,163	4.44
33	Petroleum, petroleum products, and related materials	3,21,83,91,664	3.6
74	General industrial machinery and equipment, nes, and parts of, nes	3,05,96,89,578	3.42
66	Non-metallic mineral manufactures, nes	2,15,69,06,936	2.41
	Total export	89,39,59,88,302	

Table 5.5 Change in export products in China during 1990–2019

SITC code	Top 10 export products in 1990	Value in USD	% share
84	Articles of apparel and clothing accessories	9,66,91,89,140	15.57
65	Textile yarn, fabrics, made-up articles, nes, and related products	7,21,94,45,732	11.63
33	Petroleum, petroleum products, and related materials	4,47,21,05,945	7.2
78	Road vehicles	3,81,43,51,872	6.14
89	Miscellaneous manufactured articles, nes	3,72,62,62,507	6
76	Telecommunications, sound recording and reproducing equipment	2,62,33,30,912	4.22
85	Footwear	1,95,66,19,745	3.15
5	Vegetables and fruit	1,75,95,21,792	2.83
72	Machinery specialised for particular industries	1,48,03,00,091	2.38
69	Manufactures of metals, nes	1,43,72,87,128	2.31
	Total export	62,09,13,91,501	

SITC code	Top 10 export products in 2019	Value in USD	% share
77	Electric machinery, apparatus and appliances, nes, and parts of nes	3,58,75,71,42,688	14.36
75	Office machines and automatic data processing equipment	2,77,37,00,14,229	11.1
76	Telecommunications, sound recording and reproducing equipment	2,23,01,25,15,769	8.93
89	Miscellaneous manufactured articles, nes	1,53,91,25,59,769	6.16
84	Articles of apparel and clothing accessories	1,51,85,17,09,333	6.08
74	General industrial machinery and equipment, nes, and parts of, nes	1,23,00,22,67,760	4.92
65	Textile yarn, fabrics, made-up articles, nes, and related products	1,19,94,82,79,199	4.8
78	Road vehicles	1,12,86,78,64,885	4.52
69	Manufactures of metals, nes	1,02,82,47,64,529	4.12
87	Professional, scientific, controlling instruments, apparatus, nes	84,75,19,88,747	3.39
	Total export	2,498,569,865,637	

Table 5.6 Change in export products in India during 1990–2019

2-digit SITC code	Top 10 export products in 1990	Value in USD	% share
66	Non-metallic mineral manufactures, nes	2,79,56,94,080	15.58
84	Articles of apparel and clothing accessories	2,53,27,93,088	14.12
65	Textile yarn, fabrics, made-up articles, nes, and related products	2,17,98,97,600	12.15
07	Coffee, tea, cocoa, spices, and manufactures thereof	84,41,46,816	4.71
61	Leather, leather manufactures, nes, and dressed furskins	83,23,42,528	4.64
28	Metalliferous ores and metal scrap	76,28,65,152	4.25
03	Fish, crustacean and molluscs, and preparations thereof	52,38,12,128	2.92
33	Petroleum, petroleum products, and related materials	51,76,30,240	2.89
26	Textile fibres (not wool tops) and their wastes (not in yarn)	50,89,89,152	2.84
54	Medicinal and pharmaceutical products	45,28,11,744	2.52
	Total export	**17,940,182,785**	
	Top 10 export products in 2019	Value in USD	% share
33	Petroleum, petroleum products, and related materials	43,53,52,11,983	13.47
66	Non-metallic mineral manufactures, nes	27,27,35,35,619	8.44
89	Miscellaneous manufactured articles, nes	18,82,86,99,937	5.82
54	Medicinal and pharmaceutical products	17,85,93,27,473	5.52
78	Road vehicles	17,25,58,09,214	5.34
65	Textile yarn, fabrics, made-up articles, nes, and related products	17,22,88,21,154	5.33
84	Articles of apparel and clothing accessories	17,16,55,97,703	5.31
51	Organic chemicals	16,73,50,99,889	5.18
67	Iron and steel	12,46,91,10,664	3.86
77	Electric machinery, apparatus and appliances, nes, and parts of nes	8,99,03,14,394	2.78
	Total export	**3,23250,726,391**	

Table 5.7 Change in export products in Indonesia during 1990–2019

2 digit SITC code	Top 10 export products in 1990	Value in USD	% share
33	Petroleum, petroleum products, and related materials	7,40,38,69,184	28.84
34	Gas, natural and manufactured	3,66,72,92,928	14.28
63	Cork and wood, cork manufactures	3,05,92,24,064	11.92
84	Articles of apparel and clothing accessories	1,66,60,15,360	6.49
65	Textile yarn, fabrics, made-up articles, nes, and related products	1,26,38,87,104	4.92
3	Fish, crustacean and molluscs, and preparations thereof	97,33,73,504	3.79
23	Crude rubber (including synthetic and reclaimed)	85,49,46,368	3.33
7	Coffee, tea, cocoa, spices, and manufactures thereof	84,04,47,296	3.27
28	Metalliferous ores and metal scrap	61,92,08,896	2.41
85	Footwear	56,12,07,936	2.19
	Total export	25,675,322,728	

	Top 10 export products in 2019	Value in USD	% share
32	Coal, coke, and briquettes	21,78,26,00,163	12.99
42	Fixed vegetable oils and fats	16,50,90,60,158	9.85
84	Articles of apparel and clothing accessories	8,67,46,03,168	5.17
78	Road vehicles	8,62,92,61,780	5.15
34	Gas, natural and manufactured	8,26,10,84,244	4.93
67	Iron and steel	7,66,39,44,618	4.57
77	Electric machinery, apparatus and appliances, nes, and parts of nes	6,17,76,46,826	3.68
28	Metalliferous ores and metal scrap	5,55,90,91,018	3.32
89	Miscellaneous manufactured articles, nes	4,68,56,91,357	2.79
64	Paper, paperboard, and articles of pulp, of paper, or of paperboard	4,46,78,62,159	2.66
	Total export	167,682,997,529	

Table 5.8 Change in export products in Malaysia during 1990–2019

2-digit SITC code	Top 10 export products in 1990	Value in USD	% share
77	Electric machinery, apparatus and appliances, nes, and parts of nes	5,24,45,16,638	17.81
33	Petroleum, petroleum products, and related materials	4,38,67,36,766	14.89
76	Telecommunications, sound recording and reproducing equipment	3,20,94,52,425	10.90
24	Cork and wood	2,83,45,56,126	9.62
42	Fixed vegetable oils and fats	1,66,75,76,002	5.66
84	Articles of apparel and clothing accessories	1,31,70,36,625	4.47
23	Crude rubber (including synthetic and reclaimed)	1,12,23,99,093	3.81
34	Gas, natural and manufactured	1,01,02,54,601	3.43
89	Miscellaneous manufactured articles, nes	93,25,39,438	3.17
75	Office machines and automatic data processing equipment	67,64,00,039	2.30
	Total export	**29,453,208,697**	
	Top 10 export products in 2019	*Value in USD*	*% share*
77	Electric machinery, apparatus and appliances, nes, and parts of nes	70,99,63,58,517	29.82
33	Petroleum, petroleum products and related materials	23,63,29,32,156	9.93
75	Office machines and automatic data processing equipment	13,58,65,59,916	5.71
42	Fixed vegetable oils and fats	10,82,92,34,927	4.55
34	Gas, natural and manufactured	10,70,80,68,591	4.50
87	Professional, scientific, controlling instruments, apparatus, nes	8,51,14,56,996	3.57
76	Telecommunications, sound recording and reproducing equipment	7,76,83,66,636	3.26
58	Artificial resins and plastic materials, and cellulose esters, etc.	7,23,52,71,618	3.04
89	Miscellaneous manufactured articles, nes	7,20,07,65,254	3.02
68	Non-ferrous metals	6,85,24,30,787	2.88
	Total export	**238,088,652,077**	

Table 5.9 Change in export products in South Korea during 1990–2019

2-digit SITC code	Top 10 export products in 1990	Value in USD	% share
84	Articles of apparel and clothing accessories	8,02,02,33,216	12.34
77	Electric machinery, apparatus and appliances, nes, and parts of nes	7,65,90,68,928	11.78
76	Telecommunications, sound recording and reproducing equipment	6,27,33,42,976	9.65
65	Textile yarn, fabrics, made-up articles, nes, and related products	6,08,36,28,544	9.36
85	Footwear	4,16,40,53,248	6.40
89	Miscellaneous manufactured articles, nes	3,74,77,36,064	5.76
67	Iron and steel	3,72,59,78,880	5.73
78	Road vehicles	3,34,31,88,224	5.14
79	Other transport equipment	3,04,76,24,704	4.69
75	Office machines and automatic data processing equipment	2,70,15,97,952	4.16
	Total export	65.015,672,406	

	Top 10 export products in 2019	Value in USD	% share
77	Electric machinery, apparatus and appliances, nes, and parts of nes	1,24,74,30,45,933	23.01
78	Road vehicles	62,92,39,96,656	11.61
33	Petroleum, petroleum products, and related materials	41,83,87,99,362	7.72
75	Office machines and automatic data processing equipment	36,63,34,00,874	6.76
58	Artificial resins and plastic materials, and cellulose esters, etc.	26,49,45,62,520	4.89
67	Iron and steel	26,07,80,39,128	4.81
74	General industrial machinery and equipment, nes, and parts of nes	22,48,47,64,479	4.15
72	Machinery specialised for particular industries	21,99,62,75,993	4.06
79	Other transport equipment	21,65,39,19,928	3.99
51	Organic chemicals	20,73,26,07,372	3.82
	Total export	542,171,769,089	

Source: UN-COMTRADE, SITC, 2-digit level, Revision 2 classification

Table 5.9A Details of diversification code 77

Code 77 contains	Description
77111	Liquid dielectric transformers
77118	Other electric transformers
77121	Static converters, rectifiers, and rectifying apparatus
77122	Inductors
77129	Parts, nes of the electric power machinery falling in heading 771
77322	Electrical insulators of glass
77323	Electrical insulators of ceramic materials
77324	Electrical insulators of other materials
77326	Ceramic electrical insulator fittings
77327	Other electrical insulator fittings nes
77579	Parts, nes of the electro-domestic equipment of heading 7757
77581	Electric water heaters
77582	Electric soil and space heaters
77584	Electric smoothing irons
77585	Electric blankets
77586	Electro-p domestic appliances, nes
77587	Non-carbon electric heating resistors
77589	Parts, nes of the electro-thermic appliances
77681	Piezoelectric crystals, mounted
77689	**Electronic components, parts nes**
77811	Primary batteries and cells, and parts thereof, nes
77812	Electric accumulators
77819	Parts, nes of electric accumulators
77821	Filament lamps
77822	Discharge lamps
77824	Ultraviolet, infrared lamps, and arc lamps
77831	Ignition, starting equipment, generators, etc., parts thereof, nes
77832	Vehicles electric-lighting equipment; defrosters, etc., parts, nes
77881	Electromagnets, etc.
77882	Electric traffic-control equipment
77883	Electric sound and visual signalling equipment
77884	Electrical condensers
77885	Particle accelerators, and parts thereof, nes
77886	Other electrical appliances and apparatus, nes
77887	Electrical carbon articles for electrical purposes

References

Abass, Abdul-Fatawu and Ibrahim, Muazu (2018). Exports, exports diversification and sectoral value addition: Evidence from sub-Saharan Africa, Paper presented in 4th International Research Conference of the College of Humanities, University of Ghana.

Acemoglu, Daron and Robinson, James (2012). *Why Nations Fail: The Origins of Power, Prosperity, and Poverty* (First ed.). New York. NY: Crown Publishing Group.

Acemoglu, Daron, Johnson, Simon, Robinson, James and Thaicharoend, Yunyong (2003). Institutional causes, macroeconomic symptoms: Volatility, crises, and growth. *Journal of Monetary Economics*, Vol. 50, 49–123.

Acemoglu, Daron and Ziliboti, Fabrizio (1997). Was Prometheus unbound by chance? Risk, diversification and growth. *Journal of Political Economy*, Vol. 105(4), 707–751.

African Development Bank (2018). African Economic Outlook 2018, https://www.afdb.org/fileadmin/uploads/afdb/Documents/Publications/African_Economic_Outlook_2018_-_EN.pdf, (accessed on January 12, 2022).

Agosin, Manuel (2007). *Export Diversification and Growth in Emerging Economies.* University of Chile, Department of Economics, Working Papers wp233.

Akbar, Mohammad, Naqvi, Zareen Fatima and Din, Musleh-ud (2000). Export diversification and the structural dynamics in the growth process: The case of Pakistan. *The Pakistan Development Review*, Vol. 39(4), 573–589.

Aksoy, M. Ataman and Isik-Dikmelik, Aylin (2008). *Are Low Food Prices Pro-Poor?: Net Food Buyers and Sellers in Low-Income Countries.* Policy Research Working Paper, 4642. Washington, DC: World Bank.

Aljarallah, Ruba A. and Angus, Andrew (2020). Dilemma of natural resource abundance: A case study of Kuwait. *Sage Journals.* https://doi.org/10.1177/2158244019899701

Al-Marhubi, Fahim A. (2000). Corruption and inflation. *Economics Letters*, Vol. 66(2), 199–202.

Ahmadov, Anar K. (2014). Oil, democracy, and context: A meta-analysis. *Comparative Political Studies*, Vol. 47(9), 1238–1267.

Alsharif, Nouf, Bhattacharyya, Sambit and Intartaglia, Maurizio (2016). *Economic Diversification in Resource Rich Countries: Uncovering the State of Knowledge.* Working Paper Series, WPS 98-2016, University of Sussex.

Andersen, A. D. (2012). Towards a new approach to natural resources and development: The role of learning, innovation and linkage dynamics. *International Journal of Technological Learning, Innovation and Development*, Vol. 5(3), 291–324.

Auty, Richard M. (2001). The political economy of resource-driven growth. *European Economic Review*, Vol. 45(4–6), 839–846.

Ayoola, E. O. (2005). *Corruption in Nigeria: The Way Forward*. Paper delivered at the 50th. Anniversary of Ilesha Grammar School, Dec. 17th.

Bardhan, Pranab (1997). Corruption and development: A review of issues. *Journal of Economic Literature*, Vol. 35(3), 1320–1346.

Battaile, Bill and Mishra, Saurabh (2015). *Transforming Non-Renewable Resource Economies (NREs)*. IMF Working Paper No. 15/171.

Blomström, M. and Kokko, A. (2007). From natural resources to high-tech production: The evolution of industrial competitiveness in Sweden and Finland. In D. Lederman and W. F. Maloney (Eds.), *Natural Resources, Neither Curse nor Destiny* (pp. 213–256). Washington, DC: Stanford University Press and World Bank.

Bloomberg New Energy Finance Blog (2021). New Energy Outlook 2021, https://about.bnef.com/new-energy-outlook/ (accessed on December 21, 2021).

Cadot, Olivier, Carrere, Celine and Strauss-Kahn, Vanessa (2013). Trade diversification, income and growth: What do we know? *Journal of Economic Surveys*, Vol. 27(4), 790–812.

Cadot, O., Carrere, C. and Strauss-Kahn, V. (2011). Export diversification: What's behind the Hump? *Review of Economics and Statistics*, Vol. 93(2), 590–605.

Calderon, Cesar, Kambou, Gerard, Korman, Vijdan, Kubota, Megumi and Cantu Canales, Catalina (2019). An Analysis of Issues Shaping Africa's Economic Future, Open Knowledge Repository, World Bank Group, April 19.

Callen, T., Cherif, R., Hasanov, F., Hegazy, A. and Khandelwal, P. (2014). *Economic Diversification in the GCC: Past, Present, and Future*, IMF Staff Discussion Notes 14/12. Washington, DC: International Monetary Fund.

Cherif, R., Hasanov, F. and Zhu, M. (Eds.) (2016). *Breaking the Oil Spell: The Gulf Falcons' Path to Diversification*. Washington, DC: International Monetary Fund.

Chand, Ronal, Singh, Rup, Patel, Arvind and Jain, Devendra Kumar (2020). Export performance, governance, and economic growth: Evidence from Fiji – a small and vulnerable economy. *Cogent Economics and Finance*, Vol. 8(1), 1–16.

Chang, Ha-Joon and Cheema, Ali (2002). Conditions for successful technology policy in developing countries. *Economics of Innovation and New Technology*, Vol. 11(4), 369–398.

Charles, Ayobola, Mesagan, Ekundayo and Saibu, Muibi (2018). Resource endowment and export diversification: Implications for growth in Nigeria, Online veröffentlicht: 08 May 2018. Seitenbereich. Vol. 3 (1), 29–40, https://doi.org/10.2478/sbe-2018-0003

Cirera, Xavier, Marin, Anabel Ivana and Markwald, Ricardo (2015). Explaining export diversification through firm innovation decisions: The case of Brazil. *Research Policy*, Vol. 44(10), 1962–1973.

Cudjoe, Godsway, Breisinger, Clemens and Diao, Xinshen (2010). Local impacts of a global crisis: Food price transmission, consumer welfare and poverty in Ghana. *Food Policy*, Vol. 35(4), 294–302.

Collier, P. and Page, J. (2009). Breaking in and moving up: New industrial challenges for the bottom billion and the middle-income countries. Industrial Development Report, UNIDO.

Collier, Paul, Elliott, V. L., Hegre, Håvard, Hoeffler, Anke, Reynal-Querol, Marta and Sambanis, Nicholas (2003). *Breaking the Conflict Trap: Civil War and*

Development Policy. A World Bank policy research report 56793. Washington, DC: World Bank and Oxford University Press.

Commission on Growth and Development (2008). *The Growth Report Strategies for Sustained Growth and Inclusive Development*. Washington: World Bank.

Corden, W. Max and Neary, J. Peter (1982). Booming sector and de-industrialization in a small open economy. *The Economic Journal*, Vol. 92 (December 1982), 825–848.

Corden, W. M. (1984). Booming sector and Dutch disease economics: Survey and consolidation. *Oxford Economic Papers*, Vol. 36 (1984), 359–380.

Doki, N. O. and Tyokohol, M. Y. (2019). Export diversification and economic growth in Nigeria: Manufacturing and services exports as options. *Confluence Journal of Economics and Allied Science*, Vol. 2(1), 12–25.

Djimeu, Eric W. and Omgba, Luc (2018). *Oil Windfalls Might Not Be the Problem in Oil-producing Countries: Evidence from the Impact of Oil Shocks on Export Diversification*. Economic Working Papers No. 2018-18, University of Paris Nanterre.

Dennis, Allen and Shepherd, Ben (2011). Trade facilitation and export diversification. *The World Economy*, Vol. 34(1), 101–122.

Edwards, K. A. (1993). Water, environment, and development: A global agenda. *Natural Resources Forum*, Vol. 17(1), 59–64.

Emery, Robert F. (1967). The relation of exports and economic growth. *Kyklos International Review for Social Sciences*, Vol. 20(4), 470–486.

Feder, G. (1982). On export and economic growth. *Journal of Development Economics*, Vol. 12, 59–73.

Ferreira, Gustavo F. C. (2009). From Coffee beans to microchips: Export diversification and economic growth in Costa Rica. https://ageconsearch.umn.edu/record/47178/?ln=en

Food and Agriculture Organization (2004). *The State of Food Insecurity in the World 2004*. Rome: FAO.

Fosu, Augustin Kwasi (1991). Capital instability and economic growth in Sub-Saharan Africa. *The Journal of Development Studies*, Vol. 28(1), 74–85.

Fosu, Augustin Kwasi (2001a). Political instability and economic growth in developing economies: Some specification empirics. *Economics Letters*, Vol. 70(2), 289–294.

Fosu, Augustin Kwasi (2001b). Economic fluctuations and growth in Sub-Saharan Africa: The importance of import instability. *The Journal of Development Studies*, Vol. 37(3), 71–85.

Fuady, Ahmad Helmy (2015). Aid and policy preferences in oil-rich countries: Comparing Indonesia and Nigeria. *Third World Quarterly*, Vol. 36(7), 1349–1364, DOI: 10.1080/01436597.2015.1041490.

Gelb, A. (2010). *Economic Diversification in Resources Rich Countries*. Washington, D.C.: Centre for Global Development.

Ghani, Ejaz, Goswami, Arti Grover and Kerr, William R. (2012). *Is India's Manufacturing Sector Moving Away From Cities?* National Bureau of Economic Research Working Paper 17992. http://www.nber.org/papers/w17992.

Giri, Rahul, Quayyum, Saad Noor and Yin, Rujun Joy (2019). *Understanding Export Diversification: Key Drivers and Policy Implications*. IMF Working Paper, WP/19/105.

Global Battery Alliance (2019). A Vision for a Sustainable Battery Value Chain in 2030: Unlocking the Full Potential to Power Sustainable Development and

Climate Change Mitigation Geneva. www3.weforum.org/docs/WEF_A_Vision _for_a_Sustainable_Battery_Value_Chain_in_2030_Report.pdf

Guillou, Sarah and Treibich, Tania (2019). Firm export diversification and change in workforce composition. *Review of World Economics*, 155(4), 645–676.

Gyimah-Brempong, Kwabena (1991). Export instability and economic growth in Sub-Saharan Africa. *Economic Development and Cultural Change*, Vol. 39(4), 815–828.

Haouas, Ilham and Heshmati, Almas (2014). *Can the UAE Avoid the Oil Curse by Economic Diversification?* IZA Discussion Papers 8003, Institute of Labor Economics (IZA).

Hausman, Hwang and Rodrik (2007). What you export matter"s. *Journal of Economic Growth*, Vol. 12, 1–25.

Hausmann, Ricardo and Klinger, Bailey (2006). *Structural Transformation and Patterns of Comparative Advantage in the Product Space*. CID Working Paper No. 128, Center for International Development, Cambridge: Harvard University Press.

Hausmann, Ricardo, Hidalgo, Cesar A., Bustos, Sebastian, Coscia, Michele, Simoes, Alexander and Yıldırım, Muhammed A. (2013). *The Atlas of Economic Complexity: Mapping Paths to Prosperity*. Cambridge, MA: Harvard University, Center for International Development, Harvard Kennedy School, and Macro Connections, Massachusetts Institute of Technology. https://growthlab.cid.harvard.edu/files/ growthlab/files/atlas_2013_part1.pdf (accessed on December 22, 2021).

Heckscher, E. F. (1919). Utrikshandelns verkan pa inkomstfoerdelningen. *Ekonomist Tradskrift*, Vol. 21, Del 2, 1–32.

Helleiner, Eric (1992). Japan and the changing global financial order. *Canada's Journal of Global Policy Analysis*, Vol. 47(2), 420–444.

Herzer, Dierk and Felicitas, Nowak-Lehnmann (2006). What does export diversification do for growth? An econometric analysis. *Applied Economics*, Vol. 38(15), 1825–1838.

Hesse, H. (2008). *Export Diversification and Economic Growth*. International Bank for Reconstruction and Development / the World Bank Commission on Growth and Development Working Paper, No. 21. Washington, D.C.: World Bank.

Hidalgo, C. A., Klinger, B., Barabasi, A. L. and Hausmann, R. (2007). The product space conditions the development of nations. *SCIENCE*, 27 Jul 2007, Vol. 317(5837), 482–487, https://doi.org/10.1126/science.1144581

Huang, Kuo-Feng (2011). Technological competencies in competitive environment. *Journal of Business Research*, Vol. 64(2), 172–79.

HRSG (2015). Understanding General and Technical Competencies. https:// resources.hrsg.ca/blog/understanding-general-and-technical-competencies (accessed on January 27, 2021).

Hwang, J. (2006). *Introduction of New Goods, Convergence, and Growth*. Cambridge, MA: Harvard University Job Market Paper.

Imbs, J. and Wacziarg, Romain (2003). Stages of diversification. *American Economic Review*, Vol. 93(1), 63–86.

IMF (2014). *World Economic Outlook: Recovery Strengthens, Remains Uneven*. Washington: IMF.

Innis, H. A. (1956). *The Fur Trade in Canada: an Introduction to Canadian Economic History*. Toronto: University of Toronto Press.

Ishakq, Dele and Ogbanje, Joseph Ike (2017). Over-dependence on oil and its implication for development in Nigeria. *HUMASS: McU Journal of Humanities, Management, Applied & Social Sciences*, Vol. 1(2), 25–33, Nov. 2017.

Ivanic, Maros and Martin, Will (2014). *Short- and Long-Run Impacts of Food Price Changes on Poverty.* World Bank Policy Research Working Paper, 7011. https://papers.ssrn.com/sol3/Delivery.cfm/7011.pdf?abstractid=2484229&mirid=1.

Jama, Abdikarim Bashir (2020). The effect of institutional quality on export performance of Middle East & North-Africa Region. *International Journal of Research and Innovation in Social Science (IJRISS)*, Vol. 4(1), 14–20.

Javed, Zanib and Munir, Kashif (2016). Impact of export composition on economic growth in South Asia. *Munich Personal RePEc Archive.* https://mpra.ub.uni-muenchen.de/71519/

Keesing, Donald B. (1967). Outward-looking policies and economic development. *The Economic Journal*, Vol. 77(306), 303–320.

Khan, Mushtaq H. (2000). Rent-seeking as process. In Mushtaq H. Khan and K. S. Jomo (Eds.), *Rents, Rent-Seeking and Economic Development: Theory and Evidence in Asia.* Cambridge: Cambridge University Press.

Kilian, Lutz (2014). Oil price shocks: Causes and consequences. *Annual Review of Resource Economics*, Vol. 6, 133–154.

Kim, Sanghoon and Song, Hah-Zoong (2020). A review of industrial clusters, industrial policy, and industrialization in South Korea. In A. Oqubay and J. Y. Lin (Eds.), *The Oxford Handbook of Industrial Hubs and Economic Development*, Oxford: Oxford University Press.

Klinger, B. and Lederman, D. (2006). *Diversification, Innovation and Imitation Inside the Global Technology Frontier.* World Bank Policy Research Working Paper #3872. Washington, DC: World Bank.

Koen, Michael. (1977). *Korean Phoenix: A Nation from the Ashes* Englewood: Prentice Hall International.

Lahn, Glada and Stevens, Paul (2018). The curse of the one-size-fits-all fix: Re-evaluating what we know about extractives and economic development. In Tony Addison and Alan Roe (Eds.), *Extractive Industries: The Management of Resources as a Driver of Sustainable Development* (pp. 94–111). Oxford: OUP.

Lane, Nathan (2021). Manufacturing Revolutions: Industrial Policy and Industrialization in South Korea. http://nathanlane.info/assets/papers/ManufacturingRevolutions_Lane_Live.pdf (accessed on December 22, 2021).

Lederman, Daniel and Maloney, William F. (2003). *Trade Structure and Growth.* Policy Research Working Paper; No. 3025. Washington, DC: World Bank.

Lee, Jinsoo and Yu, Bok-keun (2019). The effects of export diversification on macroeconomic stabilization: Evidence from Korea. *KDI Journal of Economic Policy* 2019,Vol. 41(1), 1–14.

Lee, Jung Hoon, Phaal, Robert and Lee, Chihoon (2011). An empirical analysis of the determinants of technology roadmap utilization. *R & D Management*, Vol. 41(5), 485–508.

Lewis, W. A. (1955). *Theory of Economic Growth.* London: Allen and Unwin Ltd.

LiPuma, Joseph A., Newbert, Scott L. and Doh, Jonathan P. (2013). The effect of institutional quality on firm export performance in emerging economies: A contingency model of firm age and size. *Small Business Economics*, Vol. 40(4), 817–841.

Lussier, Y., Sabourin, S. and Wright, J. (1993). On causality, responsibility, and blame in marriage: Validity of the entailment model. *Journal of Family Psychology*, Vol. 7(3), 322–332.

Martone, David (2003). A guide to developing a competency-based performance – Management system. *Employment Relations Today*, Vol. 30(3), 23–32.

Matthee, Marianne and Naudé, Wim (2007). *Export Diversity and Regional Growth: Empirical Evidence from South Africa*. WIDER Research Paper, No. 2007/11. Helsinki: UNU-WIDER.

McMillan, M. S., Rodrik, D. and Verduzco-Gallo, I. (2014). Globalization, structural change, and productivity growth, with an update on Africa. *World Development*, Vol. 63, 11–32.

Mehlum, Halvor, Moene, Karl and Torvik, Ragnar (2006). Institutions and the Resource Curse. *The Economic Journal*, Vol. 116(508), 1–20.

Michaely, Michael (1977). Exports and growth: An empirical investigation. *Journal of Development Economics*, Vol. 4(1), 49–53.

Miguel, Edward, Satyanath, Shanker and Sergenti, Ernest (2004). Economic shocks and civil conflict: An instrumental variables approach. *Journal of Political Economy*, Vol. 112(4), 725–753.

Nguyen, Son Thanh and Wu, Yanrui (2020). Governance and export performance in Vietnam. *Journal of Southeast Asian Economies*, Vol. 37(1), 1–25.

North, D. C. (1990). *Institutions, Institutional Change and Economic Performance*. Cambridge: Cambridge University Press.

Oh, Jung Eun "Jen", Đuc, Pham Minh, Kunaka, Charles and Skorzus, Roman Constantin (2020). *Vietnam Development Report 2019: Connecting Vietnam for Growth and Shared Prosperity*. Washington: International Bank for Reconstruction and Development/World Bank.

Ohlin, B. (1933). *Interregional and International Trade*. Cambridge, Mass.; Harvard University Press.

Olson, David H. (2000). Circumplex model of marital and family systems. *Journal of Family Therapy*, Vol. 22(2), 144–167.

Omgba, Luc Desire (2014). Institutional foundations of export diversification patterns in oil-producing countries. *Journal of Comparative Economics*, Vol. 42(4), 1052–1064.

Onodugo, Amujiri and Nwuba (2015). Diversification of the economy: A panacea for Nigerian economic development. *International Journal of Multidisciplinary Research and Development*, Vol. 2(5), 477–483.

Osakwe, Regina N. (2015). Entrepreneurship education in Delta State Tertiary Institutio as a means of achieving national growth and development. *International Journal of Higher Education*, Vol.4 (1), 182–186.

Oyelaran-Oyeyinka and Gehl-Sampath, P. (2010). *Latecomer Development: Knowledge and Innovation for Economic Growth*. UK: Routledge.

Oyelaran-Oyeyinka, Banji and Lal, Kaushalesh (2006). *SMEs and New Technologies: Learning E-business and Development*. New York: Palgrave Macmillan.

Oyelaran-Oyeyinka, Banji and Lal, Kaushalesh (2017). *Structural Transformation and Economic Development: Cross Regional Analysis of Industrialization and Urbanization*. London: Routledge.

Palma, José Gabriel (2005). The seven main "stylized facts" of the Mexican economy since trade liberalization and NAFTA. *Industrial and Corporate Change*, Vol. 14(6), December 2005, 941–991, https://doi.org/10.1093/icc/dth076

Patel, Pari and Pavitt, Keith (1997). The technological competencies of the world's largest firms: Complex and path-dependent, but not much variety. *Research Policy*, Vol. 26(2), 141–156.

Perkins, Dwight H. and Anh, Vu Thanh Tu (2010). *Vietnam's Industrial Policy : Designing Policies for Sustainable Development*. UNDP Dialogue Series 3: United Nations Development Programme, Vietnam Center for Business and Government. Cambridge: Harvard Kennedy School Ash Center for Democratic Governance and Innovation.

Prebisch, R. (1950). *The Economic Development of Latin America and Its Principal Problems*.New York: United Nations Department of Economic Affairs, Economic Commission for Latin America (ECLA). http://archivo.cepal.org/pdfs/ cdPrebisch/002.pdf.

Robinson, James A. and Acemoglu, Daron (2006). *Economic Origins of Dictatorship and Democracy*. Cambridge: Cambridge University Press.

Rodríguez-Duarte, Antonio, Sandulli, F.D., Minguela-Rata, B. and López-Sánchez, J.I. (2007). The endogenous relationship between innovation and diversification, and the impact of technological resources on the form of diversification. *Research Policy*, Vol. 36(5), 652–664.

Ross, Michael L. (2012). *The Oil Curse: How Petroleum Wealth Shapes the Development of Nations*. NJ: Princeton University Press.

Ross, Michael L. (2017). What Do We Know About Economic Diversification in Oil-Producing Countries? https://www.sscnet.ucla.edu/polisci/faculty/ross/papers /working/What%20do%20we%20know%20about%20exdiv.pdf

Ross, Michael L (2019). What Do We Know About Export Diversification in Oil-Producing Countries? https://papers.ssrn.com/sol3/papers.cfm?abstract_id =3432708

Sala-i-Martin, Xavier and Subramanian, Arvind (2003). *Addressing the Natural Resource Curse: An Illustration from Nigeria*. IMF Working Paper WP/03/139.

Samuelson, P. (1948). *Economics, An Introductory Analysis*. New York: McGraw Hill.

Sarel, Michael (1996). Nonlinear effects of inflation on economic growth. *IMF Staff Papers*, Vol. 43(1), 199–215.

Singer, H. (1950). The distribution of gains between investing and borrowing countries. *American Economic Review*, Vol. 40(2), 473–85.

Songwe, Vera (2019). "Boosting trade and investment: a new agenda for regional and international engagement". In Brahima S. Coulibaly (Eds.) Foresight Africa Publication, (pp. 97–116). Washington: Brookings, https://www.brookings. edu/wp-content/uploads/2019/01/BLS18234_BRO_book_007_WEB1.pdf

Stanley, Denise and Bunnag, Sirima (2001). A new look at the benefits of diversification: Lessons from Central America. *Applied Economics*, Vol. 33(11), 1369–1383.

UNCTAD (2018b). Diversification and Value Addition. https://unctad.org/system /files/official-document/cimem2d42_en.pdf (accessed on November 27, 2020).

U.S. Geological Survey (2021). Mineral Commodity Summaries 2021: U.S. Geological Survey. Reston: U.S. Geological Survey. https://doi.org/10.3133/ mcs2021.

Usman, S. O. (2011). The opacity and conduit of corruption in the Nigeria oil sector: Beyond the rhetoric of the anti-corruption crusade. *Journal of Sustainable Development in Africa*, Vol. 13(2), 294–308.

Vagliasindi, Maria (2012). *Implementing Energy Subsidy Reforms: An Overview of the Key Issues*. Policy Research Working Paper; No. 6122. Washington: World Bank.

van der Ploeg (2011). Natural resources: Curse or blessing? *Journal of Economic Literature*, Vol. 49(2), June 2011, 366–420.

Viner, J. (1952). *International Trade and Economic Development*. New York: Free Press.

Vollrath, Dietrich (2009). How important are dual economy effects for aggregate productivity? *Journal of Development Economics*, Vol. 88(2), 325–334.

Walsha, Steven and Lintonc, Jonathan D. (2001). The measurement of technical competencies. *The Journal of High Technology Management Research*, 13(1), 63–86.

Watkins, M. H. (1963). A staple theory of economic growth. *Canadian Journal of Economics and Political Science*, Vol. 24, 141–158.

World Bank (1993). *World Development Report 1993: Investing in Health*. New York: Oxford University Press.

World Bank (2011). *World Development Report 2011: Conflict, Security, and Development*. Washington: World Bank.

World Bank (2018). *The World Bank Annual Report 2018 (English). Policy Priorities for Poverty Reduction and Shared Prosperity in a Post-Conflict Country and Fragile State*. Washington, D.C.: World Bank Group.

World Bank (2019). *The World Bank Annual Report 2019: Ending Poverty, Investing in Opportunity*. Washington, DC: World Bank.

World Trade Organisation and OECD (2019). *Aid for Trade at a Glance 2019: Economic Diversification and Empowerment*. Paris: OECD. https://www.oecd .org/dac/aft/aid-for-trade-at-a-glance-22234411.htm (accessed on August 19, 2021).

Woronoff, J. (1983). *Korea's Economy: Man-Made Miracle* Arch Cape: Pace International Research.

Wright, G. and Czelusta, J. (2007). Resource-based growth: Past and present. In D. Lederman and W. F. Maloney (Eds.), *Natural Resources: Neither Curse nor Destiny* (pp. 183–212). Washington DC: World Bank.

Yusof, Najeemah Mohd (2010). Influence of family factors on reading habits and interest among level 2 pupils in national primary schools in Malaysia. *Procedia-Social and Behavioural Sciences*, Vol.5, 1160–1165.

Zheng, Y., and Aggarwal, A. (2020). Special economic zones in China and India: A comparative analysis. In A. Oqubay and J. Y. Lin (Eds.), *The Oxford Handbook of Industrial Hubs and Economic Development* (pp. 607–622). New York: Oxford University Press. https://doi.org/10.1093/oxfordhb/9780198850434.013.31

Index

Printed in the United States
by Baker & Taylor Publisher Services